Asian Arguments

Asian Arguments is a series of short books about Asia today. Aimed at the growing number of students and general readers who want to know more about the region, these books will highlight community involvement from the ground up in issues of the day usually discussed by authors in terms of top-down government policy. The aim is to better understand how ordinary Asian citizens are confronting problems such as the environment, democracy and their societies' development, either with or without government support. The books are scholarly but engaged, substantive as well as topical and written by authors with direct experience of their subject matter.

About the Editor

SAM GEALL is Departmental Lecturer in Human Geography of China at the University of Oxford and executive editor of *chinadialogue*. He is an editor of *Berkshire Encyclopedia of Sustainability 7/10: China, India, and East and Southeast Asia: Assessing Sustainability* and author of *Climate-Change Journalism in China: Opportunities for International Cooperation*. Sam has written for many international publications including the *Guardian, Foreign Policy, New Humanist, openDemocracy, Index on Censorship* and *Green Futures*. He is a Fellow of the RSA.

CHINA AND THE ENVIRONMENT

The Green Revolution

Edited by SAM GEALL

Zed Books

LONDON | NEW YORK

China and the Environment: The Green Revolution was first published
in 2013 by Zed Books Ltd, 7 Cynthia Street, London N1 9JF, UK
and Room 400, 175 Fifth Avenue, New York, NY 10010, USA

www.zedbooks.co.uk

FSC
www.fsc.org
MIX
Paper from
responsible sources
FSC® C013604

Designed and typeset in Monotype Bulmer
by illuminati, Grosmont
Index by John Barker
Cover designed by www.alice-marwick.co.uk
Printed and bound by CPI Group (UK) Ltd,
Croydon CRO 4YY

Distributed in the USA exclusively by Palgrave Macmillan, a division of
St Martin's Press, LLC, 175 Fifth Avenue, New York, NY 10010, USA

A catalogue record for this book is available from the British Library
Library of Congress Cataloging in Publication Data available

ISBN 978 1 78032 341 1 hb
ISBN 978 1 78032 340 4 pb

Contents

Acknowledgements

This book started life during a conversation between Isabel Hilton, editor and CEO of *chinadialogue*, and Paul French, series editor of Asian Arguments at Zed Books. I am hugely grateful to both. I am also extremely grateful to the authors, Jonathan Ansfield, Olivia Boyd, Liu Jianqiang and Adam Moser. I would like to thank the writers whose work for *chinadialogue* has been excerpted in these pages, particularly Xia Jun, Meng Si and Feng Yongfeng. I acknowledge the importance of *chinadialogue*, its contributors, staff, supporters and volunteers, unfortunately too numerous to name, in making this book possible. Dinah Gardner, who translated Liu Jianqiang's chapter, and Roddy Flagg, who translated the other excerpts from *chinadialogue*, were both reliable and accurate as ever. Everyone at Zed Books has been brilliant, particularly Tamsine O'Riordan, Kim Walker and Kika Sroka-Miller, as well as Lucy Morton and Robin Gable at illuminati. Finally, I am enormously grateful to Hayley Ichilcik, not only for her editing advice, but also for helping to keep me sane throughout the whole process.

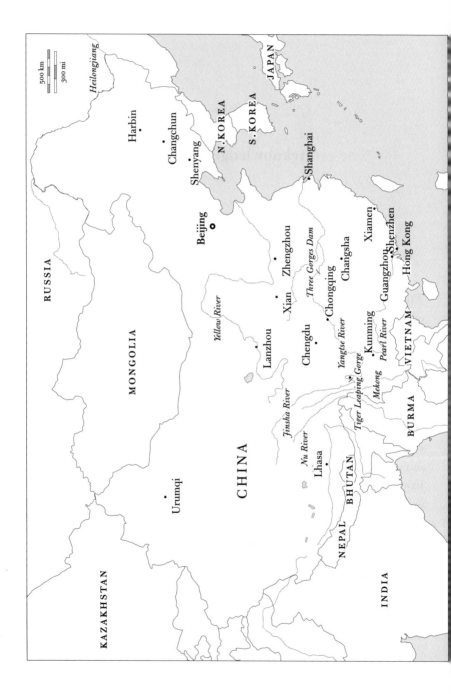

The return of Chinese civil society

ISABEL HILTON

In the early 1970s, the first batch of British students to be admitted to Chinese universities since the outbreak of the Cultural Revolution made a large, if understandable, mistake: they proposed to the authorities at the Beijing Languages Institute (now the Beijing Language and Culture University) that they should be permitted to set up a foreign students' association.

The response was swift and, to a Western eye, a little disproportionate. The normally mild-mannered Bi Laoshi ('Teacher Bi'), head of the *waiban,* the office in the institute that dealt with the foreign students, could not have made the official response plainer: he made several visits to the foreign student dormitory to ensure that the tiny spark of this idea was firmly stamped on and completely extinguished.

Teacher Bi was a diminutive, bespectacled figure who normally bore the burden of managing his tiresome flock of foreigners with a certain grace and occasional flashes of humour. On this subject, though, he was grim and categorical. There was no foreign students' association at the Beijing Languages Institute and, he explained repeatedly and firmly, there never would be. It was out of the question, probably illegal and certainly prohibited.

It seems implausible today that we could have been so naive as to imagine that the Chinese Communist Party would not see the proposal as a threat. It had established its dominance of everything that moved, thought, spoke or acted in Mao's China, and in the years since 1949 it had repeatedly directed its overwhelming firepower against any organisation that the Party did not control.

Pre-revolutionary China, on the other hand, had been rich in civil society bodies, from secret societies that ranged across the political, through social welfare to the outright criminal. There were religious associations of all denominations, business associations, clan associations and, among China's foreign residents, everything from Masonic lodges to tennis clubs. There were trade unions, welfare bodies and professional guilds. There were also numerous political organisations, including alternative communist parties and democratic parties of various stripes. None had survived in its original form and by 1973 those organisations that the Party had not destroyed or brought under control had been driven underground.

As the high point of Mao Zedong's millenarian socialism, the Cultural Revolution seemed to be the final chapter in the destruction of autonomous civil society in China. Mao saw enemies everywhere and interpreted any views that did not accord with his own as disloyalty. By the time the cult of Mao reached its apogee in the late 1960s, the space for independent thought and civic action in China had been eliminated. By the early 1970s, China could boast only a few monochrome mass organisations, such as the All-China Federation of Trades Unions, the All-China Women's Federation and the Communist Youth League of China. All claimed large membership, but they functioned to transmit the Party's message rather than to challenge its policies.

Ordinary citizens had no right to organise. Chinese citizenship conveyed no intrinsic rights at all: no guarantees of constitutional protection; no right of association; no defence against arbitrary persecution by the state; no right to observe a religious faith, other than in the shifting catechism of Marxism–Leninism–Mao Zedong Thought; and no right to set up any organisation, however innocuous the intent. It was well understood – though not by the foreign students of the day – that to try to do so would be to invite swift retribution from above. The Party had reserved to itself the right to calibrate and control everything, from matters of life and death to the most mundane activity.

More than thirty years were to pass before my next attempt to set up an organisation in China. The second venture – www.chinadialogue.net, a bilingual Chinese–English web publication on environment and climate change – met with more success. The year was 2006: Mao was long in his tomb and his arch rival Deng Xiaoping had also left the stage. The respective legacies of both leaders, each in his own way politically authoritarian, were closely entwined. Their shadows still lay across the lives of new generations of Chinese citizens. But China had also been through nearly three decades of rapid change and not just in economics and industry: society was changing too. The new century had brought new perspectives on China's rapid growth and China's citizens were no longer content to be silent on the problems that affected their lives and health. The environmental costs of China's model of development were driving people to take action; it was no longer unthinkable that foreigners and Chinese should be able to share ideas and information on China's environmental crisis.

That was what *chinadialogue* set out to do. We wanted an even-handed exchange: neither side would lecture to the other but we would aim to be honest, as well as useful and informative to both. We would commission Chinese writers to write about China and Western writers to write about international experience. We believed that there were lessons to be learned in both directions, and that it was possible to discuss climate change and environment in the spirit of trying to solve problems rather than simply blaming each other for past mistakes or present policies. Our international readers would gain a window into the Chinese experience, unmediated by a foreign lens. We would aim to be interesting for Chinese policymakers and, importantly, for the growing numbers of Chinese citizens who were beginning to find a voice and were eager to learn what had happened in other times and other places.

By 2006, when *chinadialogue* was setting out its stall, Professor Wang Ming of Tsinghua University estimated that there were 500,000 NGOs in China, most of them unregistered. It was hard to be exact, or to define what that term might mean across a wide range of options, but clearly civil society in China was bouncing back from the crushing catastrophe of the Mao era. By the end of 2011, there were approximately 449,000 legally registered civil society organisations in China. The estimate of the unregistered may be as high as 3 million. Many of them register as businesses; others do not register at all and receive little oversight, unless, in the eyes of the government, they transgress.

The return of civil society, in the environmental sphere at least, began modestly: on 31 March 1994, the organisation popularly known as Friends of Nature was officially registered with the Ministry of Civil Affairs, under the rather less user-friendly name of the Green Culture Institute of the International Academy of Chinese Culture, listing its purpose as raising environmental awareness. Technically this was not the first legally registered environmental NGO in China: an organisation was registered in Liaoning in 1991. But Friends of Nature was to play a significant role, not least because of the distinguished pedigree of the man who founded it.

The late Liang Congjie was the son of a distinguished family: his grandfather Liang Qichao had led an ill-fated reform movement at the end of the nineteenth century. Congjie's father, Liang Sicheng, was a planner and architect who had fought valiantly, if unsuccessfully, to save historic Beijing from destruction in the 1950s and 1960s. He had first tried to persuade Mao Zedong that the city, with its nesting walls and intimate historic spaces, was unsuitable for the needs of a modern state and that the new People's Republic might care to build its capital outside the walls. Later, in the Cultural Revolution, he fought again to save Beijing's magnificent city walls from destruction. They were pulled down, despite his protests and Mao ordered them replaced with Beijing's first ring road. Liang Congjie represented the third generation of a family with a keen sense of civic responsibility and reason to understand the art of confronting power with care.

Friends of Nature was influential but necessarily cautious. The revival of civil society that its registration heralded was part of the long transformation from Mao's China to today's hybrid society – an authoritarian, semi-market economy with a substantial quotient of 'Chinese characteristics'. The retreat of the state from many aspects of life in China, a necessary prerequisite for marketisation and opening up to the outside world, created both the need and the opportunity for non-state organisations in everything from policy advice and formulation to the delivery of welfare. At the same time, the retreat of the Party from its earlier efforts to dominate all thought and action has opened up space for more pragmatic, reality-based approaches and for discussion. But although the government recognises the need for civil society organisations, and the contribution they can make to China's modernisation, environmental protection and sustainable development, it has been slow to create the legal and regulatory conditions that would allow civil society to fulfil its potential. At the root of this much-delayed institutionalisation lies mistrust.

Through the 1990s and the first decade of this century, China became an industrial powerhouse, a transformation that profoundly impacted the environment, but also every aspect of life and governance: the law, labour conditions, education, consumerism, land use and migration – all were affected.

Building the institutions to support China's transition is a continuing undertaking. It began with a revision of the constitution and the enactment of thousands of new laws and regulations to govern the international business and commercial relations that China needed to open its economy for foreign investment, manufacture and trade, and to manage the retreat of the Party from the day-to-day management of Chinese society. New domestic laws and regulations were drawn up, including those intended to govern non-Party and non-state organisations.

The first regulation, Regulations on Foundation Management, were issued in 1988, when the officially sponsored non-profit sector began to emerge. The Regulations on the Registration and Management of Social Organizations followed in October 1989. These regulations required independent organisations to find a government sponsor if they wanted to register, a requirement that remains in place and is an insuperable obstacle for most grassroots organisations.

These regulations were revised in 1998, along with Provisional Regulations for the Registration and Management of Popular Non-Enterprise Units (PNEUs). In the early 2000s, some independent non-profits were able to register as PNEUs, but many more remained unregistered, or registered as businesses. New regulations have been promised and some limited experimentation in a more relaxed approach is under way, but until now the regulatory regime heavily favours state control and is widely thought to inhibit, rather than to enable, a well-functioning civil society.

It was clear by the early 1990s that the transition to a more market-oriented economy was going to entail a civil-society revival, if only to facilitate services that the government itself was no longer able to deliver. It was equally clear that the Chinese authorities remained extremely nervous of allowing autonomous institutions to function in China. The danger that the Chinese government had in mind — and one it was anxious to avoid — was the fate of Soviet Communism, in the USSR itself and in the countries of the Warsaw Pact.

The year of China's Tiananmen trauma, 1989, began with martial law in Tibet. It ended with the collapse of the Berlin Wall, the end of state socialism in Europe and the end of the Cold War that had defined world politics for forty years. Three years later, the USSR itself imploded, shrinking down to the rump of the Russian Federation and spawning a shoal of revived states from the Baltic to the Black Sea. Watching from the sidelines, the Chinese Communist Party was determined neither to lose political power, as in Europe, nor to allow China to follow the example of the USSR and break up.

The role of ordinary people on the streets in bringing down communism was not lost on Beijing. The countries of the Warsaw Pact, like China, had allowed little space for independent civil society, but it did not escape Beijing's notice that there had been enough – in the Lutheran and Catholic churches, in embryonic environmental movements, in the writers' and artists' organisations and the trade unions – to allow people to mobilise around a common purpose. When the popular purpose became to change governments – or entire political systems – people were prepared.

The aftershocks of 1989, both within and outside China, were felt for many years. Further waves of civic action swept across the post-Soviet world and beyond in the 1990s and again in the early twenty-first century, with the colour revolutions that touched Georgia, the Ukraine, Kyrgyzstan, Lebanon and Iran. By 2010, to the surprise of many, protest even spread to the Arab world. Demonstrations in neighbouring Myanmar in 2008 had not brought down the dictatorship, but no doubt contributed to the tentative liberalisation that began three years later with the release of scores of political prisoners, the lifting of Aung San Su Kyi's house arrest and a cautious step in the direction of democracy.

Viewed from Beijing, these events owed much to the actions of indigenous civil-society organisations that relied on international funding and logistical support. For some observers in Beijing, it was evidence that foreign money and ideas conspired to bring down governments.

A debate developed: on one hand, important voices in the government, and even more in the academy, argued that an active civil society was a necessary part of social and economic modernisation and that civil society was at its most useful where it was independent and properly funded.

Against this, elements of the state apparatus argued that legal independence and funding were the two factors that would enable uncontrolled entities to be created that could threaten the Communist Party. These opposing perspectives persist, and may account for the government's failure to enact long-awaited new regulations governing NGOs in China. Until new regulations appear, NGOs face continuing obstacles: they have great difficulties in obtaining legal registration, without which they cannot open bank accounts or legally receive foreign or domestic funding. Whilst tens of thousands operate in the unregistered grey zone, they have no protection from prosecution or other official sanctions.

In 2006, in the same week that Professor Wang Ming told me that there were 500,000, mostly unregistered, NGOs in China, I sat in a hotel lobby in Beijing with a group of China's most prominent environmental activists. None worked for, or with, a state-sponsored organisation. All, by then, had a track record of opposition to the dam building that was threatening China's last unspoiled rivers in the west and south-west. None had been able legally to register the organisations that they had cooperated with and, in some cases, founded.

These fledgling organisations were facing a bewildering set of problems, the scale of which had been summed up the year before by Pan Yue, a vice minister in the Environmental Protection Agency, later upgraded to the Ministry of Environmental Protection. In what must count as the most outspoken interview ever given by a Chinese official to a member of the foreign press, he described the threat that China's environmental crisis posed to China's future prosperity. He said:

> This miracle will end soon, because the environment can no longer keep pace. Acid rain is falling on one third of the Chinese territory, half of the water in our seven largest rivers is completely useless, while one-fourth of our citizens do not have access to clean drinking water. One-third of the urban population are breathing polluted air, and less than 20 per cent of the trash in cities is treated and

processed in an environmentally sustainable manner. Finally, five of the ten most polluted cities worldwide are in China.

He continued:

> Because air and water are polluted, we are losing between 8 and 15 per cent of our gross domestic product. And that doesn't include the costs for health. Then there's the human suffering: in Bejing alone, 70 to 80 per cent of all deadly cancer cases are related to the environment. Lung cancer has emerged as the number one cause of death. ... the western regions of China and the country's ecologically stressed regions can no longer support the people already living there. In the future, we will need to resettle 186 million residents from 22 provinces and cities. However, the other provinces and cities can only absorb some 33 million people. That means China will have more than 150 million ... environmental refugees.[1]

The vice minister might have added desertification and greenhouse gases to his list, or the predicted impacts of climate change on China's food security. It was clear that there was a huge mismatch between the scale of the problems and the ability of China's vulnerable civil society organisations to address them.

All of the activists gathered that day were nervous: environmental activism was well established by 2006 and actively encouraged by some elements in the Chinese government. But that did not change the fact that major economic interests were at stake and this group had come under severe pressure. In China's compressed development, these men and women represented the next generation of environmental activism from Liang Congjie's Friends of Nature: they were younger and more activist; some were more confrontational; many had backgrounds in journalism and had moved from writing about China's environmental crisis to trying to mobilise others. They reached for any tools that were to hand and played an important role in fashioning new ones, such as the regulations on transparency, the public right to know and public participation that offered environmental activists a field of action that went beyond protest.

In January 2007, the State Council introduced new Regulations on Open Government Information that gave citizens the legal right to obtain government information. These came into force on 1 May 2008, along with the rather clumsily named Measures on Open Environmental Information (for Trial Implementation). Ma Jun, one of China's most celebrated and effective environmental activists, hailed the new regulations as 'an important milestone for freedom of information in China', and a 'powerful lever for the public to monitor companies' environmental performance'.

Taken together, these measures gave environmental activists – and ordinary citizens – the means to monitor pollution and bring polluters to public attention. It gave them the right to demand information on violators, including what action they might have taken. As Ma Jun wrote on *chinadialogue*:

> If an environment agency turns down the public application for disclosure, the public may report this to the superior environmental authorities, which shall then urge the subordinate agency to fulfil their disclosure duties. The public may apply for administrative review or file administrative suits if they believe that the rejection of disclosure has infringed upon their legal rights.[2]

On paper at least, the measures represented an important step forward in public trust and empowerment.

Curiously, despite the government's reservations about the dangers of foreign interference, the period of reform has also been marked by a significant growth in the activities of foreign NGOs operating in China. According to the Ministry of Civil Affair's China Charity and Donation Information Centre in March 2012, 1,000 US NGOs were operating in China, mainly working in humanitarian aid, environmental and animal protection, and gender and labour rights. American NGOs, according to the report, have donated nearly 20 billion yuan (US$3.18 billion) to China since 1978, much of it into education and research.

Increasing trans-boundary contact is an inevitable side effect of China's transition and one that also affects China's civil society.

As China opens to the outside world, Chinese citizens come into contact with images of global civil society; they are influenced by international events and by a growing sense that global civil society has the capacity to organise around global problems, especially in the environment. Environmental imagination draws on the image of one planet; climate change offers the concept of a single global eco-system.

These connections may stimulate China's domestic NGOs but they do not directly foster their development, or help them overcome the obstacles to financial survival that the Chinese government puts in their path. On 1 March 2010, for instance, new regulations came into force that placed additional obstacles to receiving international funding, with new requirements for notarised agreements and de-tailed application forms. These regulations represent a large burden for independent NGOs, and leave them vulnerable to interference by government agencies through the uncertainties they create.

In 2011, there were again hints that the impasse over regula-tion might be resolved. Although the year began with the govern-ment's extraordinary attempt to prohibit the use of the term 'civil society', later in the year experiments in liberalising registration in Guangdong province, in southern China, and in Beijing were given official endorsement. In Guangdong, eight types of civil society organisation were permitted to register without official sponsors; in Beijing, social organisations were permitted to use the local Ministry of Civil Affairs bureaus as both registering and oversight bodies. In another sign of change, the One Foundation, a private foundation set up by the film star Jet Li, was allowed to register in Shenzhen, also in Guangdong province, which made it the first private foundation in China that was permitted to raise funds from the public – a move perhaps inspired by a series of scandals in China's public, government-sponsored foundations that has made Chinese citizens reluctant to donate.

A proposed Charity Law, currently on the legislative agenda of the Standing Committee of the National People's Congress (NPC),

may move to a first reading in March 2013, and the 12th Five Year
Plan envisages a growing role for civil society in the delivery of social
services. The institutionalisation that this would demand could also
benefit activist and environmental groups, but in a year of political
transition much remains uncertain.

In one sense, the 12th Five Year Plan marks the moment that
the ideas voiced from the political and social margins ten years
earlier entered the mainstream, enthroned within the state's core
declaration of values and developmental intentions. When they were
first voiced, these ideas were thrown down as a challenge to the
top-down orthodoxy of 'develop first, clean up later'. Today, they are
encompassed within the new official orthodoxy, one of sustainability
and circular economy, of inclusion and a more rounded growth.

What does that mean for the legitimacy of the civil society that
threw down that challenge, and that had tried to develop its inspira-
tion and its methodology outside the state system, albeit frequently
in an uneasy dialogue with power? Its ideas may have been incorporated, but that does not mean that its standing as a legitimate sector
has been vindicated. The state may have modified its understanding
of the environmental costs and benefits of competing development
models, but the approach to adjustment remains as top-down as
ever. And, ironically, the very cause that gave birth to the present
generation of Chinese environmental NGOs – the construction of
big hydro, in virtual abeyance under the 11th Five Year Plan – is set
to resume with increased force with the departure of premier Wen
Jiabao. By the end of the 12th Five Year Plan it is likely that not
a river in China will remain undammed, the protests of residents
and of civil society notwithstanding. The state might have changed
its views, but its methods, and its view of the subordinate role of
non-state and non-Party actors and organisations, have scarcely
altered.

How China resolves the ambiguities that currently weaken the
position of its civil-society organisations will be an important signal
of the direction of Chinese society in the coming years. Will the

recent trend continue of greater access to information for a liberalised media with its environmental journalists, which Sam Geall explores in Chapter 1? Will the kind of organisation that Olivia Boyd explores in Chapter 2 be allowed to develop and grow? Greater independence and more robust protection for civil-society organisations would indicate a maturity of Chinese society and a confidence in the rule of law that would help to equip China to cope peacefully with its difficult next phase of development. Adam Moser's chapter on legal activism illuminates what is possible, but also the continuing difficulties of using the law to support environmental activism. Liu Jianqiang leaves us in no doubt that China's civil society will continue to find ways to amplify the effectiveness of its actions, but how far will the authorities allow this to develop?

Continuing restrictions and harassment of individuals and organisations, of the kind that is also chronicled in the following pages, could be a disturbing signal of a return to authoritarianism, and could lead to more social unrest and street protest, like the Xiamen PX protests so brilliantly explored by Jonathan Ansfield. From the following chapters the potential for a robust and vibrant civil society is clear. Whether it is allowed to come into being is less certain.

Notes

1. 'Interview with China's Deputy Minister of the Environment: "The Chinese Miracle Will End Soon"', *Der Spiegel*, August 2005, www.spiegel. de/international/spiegel/spiegel-interview-with-china-s-deputy-minister-of-the-environment-the-chinese-miracle-will-end-soon-a-345694.html.
2. Ma Jun, 'Your Right To Know: A Historic Moment', *chinadialogue* 1 May 2008, www.chinadialogue.net/article/show/single/en/1962.

Further reading

Elizabeth Economy, *The River Runs Black*, Ithaca and London: Cornell University Press, 2004. (One of the first accounts of the roots and evolution of China's ecological crisis, including an introduction to the key figures and the early campaigns of the environmental movement.)

Mark Elvin, *The Retreat of the Elephants*, New Haven CT: Yale University Press, 2004. (An exhaustive, scholarly and highly readable environmental history of China, covering around 4,000 years of development and environmental degradation.)

Ma Jun, *China's Water Crisis*, Hong Kong: Pacific Century Press, 2003. (First published in 1999, Ma Jun's book is often compared to Rachel Carson's *Silent Spring*, as the country's first major book drawing public attention to the environmental crisis.)

Katherine Morton, *International Aid and China's Environment: Taming the Yellow Dragon*, London: Routledge, 2012. (An analysis of the relationship between international and local responses to environmental problems in China.)

Judith Shapiro, *Mao's War Against Nature: Politics and the Environment in Revolutionary China*, Cambridge: Cambridge University Press, 2001. (Compelling exploration of the disastrous environmental policies of Mao-era China, an important backdrop to the problems and campaigns of today.)

CHAPTER 1

China's environmental journalists:
a rainbow confusion

SAM GEALL

> There are fish like
> snake-fish and trout, perch and tench,
> red-eye and yellow-gill, dace and carp,
> bream, sturgeon, skate, mandarin-fish,
> flying-fish, bass, mullet and wax-fish:
> a rainbow confusion of colours blurred,
> glistening brocade, cloud-fresh schools
> nibbling duckweed, frolicking in waves,
> drifting among ghost-eye, flowing deep.
>
> Xie Lingyun (trans. David Hinton)[1]

These lines are from 'Dwelling in the Mountains', described as the first environmental poem in Chinese. Its fifth-century author, Xie Lingyun, puzzled over and catalogued myriad species in the waters of eastern China, with what historian Mark Elvin called 'a flicker of proto-Darwinian insight',[2] almost as biologists would centuries later.

In early 2010, some two centuries after Charles Darwin's birth, my interest in Xie's heirs – the environmental writers of contemporary China – first led me to an unassuming, squat grey building by the 4th Ring Road in north-western Beijing. This is home to an ambitious non-governmental group known in Chinese as 'Darwin

Nature University'. In English, the organisation goes by the name Green Beagle, referring to HMS *Beagle*, the sloop-of-war on which the great naturalist sailed.

Green Beagle brings together amateur naturalists, students, journalists and environmental activists for walks, talks and free-ranging discussions on topics from wildlife photography to grasslands preservation and the deterioration of Beijing's waterways. In the spirit of Darwin himself, whose prolific letter-writing meant that he could marshal amateur enthusiasm to effectively 'crowd-source' scientific evidence for natural selection from a great many volunteers, the NGO uses 'citizen science' to support popular participation in environmental protection across Beijing.

When a public controversy erupted at the end of 2011 about the yawning gulf between Beijing's official and unofficial air-pollution statistics (see Chapter 2), it was Green Beagle that helped organise the capital's residents to use home-testing kits and post their own air-quality readings online.

Green Beagle is the vision of Feng Yongfeng, one of China's best-known environmental journalists, who has gone to considerable lengths to shine a light into China's waters, even if what he overwhelmingly finds today is not, like Xie Lingyun, a 'rainbow confusion' of bright-hued fish, but pollution – and the murk of censorship and obfuscation.

Feng is a campaigning journalist affiliated to *Guangming Daily*, an influential state-owned newspaper traditionally associated with China's intellectuals and the country's registered minority parties. (The People's Republic technically has a multi-party government, which allows eight parties to exist under the political control of the Communist Party. These include the Revolutionary Committee of the Kuomintang, the Jiusan Society and the China Democratic League – not to be confused with banned parties such as the Democracy Party of China.)

This is not entirely unusual: China's growing citizen environmental movement has emerged with its changing media environment.

A great many of China's most prominent ecological campaigners – the first generation of Chinese environmentalists in the reform era – were also the first investigative journalists to operate in that more open media environment.

Liu Detian, a journalist at *Panjin Daily News*, founded China's first legal environmental NGO in 1991, dedicated to protecting the black-beaked gulls of north-eastern China. Liao Xiaoyi, who founded Global Village of Beijing in 1996, is a journalist and documentary-maker. Ma Jun, director of the data-focused Beijing-based NGO the Institute of Public and Environmental Affairs and winner of the 2012 Goldman Environmental Prize, started his career as an investigative reporter at the *South China Morning Post*. Wang Yongchen, who founded Green Earth Volunteers – one of China's biggest environmental NGOs and an influential force in the movements against dam-building in China's south-west (see Chapters 2 and 5) – was a radio broadcaster. The list goes on.

However, Green Beagle also actively encourages ordinary people to write about their environment – the group runs regular 'citizen journalism' training workshops, for example – and this helps to demonstrate the link between China's more open media environment and its growing citizen environmental consciousness.

Feng has a long-standing interest in how China's deteriorating environment is understood by ordinary people around the country. In his writing, he has championed the cases of local citizens engaging with their environments, such as Liu Zhenxiang, a 48-year-old taxi driver who came up with his own solution for Beijing's chronic drought. In 2007, when the Beijing Environmental Protection Bureau called for public suggestions on creating a green Olympic Games the following year, Liu submitted an article – 28,000 characters long, equivalent to around 14,000 words – titled 'Drought in Northern China: Its Causes and Solutions'. Feng wrote in *chinadialogue* that Liu's essay had identified the origins of the drought as being a vicious cycle: decreasing precipitation, declining groundwater, less evaporation and continuing drought across the region.[3] Liu proposed a three-step solution: a programme of reforestation; letting water out of reservoirs to boost groundwater reserves; and storing water in wetlands, marshes, ponds and pools across the farmland around Beijing.

The cabbie told Feng that he saw the land 'as a person', with the rivers 'as blood vessels', and pools that 'keep the blood circulating'. Beijing was massively overexploiting its groundwater. In the suburb of Shunyi, said Liu, residents had to dig wells 70 metres deep before they saw any water. 'If my water storage plan were put into action,' he continued, 'we could stop these plummeting groundwater levels.' But Liu Zhenxiang's plan was never adopted – and Beijing's water troubles have continued beyond the Olympics.

Feng also helped to bring to public attention the efforts of Liu Futang – 65 years old, no relation to Liu Zhenxiang – who more recently took to using his Sina Weibo account (a Chinese equivalent of Twitter, which is blocked by the nationwide internet censorship system popularly known as the 'Great Firewall') to expose environmental destruction in the island province of Hainan, in the South China Sea.

Liu Futang is a retired forestry official who had once piloted fire-spotting planes in north-eastern China. Liu only started his microblog upon retirement in 2011. He had become concerned about the environmental and social impacts of the island's transformation into a playground for elite tourists from overseas. (The island is famous for its beaches, and perhaps best known for the Boao Forum for Asia, an international gathering of business and government leaders modelled on the World Economic Forum at Davos.)

The development of Hainan island meant that farmers were resettled and fields and bays were ruined. So when Liu discovered that a state-owned property developer planned to build a marina on the south-eastern coast which would destroy a mangrove forest of nipa palms, an important element of the coastal ecological balance, he became worried. Not a word about the planned marina project had appeared in the local media. So, using the handle 'Hainan Liu Futang', Liu started microblogging about the proposal. The story soon went viral: the day after Liu first posted about the story, a reporter from Beijing had arrived in Hainan to speak to him. Soon, Liu had given nearly a hundred interviews. When government officials came to speak with Liu about the controversy, he posted their conversations online.

In the end, Liu's campaign didn't save the mangrove forest, though subsequent developments in the region were stalled. But in spring 2012, Liu used his microblog to voice criticism of the proposed construction of a coal-fired power station on the southwestern tip of the island. In March and April, thousands of people demonstrated against the plans, and Liu was there to microblog their progress. Significantly, Liu included some of this online commentary in a book, which he published at his own expense. Feng wrote that Liu and other citizen journalists 'embody the environmental responsibilities of the citizen and demonstrate that today it is becoming easier for anyone to protect the environment'.[4]

On 5 December 2012, the Longhua District People's Court in Hainan found Liu Futang guilty of 'illegal business activities'. The court imposed a 17,000-yuan (around US$2,727) fine and a three-year prison sentence, which was suspended. His crime? Privately printing, giving away and selling a number of books, based on his blogs, about his local environmental protection efforts.

To really understand the role that citizens can play in defending China's natural world, we will need to consider this changing media landscape, and its ability, or not, to respond to important environmental issues and scientific debates. In this chapter, I will introduce some of China's most pioneering journalists – including some of the authors that appear in this book and have appeared in *chinadialogue* over the past years – and how they report often complex and politically sensitive environmental issues. I will explore some of the contours, the limits, the obstacles and the institutions that shape reporting about environmental issues in China, and ask what this might tell us about the country's changing society and government.

BOX 1.1   A tale of resistance in Sichuan

In 2011, concerned locals formed a grassroots movement to protect forests in Sichuan province, in western China, from destruction. FENG YONGFENG reported from Dege county, in the Kardze Tibetan Autonomous Prefecture west of the province, for *chinadialogue*. What follows is an extract from one of his despatches.

Dawa Zhuoma always looks forward to getting home to the area known as Maisu in Sichuan's Dege county and the large forest that will welcome her there. She collects folk songs and knows that, without the trees, those songs would never have been sung – the music is like the river flowing through the forest: it needs to be protected and nurtured by the trees.

But on a trip home several months ago, Dawa was first shocked and then angered by what she found: the forest she had been looking forward to seeing appeared to have moved, and the roadside was littered with felled trees. A chainsaw can cut down centuries-old spruce and fir in mere seconds – and chop it up into pieces in minutes.

And then the trucks started passing. Each of these enormous vehicles can carry many trees. It takes about an hour to completely fill one, after which it drives its load away to an area with a timber shortage, where it is used to build houses and make furniture.

The other villagers were just as shocked as Dawa. In early 2010, teams of workers – who seemed more like bandits to the locals – turned up in the valley and started to fell, chop up and transport trees. This has continued ever since.

Dege's trees grow on steep, unstable mountainsides. Once the trees are felled, areas of mountainside slump into the river like a wounded man, blocking roads and becoming a potential cause of disasters such as mudslides and flash floods.

One day in June last year, the people of Maisu decided they weren't going to stand for it any longer: they stormed the camps, sabotaged the chainsaws and chased away the loggers, putting an end to the felling.

Then they built a simple hut at the entrance to the forest and erected a crude roadblock: this was the villagers' timber checkpoint. The Maisu area is made up of three villages – Puma, Dama and Yueba – and each village sends three people a day to man the checkpoint. Without their say-so, no one can remove a single tree; nor can the trucks get in. In the year since they set up this system, the villagers have stuck to their guns: 'No trees will be taken, even if I have to die', said one.

The media environment

One of the factors that has transformed Chinese society over the past three decades has been a great increase in access to information. In turn, this has helped to transform attitudes to China's environment and the problems it faces.

In the Mao era, information was heavily controlled by the state and great catastrophes occurred without being reported in the national media. In August 1975, the worst dam failure in world history occurred in Henan province, after a typhoon hit the south-eastern province of Fujian and gathered strength as it twisted and turned up through China's central plains. The 25-metre-high Banqiao Reservoir Dam collapsed, triggering the failure of a second dam and a cascade of destruction that wiped out entire villages. Survivors recalled the bursting dam sounding like the sky collapsing. Houses and trees disappeared in an instant as human and animal corpses floated to the surface of the floodwaters.

The terrible death toll remained a state secret until 2005. Records now state that 26,000 people died from flooding and a further 145,000 people died in the epidemic disease and famine that then blighted the region. But even three decades later, the state newspaper *People's Daily* wrote euphemistically of a disaster that had 'long been ignored', rather than concealed.[5]

Until the 1990s, all newspapers were subsidised by the government, either as official publications of the Party or specialised papers affiliated to mass organisations. However, following the authorisation of advertising in newspapers in 1979, non-Party papers started to gain in importance. Local papers started punching above their weight. Government-run newspapers began to spawn so-called 'child' papers as moneymakers. Some became known for their reporting about anywhere except their home province. Media outlets multiplied rapidly – and, crucially, they increasingly competed for audiences by covering issues of public concern.

Environmental reporting grew to become an important and dynamic part of the media landscape. Coverage of Green issues in Chinese newspapers grew steadily through the 1990s[6] and accelerated through the following decade. Around 2007, coverage of climate change exploded after the publication of the Fourth Assessment Report by the Intergovernmental Panel on Climate Change – a major global report that underscored the scientific consensus on global warming.[7]

In the past few years, many Chinese newspapers have launched environment sections. Most popular websites, portals and online messaging services now have Green channels. Many of the more independent publications in China – including *Caijing*, *New Century Weekly*, *Economic Observer* and *Southern Weekend* – have become known for their hard-hitting reports on environmental issues. Since these stories are seen as less politically sensitive than, for example, stories directly concerned with rights and governance, articles about sustainability-related topics have increasingly been used as vehicles for addressing social issues, from institutional corruption to the lack of transparency or public participation in policymaking.

Liu Jianqiang, one of China's best-known environmental journalists and a contributor to this volume (see Chapter 5), said about this phenomenon in a 2010 interview: 'The environment in China is not politics; politics is very sensitive. Journalists do find it easier to report about the environment.' He continued: 'my question has always been who is really harming China's environment? It's not you, me or the common people. It's the huge interest groups out there. From local governments to companies and corporations, there are huge stakes in maximizing profit.[8]

Control, change and confusion

Qian Gang, former managing editor at the liberal Guangzhou-based newspaper *Southern Weekend* and an academic at Hong Kong University, has described the contemporary Chinese media as characterised by three 'C's: control, change and chaos. His colleague David Bandurski suggests an alternative variation for the last characteristic: confusion.[9] However you choose to render it, any survey of environmental reporting in China is likely to turn up all of the Cs.

First is control. To see evidence of that paradigm, one can look to the continuance of periodic media blackouts around environmental incidents. For example, consider in late 2009, when *chinadialogue* tried to conduct an investigation in the city of Dongguan, a manufacturing hub in southern China's Pearl River Delta – which is reported to have high rates of occupational and pollution-related diseases. The researchers were continually rebuffed. Time and again, requests for interviews were refused; the environmental protection bureau, the local hospital, oncologists and environmental scientists all remained tight-lipped; even the proceedings of public academic conferences on environmental medicine were said to be confidential. One soil expert who agreed to an interview had to consult government officials first, who told him not to make any data available to the researchers.[10]

Or consider the nine days in July 2010, when the Zijin Mining Company managed to suppress media reports about a massive leak from one of its copper mines into the Ting River in Fujian province. The leak caused the death of more than 1,500 tonnes of fish. A month after the disaster (1 September 2010), villagers told the *Southern Metropolis Daily* that they used to catch turtles, grouper, beard fish and eels in the river. Now it was mostly dead, and eating what you caught was said to be 'as dangerous as taking poison'.

On 21 June 2011, users of the microblogging service Sina Weibo read this short post: 'Two wells at a Bohai oil field have been leaking for two days. I hope the leaks are controlled and pollution prevented.' Censors worked fast to delete the original post, but it spread even faster. It was likely written by a whistle-blower at China National Offshore Oil Corp (CNOOC), the state-owned Chinese company that forms half of a joint venture with ConocoPhillips at an oilfield in the Bohai Sea, off China's north-eastern coast. It turned out to have been true. In the end, the size of the oil sheen officially reached about 2,500 barrels, polluting around 4,250 square kilometres of sea. However, the State Oceanic Administration did not confirm the leak until an entire month later. Later that same summer, nearby in the north-eastern coastal city of Dalian, residents took to the streets to oppose a planned paraxylene (PX) factory (see Chapter 4). Microblog posts containing slogans and pictures of the protests were quickly scrubbed from the Internet. Censors filtered the word 'stroll' (*sanbu*), which was employed by activists to describe the demonstrations.

Asked what the greatest obstacle is to reporting climate change in China, one journalist told me: 'Information is not transparent enough. The government contacts the media only when the government needs to express something in the media, but the government rarely grants interview requests – and officials often just speak in official language' (Beijing, 23 June 2010). So, traditional forms of media control still exist. But what about the second C: change?

Here I have already begun to outline one set of changes: the increasing commercialisation and diversification of the media industry in China. The huge growth of online media has another important factor – although print publishing is far from dead in China – since the Internet allows far more news and information to proliferate across regions, often faster than the censors can catch up. China now has more than 500 million Internet users. Its most popular microblogging platform, Sina Weibo, boasts more than 300 million users and has transformed the media landscape. Despite an elaborate censorship apparatus that filters politically sensitive terms, the political conversations on Weibo are lively; users find ingenious methods to get around censorship, using humorous and elaborate code-words, images and by substituting sensitive characters for sound-alikes; and journalists find numerous tips and leads online.

The Internet also means access to translated materials from around the world on global environmental challenges. Some of *chinadialogue*'s most-read articles have not been about China's environmental problems, but stories from elsewhere: about the introduction of the Clean Air Act in the United Kingdom, water issues in America, or dam failures in Italy. A shared and plural world-view has become palatable: the narrow orthodoxy that once suggested China's situation could only be properly understood from the vantage point of the central government in Beijing has been largely discredited. For example, communities of volunteers using crowd-sourced translations regularly upload online a Chinese edition of the British weekly *The Economist*, complete with picture captions. World news is consumed and debated voraciously across the online social networks.

These innovations pose new challenges for media control, so it's not surprising that the government is keen to get in on the act, too. At all levels, the authorities have increasingly attempted to use social media, not only as a gauge of public opinion, but also as a way to try to influence it, leading to a situation that Internet-freedom expert Rebecca MacKinnon has described as 'networked authoritarianism'.[11]

Finally, the rise of journalism as a professional aspiration for young people – many of whom do not view it as an official propaganda role, as in previous generations – has significantly affected China's media landscape. But professionalism can take different forms. In a 2011 article in *China Quarterly*, the political scientist Jonathan Hassid identified four different 'ideal-types' for professional journalists in contemporary China.[12]

The first group he described were the 'American-style profession-als': journalists who aspire to represent 'objective facts' and 'balanced opinions'. One report cited by Hassid said that younger reporters were more professional than older ones because they had more formal training and were 'more influenced by America'. Presenting an article as being 'nothing but the facts' can sometimes be a powerful way of carrying out watchdog journalism – but there is also, Hassid noted, a tendency towards 'political passivity' among these reporters.

The second are the so-called 'throat and tongue' of the Chinese Communist Party. These 'communist professionals' might aspire to the same notions of journalism-as-propaganda that were enforced more rigidly in the Mao era, but they are not relics of a bygone age, as a brief look through an official media organ like *People's Daily* quickly reveals. For example, around the time of the Copenhagen climate-change conference, China's state media went into overdrive extolling the Chinese leadership's role in climate-change diplo-macy. Wrote one newspaper: 'In the days leading up to his flight to Copenhagen, Premier Wen Jiabao has been on a marathon run of telephone diplomacy with major global leaders, a key indicator that the nation is vigorously pushing for a climate change treaty at the United Nations conference.'[13]

The third are the 'workaday journalists': the reporter who will do almost anything for the right price. Corruption among journalists in China is widespread, from payments or bribes in the form of 'car fares' and 'red envelopes' – companies and local governments underwriting reporters' travel, and throwing in a cash-stuffed enve-lope for good measure – to cases of outright blackmail. For example, one broadcast journalist at a Beijing television station – ironically, working for a programme called *Transparency* – was exposed in 2007 for faking a story about cardboard being included as a meat substitute in steamed buns, a popular street snack. The reporter had in fact hired four migrant workers to make the buns – supposedly three parts caustic soda-soaked cardboard to two parts meat – and filmed them. It is notable that some of China's most independent and daring publications, such as the business magazine *Caijing* – founded by investigative journalist Hu Shuli, now the editor of *New Century Weekly* – are the only outlets to enforce a strict code of ethics for their journalists, including refusing the red envelopes.

Finally, and most significantly in this chapter, is the fourth type of journalist – the writer like Feng. Hassid called them the 'advocate professionals', and their aim is to advance a social, ideological or economic viewpoint in their stories; to push the envelope and explore the boundaries of China's public sphere. It is this last type I have mainly found represented among Chinese environmental journalists. Yet rather than advocating a specifically environmentalist or Green ideology – reporters' views on climate change and the environment often differ a great deal – the commitment I most often found among Chinese environmental reporters was to the ideals of transparency, openness and public participation.

Perhaps it is these sorts of advocate professionals that can survive best among the last C: chaos or confusion; for, as Bandurski said, confusion 'actually represents an opportunity, as enterprising professional journalists can exploit the gaps in this complex environment and push coverage further than the authorities might formally allow'. One vivid metaphor for those strategies used by savvy journalists to navigate this often dangerous and perplexing media environment is the 'edge ball'. It is attributed to Qin Benli, then editor of *World Economic Herald*, a Shanghai-based newspaper that was a key source of information and support for Chinese democracy protesters in 1989. In an interview, Qin said: 'It's like playing ping-pong. If you hit the ball and miss the end of the table, you lose. If you hit the near end of the table, it's too easy. So you want to aim to just nick the end of the table. That's our policy.'[14]

Hidden faces

However, it would also be a mistake to assume that investigative Chinese journalism started with the reform era – or, as some have suggested, that it has only arisen thanks to openings created by the central government. The life and work of Liu Binyan, one of China's most important journalists, presents some interesting parallels with today's environmental writers.

Liu Binyan was born in 1925 and joined the Communist Party underground in 1943, before Mao Zedong came to power. After the revolution in 1949, Liu worked as a reporter and editor for the state-controlled *China Youth Daily* – still an influential newspaper today. Many years later, in an interview with the writer Perry Link, Liu said that he found this work 'fairly unappealing'. 'There was lots of recording of the words of the leaders and mechanical passing of them down to the readers.'[15]

Liu tired of working as the 'throat and tongue' of the CCP. As his reportage strayed into pioneering criticisms of censorship and corruption under the communist regime, journalists and editors initially praised his daring. By 1957, however, Liu had been labelled a 'rightist' during Mao's notorious first crackdown on critical intellectuals, the Anti-Rightist Campaign – an act of brutal suppression that came on the heels of the supposed liberalisation of the 'Hundred Flowers' movement. He was expelled from the Party and sent down to the countryside for 're-education'.

Soon after the end of the Cultural Revolution – and after a period of rehabilitation followed by eight years spent in a detention camp through much of the 1970s – Liu Binyan delivered a talk, on 9 November 1979, at the Fourth Congress of Chinese Literature and Art Workers in Beijing, recounting a powerful tale of official and unofficial narratives, or, as he called it, two kinds of truth:

> In my own personal experience, the most unforgettable years were 1958–1960, when I shared a bed and even sometimes a quilt with poor peasants. The things I saw in the villages, and the plaints I heard from the peasants, were all vastly different from what was being spread by the authorities and the press … For example, the higher authorities told us that our impoverished gully of a village ought to build a zoo and a fountain … With no water source – with

man and beast still drinking rainwater – how were they to build a fountain? A struggle began to rage deep inside me: how could two diametrically opposed 'truths' coexist in the world?

The speech was met with rapturous applause. But nine years later, Liu was forced to leave China. He died in the United States in 2005. The writer Su Xiaokang wrote upon his death: 'Banishing him was like tearing him from the breast of China; the hardship of his survival is not adequately expressed by a pallid term such as "exile".'[16] However, Liu's ethos, which he held to even during the repression of the Maoist era – of the reporter as witness and unmasker of the truths behind official propaganda – burns bright in the work of investigative environmental writers today.

Take, for example, the case of Meng Dengke, who won a prize in 2010 at the China Environmental Press Awards for 'best investigative report'. That article centred on an obscure-sounding meeting in Guangzhou, southern China, in March 2009 called the '7th Solid Waste Advanced Salon'. The 'salon' concerned rubbish incinerators, which are often described as 'green energy' and have been supported under the 12th Five Year Plan, but are also sited in urban neighbourhoods and have been opposed by residents for health and environmental reasons across China.

For example, since 2010, Nantong resident Xie Yong has been battling the environmental authorities for access to emissions data that might provide evidence of a link between his son's cerebral palsy and toxic pollutants, including dioxins, from a nearby waste-to-energy plant. He believes that he lives in a cluster of such cases, and he is being supported in his quest by the Center for Legal Assistance for Pollution Victims. Currently only about 10 per cent of China's municipal solid waste is burned, but a central target calls for this to increase to 30 per cent by 2030, and the industry has boomed since the government offered a generous subsidy for power from incinerators.

The regulations on emissions from such plants are more lax than for conventional power plants, and the facilities often operate without running their pollution-control systems, even where these are mandated. Perhaps worst of all, the plant operators often add coal to the burning waste. According to researcher Elizabeth Balkan, in private interviews 'plant operators admitted to using a feedstock mix comprising equal parts coal and rubbish, which far exceeds the 20% coal limit mandated by the central government.' She continued: 'Under these conditions, plants are operating essentially as small coal-fired power stations – exactly the kind of facility that Beijing is trying to eliminate on public health grounds.'[17]

In Meng's article for *Southern Weekend* (3 December 2009), the links between the waste-burning industry and the pro-incineration experts who have secured government support for such schemes came under scrutiny. At the salon, the invited academics simply showed contempt for public concerns. Meng wrote that the industry experts claimed that 'the public are ignorant and obstructionist' and that 'the government should make full use of the legal system to put an end to local disruptions in the interests of the wider good, if necessary relocating residents rather than the incinerators'. It caused an uproar: Meng suggested that while this appeared to be an academic meeting, it was in fact a one-sided industry-lobbying event.

Meng told me later in a video interview (13 May 20 10), which was broadcast on the Green channel of the popular Chinese online portal *Tencent QQ*, that there were many protests about incineration in China. However, he said:

> Due to media controls, we cannot write reports in certain areas. We wanted to find another angle to write about waste incineration, therefore we opted for these experts. Why did we choose them? The reason was a public consulting conference hosted by the Guangzhou government, to which all the experts were invited. They are the 'incinerationists' mentioned in my article. After collecting more information, we found that those experts had many titles and roles... We wanted to find out their true face, the one hidden behind their 'expert' identity.

Another investigative journalist who has found novel ways to peer behind the curtain is Feng Jie, 30, from the north-western province of Ningxia. Feng won the 'Journalist of the Year' category at the 2012 China Environmental Press Awards for three stories written for *Southern Weekend*, including a series about the oil spillage and cover-up in the Bohai Sea in 2011. A year earlier, immediately after the Deepwater Horizon spill in the Gulf of Mexico, Feng wrote that the 'technological challenges of deep-sea exploration and extraction are stretching human knowledge to its limits'. Presciently, she noted that CNOOC was 'assessing risk factors in the Bohai' and quoted a technical consultant at the company, who warned that 'the Gulf of Mexico leak was a wake-up call'.[18]

Feng Jie arrived on the scene of the Bohai spill on 30 June 2011, several days after the first microblog 'rumours' of a leak had started to circulate and long before the State Oceanic Administration had confirmed the accident. Nevertheless, Feng found confirmation from insiders at the organisation – and became the first to publish in print what many on Weibo suspected. She then followed the story closely for the next six months. When a number of media reports pointed the finger at the US company ConocoPhillips, one half of the joint venture that ran the oil platform, she suggested that Chinese state-owned company CNOOC was shirking responsibility – and that the government regulators were not doing their job.

Crucially, and perhaps surprisingly, her perceived professionalism seemed to earn her the respect and trust of the regulators, and she was able to interview key SOA officials before other journalists. Feng had previously worked at the *China Economic Herald*, a heavyweight financial newspaper managed by the country's top economic planner, the National Development and Reform Commission. There, she developed the deep contacts and the know-how that would later help her. Feng reportedly went so far as to barge into an SOA department head's office. 'My editor's always asking which key people I've interviewed or what facts I've got,' she told Beijing-based journalist Liu Yuan. 'We all agree that catching the public mood is important, but you need to get as close as possible to the actual sources of information if you're going to give your readers the facts they want.'[19]

Giving the readers the facts is difficult without official transparency, but the fallout from one effort from the top – to introduce open government information laws – has produced another 'rainbow of confusion' in which enterprising journalists could begin to make some headway.

Testing the limits of openness

Being open with environmental information is not only admirable in principle. The evidence shows it is a cost-effective method for policymakers concerned about pollution control: it can harness social participation and public pressure to improve the environment, often more effectively than top-down measures, such as tightening emissions standards.

Some in the Chinese government have clearly taken this on board. After a period of policy experimentation, including local-level pilots and several years of research by the Chinese Academy of Social Sciences, an influential think-tank, the government introduced legislation in 2008 not dissimilar to the UK's Freedom of Information Act: the Regulations of the People's Republic of China on Open Government Information. Many Chinese government officials, particularly at the centre, clearly believe there are benefits to greater transparency, such as keeping tabs on local inefficiency and corruption: one official from the State Council told reporters that the regulations would 'help curb corruption at its source, largely reducing its occurrence'.[20]

But in the hands of China's grassroots environmentalists, it could also be a powerful tool to hold polluters to account. Article 1 clearly states that the purpose of the regulations is to 'ensure that citizens, legal persons and other organisations obtain government information in accordance with the law, enhance transparency of the work of government, promote administration in accordance with the law, and bring into full play the role of government information in serving the people's production and livelihood and their economic and social activities'.

The regulations, issued by China's State Council – an executive body chaired by the premier, which coordinates government ministries and helps to bind the Chinese Communist Party (CCP) with the central government, as well as, in effect, extending the regulations downward to provincial and local governments – establish two basic types of open government information. The first is that which should be proactively disseminated by government agencies at various levels – for example, on their official websites; this includes reports on 'financial budgets and final accounts'; emergency plans and early-warning information 'against sudden public events'; and information 'on the supervision and inspection of environmental protection, public health, safe production, food and drugs, and product quality'. The second is that which should be disclosed in response to requests from the public, usually free of charge (although the requester has to cover the costs of producing the information), within fifteen to thirty days.

As with similar legislation in other countries, there is a clause that stipulates the exemptions from disclosure – Article 8: 'The government information disclosed by administrative organs may not endanger state security, public security, economic security and social stability.' There is also Article 17, which states that if other laws or regulations 'have different provisions on the scope of authorisation to disclose government information, those provisions shall be followed'. This means that other laws, such as the state secrets law – which is frequently used in China, not only to keep controversial information from public view, but also as a means of silencing individuals critical of the government – can trump the regulations.

The first government department to implement the national regulations as a more specific decree was the Ministry of Environmental Protection (MEP). The result was the Environmental Information Disclosure Decree, which requires, for example, that enterprises identified as 'major industrial polluters' should disclose and report emissions data within thirty days of a request from the public. It also sets out guidelines for the proactive disclosure of seventeen types of government-held environmental information. It is on these latter measures that there has been the most progress. The website of Beijing's municipal environmental protection bureau, for example, clearly discloses these seventeen categories of information, including environmental laws, regulations, standards and administrative permits.

However, a report by free-expression campaigners Article 19 found that the Beijing bureau, despite its comprehensive website, was poor at responding to requests for information from the public. According to the report's author, Amy Sim, 'A lot of officials interpret [the regulations]: as long as it's not within the 17 types of proactive disclosure, they will not disclose.'[21] Reading the study, it's clear that more sensitive information of relevance to campaigners – for example, on the disposal and discharge of hazardous waste – is still very difficult to obtain. Alex Wang, a Chinese environmental law expert at the University of California, Berkeley, said in an interview: 'China has made great strides in environmental disclosure in recent years, but right now the types of information that are most critical to uncovering environmental problems – emissions data, records of violations, environmental impact assessment reports – are still difficult, if not impossible, for the public to obtain.'

But with these regulations in place, on what grounds is sensitive information still being withheld? Speaking at a seminar, Wang Canfa, director of Beijing's Centre for Legal Assistance to Pollution Victims, said: 'Although the regulations list 17 types of information that should be disclosed and only one short clause on exemptions, that one short clause has become a catch-all' (27 April 2011). The reference here is to Article 8, the exemption clause in the national regulations regarding national security and social stability, which also applies to the environmental decree.

Open information legislation across the world contains similar exemptions. The extent to which governments rely upon these can give a good indication of their commitment to their own openness policies. But in China the situation is a little more complicated. In an authoritarian country you might expect to see 'state security, public security, economic security and social stability' relied on frequently as grounds to refuse requests for information. But although refusals from Chinese government agencies to release information are frequent, Sim, in her study of environmental information requests, discovered that such justifications were not cited as much as other explanations that, in fact, had no legal basis whatsoever. The grounds for rejection, she found, were generally 'not very clear': many officials replied that the information was simply 'inconvenient to disclose' or that it was 'liable to be sensationalised by the media'. As with much regulation in China, the existence of the legislation – which, on the books, looks to be in line with international norms – doesn't mean that it is being effectively, consistently or accurately enforced.

The press in China has taken an active interest in the poor implementation of transparency rules. In 2009, it became headline news in the country when two journalists from the government news agency Xinhua were stopped from photographing documents listing pollution violators, information that the authorities are supposed to disclose, at a provincial government meeting in Heilongjiang, north-east China. (It was this province that was most affected in 2005, when a series of explosions at a petrochemical plant created an 80-kilometre-long toxic slick in the Songhua River. The State Environmental Protection Administration, the predecessor of the MEP, only admitted the serious pollution of the river ten days after the explosion and one day after water was cut off in the provincial capital of Harbin.) When an official told them the information was 'confidential' and the media already had 'enough' information about pollution, the reporters walked out of the meeting in protest – a gesture that earned them widespread sympathy from Chinese media commentators.

However, despite their interest in the implementation of the regulations, Chinese journalists have not made much use of the legislation itself. Surprisingly few Chinese journalists that I have interviewed in my research are aware that open information laws even exist in China. In early 2009, *Southern Weekend* published on its website an environmental impact assessment, obtained using open government information laws, which approved the construction of a controversial petrochemical plant in Fujian Province. But such cases are still rare.

In China, the pressure for open information has come not as often from the press as from civil society organisations. Friends of Nature (FON) has been campaigning since 2009 for the government to disclose information about proposed boundary changes at a protected area for rare and endangered fish species on the Yangtze River – decisions that it suspects are intended to make way for the planned Xiaonanhai Dam project, near the city of Chongqing in south-west China. The boundary change 'basically means a death sentence for these endangered species,' said Chang Cheng, a Beijing-based campaigner for FON. The species include the Chinese paddlefish and the Yangtze sturgeon, a so-called 'living fossil' that has survived for some 140 million years, since the time of the dinosaurs.

The Yangtze sturgeon has been referred to as the 'underwater panda': it is a protected species, which can measure up to 4 metres in length and reach a weight of 450 kilograms, and is regarded as a Chinese national treasure. The Upper Yangtze Rare and Endemic Fish Nature Reserve, created in the 1990s as a refuge for species threatened by the Three Gorges Dam, is its last hope for survival. The reserve also protects four species of wild carp – another population that has crashed with dam building, river pollution and increased shipping traffic – which helps to provide the genetic diversity crucial for fish farming. In an interview with the *Guardian*, environmentalist Ma Jun observed: 'Part of the problem is that unlike pandas, snub-nosed monkeys or Tibetan antelopes, most people have not heard of or seen the fish affected.'[22] Not only is he right about that, but even local memories are fading fast. In 2010, a team of conservation biologists studied the social phenomenon known as 'shifting baseline syndrome' on the Yangtze River: the loss of perspective about past ecological conditions caused by lack of communication between generations of people. The scientists found that young people along the river had begun to see degraded environmental conditions and declining catches as the norm – and even species millions of years old were being forgotten as soon as they ceased to be encountered on a regular basis.[23]

This makes attempts to write and report accurately about the species – and the threats to its remaining habitat – all the more important. Using open government information laws, FON requested a copy of the government's on-site investigation report and the declaration of the boundary change, which includes an impact assessment. But the Ministry of Agriculture refused these on the grounds that 'procedural' data is not covered by transparency legislation. Chang told me in an email: 'This is like a "Catch-22" situation for the public who wish to supervise and participate in the government's decision-making.' He has a point: if the government isn't willing to disclose how its decisions are made, and if its procedures aren't being correctly followed, it's difficult to see how freedom of information can be used to hold the government to account at any time other than after the event. Or to put it another way: it won't be much help to find out that procedures were carried out incorrectly after the Yangtze sturgeon is declared extinct. The Green group has teamed up with the China University of Political Science and Law to demand an administrative review that challenges the legality of this 'Catch-22' situation. They are still awaiting the result.

The state of open government information reflects the delicate balancing act that defines governance in China today: between pressure for greater openness and public oversight, while maintaining stability (or 'harmony', as it is known in propaganda) through high rates of economic growth, enhancing 'social management' and safeguarding the unchallenged political authority of the CCP. Yet there is a glimmer of hope in the dynamic way that some groups – and the next chapters look in greater detail at the broader growth of China's environmental movements', including NGOs', legal attempts at reform, urban and rural protests – have taken up the greater openness of government information in China.

Whether due to continued government repression – which the case of Liu Futang so vividly illustrates – or other, more subtle constraints, the press has yet to fully embrace the potential of the transparency regulations. But environmental journalism nevertheless has helped to create more environmentally aware citizens, bring light to murky back-room politics and foster a feistier, more responsive public sphere. The crowd at Green Beagle's headquarters, is young, well-informed, inquisitive – and may point a different way forward. It is perhaps a bittersweet upside to a dire environmental situation. As Feng Jie said: 'It's as if this is a golden age for China's environmental journalists. But it's not something I'm happy about.'

Notes

1. Xie Lingyun, *The Mountain Poems of Hsieh Ling-Yün*, trans. David Hinton, New York: New Directions, 2001.
2. Mark Elvin, *The Retreat of the Elephants,* New Haven and London: Yale University Press, 2004, p. 356.
3. Feng Yongfeng, 'China's Drought: A Taxi Driver's Response', *chinadialogue,* 27 July 2007.
4. Feng Yongfeng, 'Citizen Journalists in China', *chinadialogue,* 11 April 2012.
5. 'After 30 Years, Secrets, Lessons of China's Worst Dams Burst Accident Surface', *People's Daily,* 1 October 2005.
6. For a quantitative basis for this assertion, see Yang Guobin, 'Brokering Environment and Health in China: Issue Entrepreneurs of the Public Sphere', *Journal of Contemporary China*, vol. 19, no. 63, 2010, pp. 101–19.
7. See Sandy Tolan, 'Coverage of Climate Change in Chinese Media', *Human Development Report 2007*, Occasional Paper, 2007, http://tinyurl.com/6gmevvs.
8. From 'China's Environmental Movement: A Journalist's Perspective', interview with Neha Sakhuja on the website of the Asia Society, http://asiasociety.org/policy/environment/climate-change-and-energy/china%E2%80%99s-environmental-movement-journalist%E2%80%99s-perspective.
9. From 'Monitoring Changes in China's Media', interview with Bandurski by Emilie Frenkiel, *Books and Ideas*, 30 September 2011.
10. *Report on Environmental Health in the Pearl River Delta,* EU–China Civil Society Forum, www.eu-china.net/web/cms/upload/pdf/materialien/11–06–09_2011_06_09_chinadialogue_environmental_health.pdf.
11. Rebecca MacKinnon, *The Consent of the Networked*, New York: Basic Books, 2012.

12. Jonathan Hassid, 'Four Models of the Fourth Estate: A Typology of Contemporary Chinese Journalists', *China Quarterly* 208, 2011, pp. 813-32.

13. Fu Jing and Cheng Guangjing, 'Wen on Whirlwind Phone Diplomacy for Climate Change', *China Daily*, 14 December 2009.

14. Emilie Frenkiel. 'Monitoring Changes in China's Media', *Books and Ideas*, 30 September 2011; Nicholas D. Kristof, 'Shanghai Journal: At the Cutting Edge of China's New Journalism', *New York Times*, 16 January 1989.

15. Liu Binyan and Perry Link, *Two Kinds of Truth*, Bloomington: Indiana University Press, 2006.

16. Su Xiaokang, 'Unnatural Exile: In Memory of Liu Binyan', *China Rights Forum* 1, 2006, p. 59.

17. Elizabeth Balkan, 'The Dirty Truth about China's Incinerators', *chinadialogue*, 4 July 2012.

18. Feng Jie, *Southern Weekend*, 8 July, 2010; republished as 'Dangers of the Deep' in *chinadialogue*.

19. Liu Yuan, 'Delving behind the Headlines', *chinadialogue*, 12 April 2012.

20. An earlier version of this section appeared as Sam Geall, 'Data Trap', *Index on Censorship*, vol. 40, no. 4, December 2011, pp. 48-58.

21. *Access to Environmental Information in China: Evaluation of Local Compliance*, London: Article 19, December 2010.

22. Jonathan Watts, 'Last Refuge of Rare Fish Threatened by Yangtze Dam Plans', *Guardian*, 18 January 2011.

23. S.T. Turvey et al., 'Rapidly Shifting Baselines in Yangtze Fishing Communities and Local Memory of Extinct Species', *Conservation Biology*, vol. 24, no. 3, 2010, pp. 778-87.

Further reading

David Bandurski and Martin Hala, *Investigative Journalism in China*, Hong Kong University Press, 2010. (Insider accounts from reporters who covered some of China's biggest investigative stories.)

Sam Geall, 'Climate-change Journalism in China: Opportunities for International Cooperation', *chinadialogue*, Caixin and International Media Support, 2011, http://tinyurl.com/climatechina. (Based on interviews with Chinese journalists, explores how climate change is covered in China's media.)

Liu Binyan and Perry Link, *Two Kinds of Truth*, Bloomington: Indiana University Press, 2006. (Essays and an in-depth interview with Liu, the pioneer of Chinese reportage.)

Susan Shirk, ed., *Changing Media, Changing China*, Oxford: Oxford University Press, 2011. (Surveys China's emerging public sphere.)

Yang Guobin, 'Brokering Environment and Health in China: Issue Entrepreneurs of the Public Sphere', *Journal of Contemporary China*, vol. 19, no. 63, 2010, pp. 101-19. (Explores how public controversies are created.)

CHAPTER 2

The birth of Chinese environmentalism:
key campaigns

OLIVIA BOYD

At the crack of dawn one winter morning in Beijing, Meng Si woke
to a disturbance in her flat. Investigating its source, the 25-year-old
journalist found her boyfriend at his computer, wide-eyed, ordering
face masks online. 'He was panicking,' she later told me. 'There was
so much information circulating about PM2.5 and he realised that
the air pollution problem affects him as well.'

He was not alone. This was December 2011, and an extraordinary
citizen-led campaign over urban air pollution in China – played
out largely on the country's microblogs – was reaching its apex.
A particularly toxic few weeks in the capital had seen aeroplanes
grounded, roads closed and air-purifier sales soar, as thick smog
descended, obscuring all but the lowest of buildings.

Frightening statistics about the health effects were also making
the headlines: the English-language newspaper *China Daily* reported
that lung cancer cases in Beijing had increased by 60 per cent in
the past decade. People were afraid and angry – and they funnelled
those emotions into an online protest on an enormous scale. Millions
of urbanites took to blogging platforms to express outrage at the
environmental conditions of their cities.

It was not just the severity of the pollution that prompted the uproar. The outpouring was also a sign of how paper thin the public patience with fudged government statistics – which excluded data on key pollutants and painted a determinedly rosy picture of Chinese urban air quality – had worn.

Every year since 1998, when public reporting on air quality began, the Beijing government claimed to have increased the number of 'blue sky days'. This metric was based on the city's air pollution index, produced by monitoring coarse particulates (PM10), sulphur dioxide and nitrogen oxide. Anything below 100 on that index was classed as a 'blue sky day'. In 2009, the number was 285; the following year it climbed to 286.

It was a poor choice of labels. As Beijingers were effectively told day after day that the grey haze outside their windows was in fact a totally different colour, anger began to build. 'People can feel that the air is bad, and see that the sky isn't blue,' said Meng Si. 'When you see that gap, it's easy to feel disgusted that the government is treating us like idiots.'

Alternative data streams contributed to the growing mistrust. In February 2011, for example, two young Beijingers, Lu Weiwei and Fan Tao, shared the results of their year-long visual diary, suggesting the capital had seen just 180 genuine blue sky days between 2009 and 2010, 100 fewer than the official assessment. People began to complain about having been 'blue-skied' – an echo of the popular slang for having one's online postings censored, being 'harmonised'.

Then the Americans got involved, thanks to the Twitter feed releasing hourly data on fine particulates (PM2.5) from an independent air-quality monitor atop the US embassy. PM2.5 – at that time excluded from official data sets – is shorthand for particulate matter measuring 2.5 microns or less in diameter, a pollutant small enough to enter human blood and lung tissue that can cause asthma, heart disease and cancer. Set up initially to provide information to embassy staff, the feed sent out raw measurements along with explainers like 'unhealthy', 'very unhealthy' and, once, famously, 'crazy bad' (the last one an accident, the embassy said).

Towards the end of 2011, Beijing-based consultant Steven Q. Andrews analysed the US embassy data, producing a damning comparison with official statistics: over 80 per cent of days in Beijing had unhealthy levels of pollution, and the air quality was hazardous more often than good. In the analysis, which was published on *chinadialogue*, Andrews concluded that the city authorities had artificially deflated air pollution statistics by adding new stations in the city's cleaner suburbs.

The revelations were explosive. Not only did people finally have access to PM2.5 data, albeit limited to one small section of Beijing, but they could see stark discrepancies between the portrait of air quality painted by a foreign embassy and their own government. Once a technical term, 'PM2.5' – like 'PX' before it (see Chapter 4) – became an unlikely rallying point for citizens calling for greater official honesty and openness.

'We firmly demand that Beijing's environmental protection administration starts publishing PM 2.5 levels in 2012! Otherwise provide all Beijingers, including the transient population, with gas masks!' wrote one NGO worker, Guo Xia.[1] An online poll started by the well-known property developer Pan Shiyi saw tens of thousands call for the government to release more accurate measurements.

Their calls were heard. By January 2012, Beijing had started to release trial PM2.5 data from one monitoring station in an area called Chegongzhuang. Then, in March, the State Council – China's highest administrative body – announced revised national air quality rules following a meeting chaired by premier Wen Jiabao. As well as mandatory PM2.5 and ozone measurements, standards would be tightened to be more in line with World Health Organization levels. The new regime would come into force in Beijing, 27 provincial capitals and 3 key industrial regions in 2012, followed by 113 cities in 2013 and most other cities by 2015. Meanwhile, Beijing's environmental authorities quietly dropped the term 'blue sky day' from their updates.

It was a big result, and one with potentially far-reaching implications for public participation in environmental governance in China. The voice of an angry citizenry had reached the highest levels of government and triggered concrete changes in national pollution policy. It was a result hailed by environmentalists as a 'milestone' for public participation in environmental governance.

China's leading voice on transparency, Ma Jun, whose NGO the Institute of Public and Environmental Affairs (IPE) runs a pioneering project to map water and air pollution violations in China, called it a 'huge step'. Perhaps more surprisingly, the authoritarian government also acknowledged the role of public pressure. Announcing the new regulations, state news agency Xinhua praised the 'stirring campaign' played out on social networks, which had gained a 'satisfying response' from policymakers.

The 'PM2.5 campaign' was one of the clearest examples yet of public participation in environmental decision-making in China. But there are many other cases of citizen attempts to engage in and campaign on the country's environmental crises: from protection of the Tibetan antelope on the high plateau, to crusades against dam-building in south-west China, NGOs, volunteers and concerned citizens have shown their commitment to the environment over the past two decades. Sometimes they have triumphed, sometimes achieved mixed results and sometimes experienced bitter failure.

This chapter will look at the key campaigns that have characterised two decades of environmental activism and volunteerism in China; campaigns that set the conditions for the air-quality data triumph of 2012; and, perhaps, as many hope, a brighter future for public environmental supervision.

What might the emergence of a more vibrant 'civil society' signify for ordinary Chinese people? And what, indeed, does 'civil society' even mean in this case? The traditional understanding of the term as a sphere separate from government and business will only take you so far in analysing China's recent campaigning history. While Green activism has been non-governmental in the sense it has been led by and involved large numbers of people working outside of government institutions, state actors have also been closely bound up in the story. In many, if not most, cases, the 'citizen voice' would not have been heard without the support, sanction or direct participation of individuals in government. Business figures too are increasingly playing a role.

Perhaps, then, 'civil society' in China, rather than being defined exclusively by its membership, is better seen as a space where multiple actors hold a conversation about the kind of community – be it local or national – that they want to live in. That space began to open up after the reforms of the late 1970s and early 1980s slowly started to roll back the extent of state control, and environmental protection was one of the earliest movements to be supported by it.

Since then, this space has evolved and enlarged, and helped to shape the modern Chinese experience. As it has grown, a number of different actors have piled in: from local activists concerned about particular issues that affect them directly (so-called 'nimbys', from 'not in my backyard'), to increasingly professionalised campaigners who establish NGOs, as well as journalists, academics and businesspeople. What it means to be a Chinese citizen is changing – and the environment is closely bound up in that story.

The Green NGOs that started to appear in China in the mid-1990s – and proliferated in the 2000s – have played a pivotal role in building a sphere that, given its authoritarian context, enjoys relative leeway from the state. Environmentalists have not only largely escaped the repression that faces China's human-rights campaigners, for example, but also have managed to exert a certain level of influence over government policymaking. Since for more than four decades, the Chinese Communist Party had demonstrated near zero tolerance of alternative spheres of influence, it is no exaggeration to say this marked a significant shake-up.

By 2008, China had 3,539 environmental NGOs, according to the All-China Environment Federation (which includes Taiwan in these figures), involving around 300,000 people. These comprised

1,309 government-sponsored outfits (also known as 'government-organised non-governmental organisations', or GONGOs), 1,382 school environment societies, 508 grassroots organisations and 90 branches of international groups, as well as 250 NGOs in Hong Kong, Macao and Taiwan.

The first independent NGO to win official recognition was a small bird-conservation group called the Society for Protecting Black-Beaked Gulls, which registered on 18 April 1991, in Panjin city, in the north-eastern province of Liaoning.[2] However, it is the larger, Beijing-based organisation Friends of Nature (about which Isabel Hilton has written in the Introduction) which is normally credited as the environmental movement's significant pioneer. By 2000, it had 1,000 individual members and 3,000 corporate members. Picking up the Ramon Magsaysay Award – an Asian public service prize – that year, founder Liang Congjie was praised for addressing sensitive issues without alienating the government. Liang agreed with the analysis. 'The Chinese government has found in us an ally', he said in his acceptance speech. In styling itself as a friend of the centre, Friends of Nature displayed a formula that would be crucial to the expansion of China's Green civil space: in a country marked by poor local enforcement of central policies and laws – sometimes exemplary on paper – NGOs offered help to top officials trying to turn their edicts into reality.

Would-be activists were further galvanised by the Fourth UN Conference on Women in Beijing in 1995, where they got to see first-hand the advocacy of international NGOs. As Korean sinologist Namju Lee has written, Beijing's primary motivation in hosting the conference had been to boost its international influence, but 'the criticism that the international NGOs lodged against the Chinese government policies, such as its coercive birth control programme, drew far more attention than any of the conference's other events.'[3] In short, the Chinese participants saw established civil-society players from other countries at work.[4] Some of China's best-known Green organisations were launched in the summit's wake, including Global

Village Beijing, in 1995, and the Center for Legal Assistance to Pollution Victims, in 1998.

The following decade saw rapid growth of the sector and a shift in emphasis, particularly in the wake of a groundbreaking campaign against dam construction in the Nu Valley, south-west China. Civil rights and government transparency appeared on the agenda. The launch in 2000 of China's Western Development Strategy – a campaign to modernise the country's impoverished western regions (including the autonomous regions of Tibet and Xinjiang) – also triggered the creation of a new wave of organisations concerned with the ecological and social fallout of rapid development.

In eighteen short years, independent environmental organisations have gone from near non-existence to numbering in their thousands. Despite numerous setbacks, many campaigns have contributed to a complex and fast-evolving environmental sector that has won some significant victories.

Conservation battles

Today, China's environmental movement is broad in its subject matter. Pollution campaigns – like the one outlined above – are just one element in an activist world which lobbies on everything from climate change, desertification and water depletion to corporate responsibility, environmental health and dam building, and much more in between. But the list wasn't always so long. As China's earliest Green activists felt their way in the brave new world of the mid-1990s, certain topics were identified as relatively safe, and others too risky to touch. Conservation was in the first category. It became the mainstay of the early campaigning, and has remained one of the core themes of Chinese environmentalism.

One of the longest-running battles has taken place in the high mountains of Yunnan, on the border with Tibet, where a small monkey with a distinctive face has been fighting for survival. The black snub-nosed monkey – so-called because of its stumpy nose, with nostrils facing forward – feeds on lichen in the high-altitude forests of this part of south-west China. Deforestation has destroyed swathes of its natural habitat, and poaching further devastated numbers: fewer than 1,000 adults remained in 2008, according to the IUCN red list of threatened species, marking an estimated decline of well over 20 per cent in twenty-five years.

But if officials in the Baima Snow Mountain Nature Reserve are to be believed, numbers are now slowly recovering – creeping up by thirty to forty annually, and gradually bringing the species back from the brink of extinction. That the snub-nosed monkey has survived its brush with oblivion at all is in large part thanks to a small group of individuals who brought its plight to the attention of the nation some sixteen years ago.

The animal's significance stretches far beyond the borders of its south-west Chinese home. Together with the Tibetan antelope, the snub-nosed monkey has become one of the key symbols of a domestic conservation movement that grew its wings in the late 1990s, and helped lay the groundwork for a nationwide environmental charge. The story of these two famous animals in China has already been well told by many commentators, including Elizabeth Economy in her book *The River Runs Black* and Yanfei Sun and Dingxin Zhao's chapter in *Popular Protest in China*, edited by Kevin J. O'Brien. These two volumes provide much of the detail here. But no account of the growth of Chinese civil society would be complete without a description of these seminal campaigns.

It started with a nature photographer. In the early 1990s, Xi Zhinong – then in the employ of the Yunnan Forestry Department – made six visits to Deqin county to track and film the elusive snub-nosed monkey, joining a Chinese professor and US zoologist who were surveying the monkey populations in the mountains on the edge of the Tibetan plateau. In 1992, Xi became the first person to capture the species on film in the wild. Six years later, he explained his passion to *China Daily*: 'Although Yunnan ... is hailed as the kingdom of wildlife, hardly anyone knew about the monkey... But the monkey is the king of the kingdom! I vowed to document its life so that people can know more about the endangered king.'[5]

In 1995, Xi was devastated to discover the Deqin county government was preparing to hand over to loggers swathes of forest amounting to around 20 per cent of the monkey's habitat. Via a friend, he raised the issue with veteran environmentalist Tang Xiyang, a former journalist whose bitter experience of Mao-era China triggered a profound interest in the natural world that has shaped the later decades of his life. In the Cultural Revolution, his first wife, a teacher, was beaten to death by a group of violent students, and Tang sent to labour in the countryside. There he took solace in the rivers, birds and trees. 'Nature saved me', he later said. Finally rehabilitated in 1979, Tang founded *Great Nature* magazine and, working closely with his second wife Marcia Bliss Marks, an American education specialist who was working in China when they met, Tang went on to become a renowned writer, speaker and organiser in the environmental field.

Tang helped Xi to write a letter on the plight of the snub-nosed monkey to the head of the State Environmental Protection Administration (SEPA), which was republished widely in the media. Friends of Nature played a crucial, coordinating role here, using its already significant connections to get the story into the press, organise lectures and marshal student support. In the summer of 1996, Tang created yet more buzz when he took some thirty students to the forests of Deqin for the first 'Green Camp', later an annual institution. In an interview (9 December 2003) with China Central Television (CCTV), Tang described how it came about:

> Knowing how precious primeval forests and snub-nosed monkeys are, I told myself, I have to see what's going on with my own eyes... But later I thought it would be a better idea if I could take a group of college students with me. They could do some research on the environmental issue and have some field experience. Marcia asked whether I had any difficulties. I told her frankly that I didn't have any money. She then offered 10,000 yuan... With this start-up

money, I began to recruit college students as volunteers to join me. Thus the Green Camp was born.

For the budding environmental movement, the government response to the campaign was thrilling. The State Council ordered the local government to halt logging in the area and agreed to provide compensation for losses to the local economy. But it was also a lesson in the limits of central state capacity. In 1998, the environmentalists learned that logging was still happening. Illegal deforestation was documented in an investigative programme for CCTV, prompting national outrage. Premier Zhu Rongji reportedly saw the programme and phoned the Yunnan Forestry Department to complain, leading to recriminations against specific local officials and the removal from office of the county's deputy head.

In spite of top-level backing for environmentalists, the illegal timber trade has proved a stubborn foe. Against a backdrop of powerful economic interests and low public awareness in an impoverished province, efforts to stem logging in Yunnan's mountains have seen only mixed success. Reserve officials may say snub-nosed monkey numbers are growing (the International Union for the Conservation of Nature red list still classifies the population trend as 'decreasing') but the baseline is pitifully low: there are only fifteen isolated sub-populations of the species left.

The outcome of civil society efforts to protect the snub-nosed monkey nonetheless had a profound impact on the self-image of China's environmentalists. As Elizabeth Economy wrote in *The River Runs Black*: '[The campaign] transformed the landscape of environmental protection in China... It was the first time China's environmentalists had coordinated their activities and affected policy at the most senior levels of the Chinese government.'[6]

For some, it was more than a brief campaign. Photographer Xi Zhinong and his wife Shi Lihong went on to found their own NGO in Deqin, the Green Plateau Institute. Talking to *BBC Wildlife* magazine in 1999, Xi said: 'We've found college students who are very enthusiastic. We want to increase international attention for species like the Tibetan antelope and the Yunnan snub-nosed monkey.[17] The couple later returned to Beijing to run their documentary studio Wild China, becoming two of the best known figures in China's expanding Green circle.

For China's environmentalists in the 1990s, the case of the Tibetan antelope was equally momentous. It also followed a broadly similar pattern: local concerns were brought to the attention of Beijing-based activists, who, in turn, worked to get the issue onto the national media and central government agendas. At the same time, a loose partnership formed between environmentalists and top officials, both wanting to promote enforcement of existing laws at regional levels.

The Tibetan antelope, or chiru, an elegant, fawn-coloured creature with a black face and soft, thick fur, inhabits Xinjiang, Tibet and the Kekexili grassland of Qinghai. The last of these – also known as Hoh Xil – is China's least populated area, an 83,000-square kilometre expanse of the north-western Tibetan plateau that is home to hundreds of species of wild animal, twenty of them under state protection, including the brown bear, the wild yak and the chiru. More than half the grassland was declared a national nature reserve in 1995, but the designation did not stop conservation concerns and controversies. (Most recently, news that beverage company Snow Beer was offering customers trips to an area supposedly out of bounds to anyone but scientists prompted an angry row.)

This part of China has a tough climate, for which the animals are equipped. But the shaggy coat that allows the chiru to survive the plateau's bitter winter has also proved a curse: the silky underfur is woven into shawls, mainly in Kashmir, which are sold as luxury items. It takes four antelopes to make just one of these shawls, known as *shahtoosh*, Persian for 'king of wool', and known to fetch prices as high as US$17,000.

Though the species has been protected since 1979 by the Convention on International Trade in Endangered Species (CITES), to which China has been a party since 1981, commercial-scale hunting has caused its population to plummet. Numbers are believed to have fallen from around 1 million, fifty years ago, to between 100,000 and 150,000 today. As in the case of the snub-nosed monkey, however, reported success in slowing illegal hunting may hint at a brighter future. (IUCN has noted 'the potential for a possible revised uplisting' on its red list from the current 'endangered' status.) And, like the snub-nosed monkey, the antelope may owe its survival to civil society activists.

In 1992, a group of sturdy Qinghai locals formed the Wild Yak Brigade. Their mission: to defend Tibetan antelopes on the high-altitude Kekexili grassland from poachers. They roamed the harsh landscape for weeks on end in their battered jeeps, risking their health on a threadbare diet of noodles and buns as they hunted for law-breakers to detain and deliver back to city authorities, backed up by a few rifles. By 2000, the group estimated it had reduced by 20 per cent the number of antelope skins reaching the market. As if a rugged band of criminal-hunters in the wilds of western China wasn't sufficiently captivating of the public imagination, in 1994 their leader Gisang Sonam Dorje was dramatically shot dead by poachers. His brother-in-law Zhaba Dorje took the reins, but four years later was also found shot dead. The death was officially recorded as suicide, but alternative theories abound.

The Wild Yak Brigade was propelled to international fame. The *Los Angeles Times*, in an article entitled 'Heroes of China's Wasteland' (29 August 2000), called them the 'guardian angels' of the vanishing antelopes, who had 'come to personify a kind of old-fashioned heroism fast fading in a changing country obsessed with the pursuit of personal wealth.' Though the brigade was disbanded in 2001, and 'absorbed' into the official protection apparatus, its fame persisted: Lu Chuan's 2004 film inspired by their work, *Kekexili: Mountain Patrol*, picked up global awards and raised awareness both inside and outside China of the far west and its endangered species.

But the campaign's reach was not just a result of the celluloid-friendliness of this band of brothers. Even more important was their collision with well-connected and organised NGOs in Beijing – and further afield. Once again, Friends of Nature played a pivotal role. In 1996, some of its members went on an investigative trip to Kekexili, which it followed two years later with a series of conferences about the Tibetan antelope, organised in collaboration with international groups including WWF.

In 1998, shortly before Zhaba Dorje's death, Friends of Nature invited him to Beijing for a series of talks and press conferences, and to report on his work to the authorities. In October of that year, when British prime minister Tony Blair made a state visit to China, Liang Congjie used the opportunity to flag up the issue on the international stage, sending the foreign leader an open letter calling for action to stop the *shahtoosh* trade. Blair responded immediately, saying he shared the 'revulsion over the illegal slaughter', further fuelling media attention. 'Bloody Shawls Exterminating Chiru', read one headline in the *China Daily*.[8] By 1999, officials were persuaded to organise a crackdown, and in April of that year twelve groups of poachers were arrested. But again, the weakness of provincial law-enforcement reared its head: by June, the hunters were back in operation. Thanks to continued pressure from NGOs, journalists and students, however, the plight of the species has stayed on the agenda since. A Tibetan antelope named Yingying was even chosen as one of the official mascots of the 2008 Olympic Games in Beijing, along with a fish, a panda and a swallow.

By many measures, activist success in protecting the snub-nosed monkey and the Tibetan antelope has been severely limited. But its significance for China's environmental campaigners should not be underestimated. Through these efforts, the country's earliest Green groups proved their ability to bring violations of official policy at local level to the attention of the centre.

But conservation in China is still an uphill struggle. For all the small triumphs described here, the overall picture for biodiversity remains bleak in the face of rampant pollution, deforestation, desertification and the sheer force of economic interests. Often, the voice of

NGOs, concerned citizens and even well-meaning officials, is simply too weak to fight these. At Poyang Lake in south China, the country's largest freshwater lake and one of the world's most important wetlands, a network of volunteers is fighting a brave battle against bird poachers – with almost no success. In the first three months of 2012 alone, campaigners estimated that 1,000 birds, mostly young swans, were caught in the network of crude traps that criss-cross the lake. Numbers killed by less visible methods are unknown. Only a tenth as many birds now winter there as did a decade ago.[9]

Official efforts are also significant – as many as 1,200 people are said to be working in some capacity to protect the birds. But still the relentless poaching continues, driven by rocketing black-market prices that see one swan fetch as much profit as six months of fishing. With those rewards, even the threat of long jail terms and high fines have failed to stem the hunting. These days, Poyang is called 'the Kekexili of south China'.

The spectre of the baiji also continues to haunt conservationists. The 25-million-year-old species, also known as the Yangtze River dolphin, was declared 'functionally extinct' in 2006, extinguished from its only habitat by untrammelled development, river traffic and crude fishing methods, including the use of electric rods, even dynamite. In his book, *When a Billion Chinese Jump*, Jonathan Watts explains how, for many years, even acknowledging the baiji's decline was tantamount to an attack on the government.[10] Watts reports a conversation with dolphin expert Wang Ding aboard the Yangtze boat making the last scientific expedition in search of the creature: 'It would be better if we had tried to conserve them then [20 years ago],' said Wang. 'But the problem at the time was that China was very poor. The government was focused only on economic development. People didn't care about the environment at all.'

China's transformation came too late for the baiji. Now, with more money, expertise and an active and accepted Green activist community, can it do a better job elsewhere? Many hope so. Writing on *chinadialogue* in 2007, founder of NGO Green Earth Volunteers

Wang Yongchen urged the story of the baiji to prompt wider change: 'The Chinese people gave the baiji the name "Goddess of the Yangtze". But if our dreams of seeing the goddess again are to come true, our slogans about "living in harmony with nature" need to become more than words.'[11]

Dams, dams and more dams

As a lens for viewing the complex dynamics of China's evolving civil space, it doesn't get much better than the controversies over dams. For activists seeking to protect the country's rivers – and the communities who depend on them – the enormous highs and bruising lows of the last decade show not only how much citizens can achieve when conditions are right, but also how uncertain the political environment remains.

Hydropower is an emotive topic in China. Disastrous projects intended to prove the power of (socialist) man over nature litter late-twentieth-century Chinese history, giving dam building power-ful resonances and sensitivities – for both public and state. Tens of thousands of dam projects were launched during the Great Leap Forward of the late 1950s, Mao's disastrous attempt to transform China into a modern, world-beating economy through high-speed industrialisation and collectivisation. Plagued by poor planning and shoddy construction, almost 3,000 of them had collapsed by 1980, leaving devastation and death in their wake, as Judith Shapiro powerfully describes in *Mao's War Against Nature*.[12] Scientists who had warned against ill-conceived projects meanwhile found their careers in tatters.

From the social and ecological risks of the Three Gorges Dam, China's most famous – and infamous – hydroelectric project, to the threat of extinction facing rare and ancient fish species in the Yangtze River thanks to the latest dam project, history's shadows appear to be fleshed out in grim, modern-day realities. But there are some reasons for optimism. Unlike the failed opposition to the

Three Gorges scheme in the 1980s and 1990s – which helped land environmentalist and journalist Dai Qing in prison for ten months – twenty-first-century activists have seen concrete successes. Most notable among them was the mothballing of plans for a thirteen-dam cascade on the Nu River in Yunnan province, south-west China, in 2004 on the direct instructions of Wen Jiabao, though recent developments indicate this was only a temporary win.

More than that, China's environmentalists have fomented and engaged in a debate about energy policy at a national level that would have been impossible in the not too distant past (also see Chapter 3). In so doing, they have transformed their own movement: learning valuable lessons about lobbying and mobilisation, and pushing the boundaries of their remit – from the relative sanctuary of wildlife protection and tree-planting to the wilder realms of human rights and government accountability.

On first blush, hydroelectric dams may seem a strange target for Greens. After all, they generate electricity without emitting carbon dioxide. For a country still dependent on coal for 70 per cent of its energy and blessed with many river systems, this renewable power source has obvious benefits.

But the full picture is more complex. Large dams – epic engineering schemes of concrete and steel – have been built in or planned for some of China's most beautiful and ecologically sensitive landscapes, where river resources are best. Often, they are followed into these fragile environments by energy-intensive and dirty industries, keen to take advantage of the new power supply, which trigger new waves of mining. Meanwhile, whole communities are displaced, many losing their livelihoods along with their homes and receiving inadequate compensation. The immense sway of China's 'big five' energy corporations, and the financial rewards for local officials who back them, mean environmental and social responsibilities are often sidestepped.

Estimates of the numbers of people displaced by Chinese dams vary wildly, but by any measure are high. Writing in 2007, journalist-cum-activist Zhang Kejia reported in *China Youth Daily* that 16 million people have been relocated to make way for large-scale hydroelectric projects in the past half century, of which 10 million were still living in poverty.[13] Tang Chuanli, head of the Ministry of Water Resources' Reservoir Resettlement Bureau put the total relocated population at over 23 million, with one-third living below basic subsistence levels, as Liu Jianqiang pointed out on *china-dialogue* the same year.[14]

Despite this litany of concerns, China's hydro ambitions appear to be on an ever upward curve. Before 1949, there were only 22 large dams in China. By 2000, the country had almost half the world's total of 45,000. And since the Three Gorges Dam opened in 2008, it has also been home to the largest hydroelectric scheme on the planet: a 22,500-megawatt goliath over the Yangtze, said to be able to meet 3 per cent of China's energy needs, and also intended to control flooding on the disaster-prone river. Almost every river in the country is now exploited for its power-generating potential, and yet the proposals continue to grow: the 12th Five-Year Plan, published in 2011, sets out plans to boost construction in the south-west, paving the way for a new 'great leap forward' in hydropower.

This emphasis on heavy engineering as a solution to China's energy challenge has long been a source of anxiety to the country's environmentalists. The latest surge is not much of a surprise when you consider the men who have been running China for the last ten years: president Hu Jintao used to work for Sinohydro (now the largest hydroelectric firm in the world) and premier Wen Jiabao is a geologist by training.

Nonetheless, government stalling of contentious projects and acknowledgement of problems that have plagued the Three Gorges Dam since construction, such as landslides and bank collapses, have in the past decade given activists hope that they can influence policy in this sector. NGOs – and their partners in journalism, academia and officialdom – have been locked in a tug of war with proponents of large dams, competing for influence over decision-makers.

To understand the symbolic significance of the shift to a more open conversation about hydropower, you have to consider the history of the Three Gorges Dam. This US$30 billion structure in one of China's most dramatic landscapes on the Yangtze River in Hubei province, which displaced some 1.2 million people in the making, was lumbering towards completion just as the campaign against the Nu River dams was getting under way. Not only had passionate opposition failed to stop the Three Gorges scheme from going ahead, but it had also been severely punished.

The idea for a major dam over the Yangtze had been around since 1919, when it was first proposed by the founding father of republican China, Sun Yat-sen. It resurfaced under nationalist leader Chiang Kai-shek, the 1930s' Japanese occupiers and, later, Mao Zedong, who even wrote a poem about it – 'Swimming'. Coming back yet again in the 1980s, the project was finally approved by the National People's Congress, the parliamentary body that effectively rubber-stamps decisions of the most powerful officials, in 1992. Construction started two years later. Eventually, the reservoir flooded 632 square kilometres of land, altering the scenery of one of China's most dramatic landscapes, and swallowing 13 cities, 140 towns and 1,350 villages.

Opposition to the dam was personified by prominent journalist Dai Qing, a columnist for influential newspaper *Guangming Daily* for much of the 1980s. Concerned that China was repeating past mistakes with 'the most environmentally and socially destructive project in the world' Dai openly challenged the Three Gorges proposal in her book *Yangtze! Yangtze!*[15]

This collection of writings and conversations with opponents of the dam was published in 1989. After the Tiananmen Square massacre in June of that year, the book was banned and Dai Qing denounced and imprisoned for ten months. She didn't give up, however, continuing to lobby against the project throughout the 1990s (her efforts included a trip to Japan in 1996 to try to persuade the leadership not to help finance the scheme). But her hopes of halting the project were ultimately crushed.

Dai's concerns about the Three Gorges Dam have been vindicated. Since it opened in 2008, the project has been identified as the cause of a range of environmental problems, including landslides, sediment build-up and pollution – the last due to the river's compromised ability to cleanse itself and contamination from factories and mines submerged by the reservoir.

In 2010, cracks appeared in buildings and roads near the dam and local officials announced 300,000 additional people would have to move in addition to the 1.2 million already relocated. In the first five months of that year alone, ninety-seven significant landslides were recorded, and by May even state media were admitting that the Three Gorges area faced a 'grim' situation.[16] In a *chinadialogue* interview the same year, environmental journalist Jonathan Watts commented on an apparent distancing of the top leadership from the project: 'At the exhibition centre at the Three Gorges Dam, there are no pictures of the current leaders, premier Wen Jiabao and president Hu Jintao. The top leaders of the country did not attend the topping-off ceremony for the dam. This suggests to me that there are reservations about the wisdom of that project and concerns about where it is going.'[17]

Continued public acknowledgement of the problems since appears to support this position. In May 2011, an official statement released following a meeting of the State Council, China's highest administrative organ, said the project was 'greatly benefitting society,' but had also 'caused some urgent problems in terms of environmental protection, the prevention of geological hazards and the welfare of the relocated communities'.

Hydropower is still a favoured technology in China, but the leadership appears at least to have acknowledged that there are lessons to learn from the mistakes of the past. That they are willing to do so openly also hints at increased awareness of the importance of transparency. Charting the exact relationship between a scattering of civil-society campaigns and a broader shift in government's approach to its engineering schemes is a challenge, but it is hard to believe these signs of progress would have happened without the input of bold, brave and determined environmental activists.

However, more than getting government to acknowledge existing mistakes, activists wanted to stop the mistakes from happening at all. In 2004, they seemed to make a breakthrough. An alliance of NGOs, journalists, academics and on-side officials appeared to have defeated plans for a cascade of major dams in Yunnan province, south-west China – temporarily, anyway.

With its high snow-capped peaks, low plains, dense jungle and thousands of plant and animal species, Yunnan is one of China's natural treasure chests. It also enjoys abundant water assets: per capita resources are four times the national average. The Nu River (known as the Salween outside of China's borders) is one of the great rivers of this richly biodiverse region. Its name means literally 'the Angry River', thanks to its raging waters; starting high on the Qinghai–Tibetan plateau, the Nu flows in tumult down to the Indian Ocean. At the time of writing (though it was a situation not expected to last) it was the only one of China's big rivers still free of large-scale dams.

The idea to build a cascade of dams here was first put forward in the late 1970s, but it wasn't until 2003 that state-owned power firm Huadian formally unveiled its proposal for a series of thirteen hydroelectric barrages on the river, which was expected to generate revenue of 34 billion yuan ($5.4 billion) per year – a forceful figure given the intense poverty of the province. Indeed, much of the ensuing debate centred on the appropriate balance between economic development and environmental protection. In August of 2003, the State Council approved the project.

Campaigners and concerned officials got to work, arguing that the dams would forcibly displace 50,000 people, harm the flora and fauna in this biodiversity hotspot and impact downstream communities, including in Myanmar and Thailand.

Key among the opponents was Yu Xiaogang, head of Green Watershed, an NGO based in Yunnan's provincial capital Kunming,

and already a veteran observer of disastrous river management policies. First awakened to the potential impacts of dams while assessing
an ecologically devastating project at Yunnan's Lashi Lake for his
doctoral thesis, Yu went on to build an award-winning watershed
management project in the area, involving local people, NGOs and
officials that was later hailed by central government as one of the
country's top ten examples of sustainable development.

Another activist at the heart of the campaign was Wang Yongchen,
a journalist and founder of Green Earth Volunteers (GEV), a Beijing-
based NGO established in 1996. For GEV, dam-building was an
entirely new area of focus; as academic Andrew Mertha notes in
China's Water Warriors,[18] Wang's only prior experience with dams
had been when she witnessed the opposition of Thai villagers to
a controversial project during a 2001 visit to the country. But the
organisation took to the new topic with gusto: by October 2003,
a civil-society alliance against the dam proposal had formed, and
on the 25th of that month, sixty-two organisations and individuals
signed a petition, which was publicised by the media, stirring a
public outcry.

In April 2004, to the delight of the activists, Wen Jiabao ordered
that the dams be postponed while their environmental impact was
properly considered. It was only a suspension – not a cancellation
– but represented a momentous triumph for the environmental movement nonetheless.

The work of the campaigners didn't stop there. Yu made efforts
to educate the local population about the potential impacts of the
dam cascade, should it go ahead, and involve them in the campaign
to ensure it didn't. In May, he took a group by bus to observe how
dams on the Lancang River (known as the Mekong outside of China)
had changed the lives of communities. Yu explained why to the
magazine *Nanfeng Chuang*:

> The temporary suspension of the plan to dam the Nu River is a
> result of the struggle between environmentalists, the government
> and the hydropower companies. Everybody knows the last are

trying to push ahead with the schemes anyway. As it stands, NGOs, governments and power companies have all taken part in this debate, but we have heard nothing from the real stakeholders – the indigenous people living in the Nu River valley who will be most affected by these dams.[19]

The party of villagers saw how some people displaced by the Manwan Dam – the first hydropower scheme to be built on the Lancang, completed in 1996 – had been reduced to scavenging after losing their land and receiving pitiful compensation. Powerful footage as the group spoke to peasants picking through garbage and caught a glimpse of a devastating future was captured on film and later distributed on DVD among Beijing NGOs and grassroots activists in Yunnan – though distribution of the documentary was later banned. In October 2004, Yu went a step further, taking two peasant activists to a hydropower conference in Beijing, sponsored by the United Nations and attended by National Development and Reform Commission vice minister Zhang Guobao, an unprecedented move.

As well as a dynamic and effective champion of the cause, the activists had something else in their favour. This area of Yunnan had just been made a UNESCO World Heritage site, upping its status as a focus of national pride and increasing overseas interest. Campaign groups, including the International Rivers Network (IRN), worked to get the issue onto the international agenda, and on 9 April 2004 it featured on the front page of the *New York Times*.

Indeed, from the start, international involvement was crucial, teaching the activists a lesson about global support that would be carried into future areas of campaigning, such as Ma Jun's ongoing work on supply-chain management and heavy-metal pollution (profiled below). Thai organisation Southeast Asian River Network, concerned about the downstream impact of the cascade, organised a petition against the Nu scheme – signed by eighty-two organisations – which it sent to the Chinese embassy in Bangkok.

Around the same time, in 2003, another scheme was defeated. A dam planned for Yangliu Lake in Sichuan, in western China, would have flooded the ancient Dujiangyan waterworks – the oldest and only surviving no-dam irrigation system in the world, which dates back to the third century BC. Construction started in secret but soon came to light, triggering a campaign from a coalition of environmentalists, scientists, journalists and officials, and significantly strengthened by nationalistic rhetoric linked to the heritage value of the site. The Sichuan government eventually halted the project.

As with the Nu River project, the success in this case relied not only on NGOs but also on the crucial involvement of other actors, most prominently journalists and officials opposed to the dam. As in the 1990s, civil-society campaigners were using these alliances to pressure policymakers to protect the environment.

The turning point marked a shift for the environmental community, from a non-confrontational stance and exclusive focus on ecology to a broader agenda that included social justice and government transparency – issues that might previously have been near impossible to touch without reprisal.

It also revealed in grim, high-definition the nature of the beast they were dealing with – an erratic polity, which, as US river conservation advocate Kristen McDonald noted in her doctoral thesis,[20] allowed central and local governments to adopt radically different stances. While Yu Xiaogang, for instance, gained access to and praise from top officials for his contributions to sustainable development, he was at the same time coming under attack from authorities in his home province. In 2005, Green Watershed was openly condemned by the provincial government and Yu personally banned from leaving China, public speaking and organising workshops.[21]

Setbacks for anti-dam campaigners in the last two years have shown how fragile progress can be for civil-society activists operating under a government that is authoritarian, opaque and riven with factions and forces pulling in different directions. The latest reports indicate that, eight years after the Nu victory, the construction programme is gearing up to start again. In February 2011, a senior official from the National Development and Reform Commission said that hydropower development on the Nu 'is a must'.

New projects have also raised concerns. In March 2012, construction began on another Yangtze scheme, the 30 billion yuan ($4.8 billion) Xiaonanhai Dam, which will flood the last free-flowing portion of the middle reaches of the river and destroy the region's last reserve for rare fish.

'The scale and frequency of dam cascades on the Upper Yangtze [are] cutting off migration routes for many rare and unique species of fish and halting the flowing water on which they depend. This reserve is their last refuge', Sun Shan, director of Beijing-based NGO the Shan Shui Conservation Center, told *chinadialogue* in 2011.[22] Back then, environmentalists were still hopeful they could change the minds of top officials. An open letter from Friends of Nature to China's top officials just before the 2011 parliamentary season called for urgent attention to the plight of the reserve. Their calls appear to have gone unheeded.

BOX 2.1   Remembering the Nu campaign

LIU JIANQIANG is the Beijing-based deputy editor of *chinadialogue*. He covered the story of the Nu River campaign for the Chinese newspaper *Southern Weekend*, where he was working as senior reporter at the time.

In 2004, China only had two large rivers yet to be dammed. The Yarlung Zangbo in Tibet (called the Brahmaputra once it flows into India) was one; the other was the Nu River. In August 2003, Nu prefecture in Yunnan province finished the Nu River Middle and Lower Reaches Hydropower Planning Report, which proposed building a 13-dam cascade on the river's main stretch, with a total installed capacity of 21.32 million kilowatts and an annual power output of 102.96 billion kilowatt-hours.

A report in *China Newsweek* said that on 12 August 2003 an official from the State Environmental Protection Administration

(SEPA) was told to take part in a review meeting for the 13-dam cascade plan on the Nu River. This was the first time this official had heard anything about the plan. At the meeting, he realised that he was the sole person who opposed it. When the meeting was over, he strongly disagreed with the explanation given by 'every single one of the participants' and requested that his opinion, as a SEPA delegate, be recorded in the minutes of the meeting.

I found out afterwards that the official from SEPA was Mu Guangfeng. He was the department head of SEPA's supervision department. He believed that the Nu River dam project never went through legal environmental procedures and its environmental impact assessment wasn't clear. Projects like this can't be started in a rush.

Up against the NDRC and big interest groups, this mid-level SEPA official found himself outnumbered. So he told his friend, China National Radio presenter, Wang Yongchen, about what was happening.

Wang Yongchen is an active member of China's environmental civil society. Another of her identities is as the founder of Green Earth Volunteers, an environmental NGO. A report in *Business Week* said that on 3 September 2003 Wang Yongchen got in touch with a group of scholars to attend an appraisal meeting held under the auspices of SEPA, where she voiced strong opposition to the Nu River dam project. She also organised dozens of journalists to attend that meeting so they could report the story. This meeting in Beijing was later known as the occasion when the 'first shot to protect the Nu River was fired'.

On 25 October 2003, at the second representatives meeting of the China Environmental Culture Promotion Association, using just a piece of paper and a pencil, Wang Yongchen collected the signatures of sixty-two scientists, artists, media and environmental activists on a petition to oppose the dam project. Press coverage of this story caused a widespread public reaction.

At the end of November 2003, at a meeting of the World Rivers and People Against Dams held in Thailand, Wang Yongchen and other Chinese environmental NGO workers rushed about drumming up support for their campaign to protect the Nu River. In the end, they secured signatures from NGOs from more sixty nations on a petition to save the Nu River, which was then presented to UNESCO. The UN body replied in a letter headlined 'Concerns about the Nu River'.

Between 16 and 24 February 2004 Wang Yongchen led a group of twenty journalists from Beijing and Yunnan, environmental volunteers and scholars on a nine-day study trip to the Nu River. Shortly afterwards the papers were full of stories about the biodiversity and cultural diversity along both banks of the Nu River.

Wang Yongchen was able to help the media and civil society use their strengths and express them to the fullest in an environment where the media and NGOs did not have much freedom. Because of her outstanding efforts to protect the Nu River, in 2004 Wang Yongchen was named World Environment Champion and listed among the top ten Chinese environmental figures.

However, there are still many Chinese environmental activists that use more traditional methods to protect the public's interest. For example, environmentalist Li Xiaoxi, an associate professor at the official Air Force Command College and deputy to the People's Congress for Beijing's Haidian district. This 60-year-old environmentalist is famous for talking bluntly.

In January 2004, Li Xiaoxi wrote a letter to premier Wen Jiabao about the Nu River dam. Shortly afterwards, he sent the NDRC his instructions on the Nu River Middle and Lower Reaches Hydropower Planning Report: 'Major hydropower projects such as this, which attract a high degree of public attention and different views on environmental protection, must be considered carefully and decisions made scientifically.' It looked inevitable that the Nu River dam project, which had been racing along, was going to come screaming to a halt. Three days after Premier Wen's instructions, State Council leaders specially informed Li Xiaoxi of his action.

This piece of great news was immediately passed on to Wang Yongchen, who was at the Nu River doing interviews at the time.

She was moved to tears. It was the most significant victory to date in the history of China's environmental movement. It signified that China had made a complete departure from the era of the Three Gorges Dam. The country's newly born civil society had helped the public to influence the government and big business interests. This would have been unimaginable in the past.

Information is the key

If campaigns against large dams raised the stakes for China's budding environmental movement in the early years of the new century, those stakes were further increased by environmental activists with an ambitious aim: freedom of information.

Led by Ma Jun, director of the Institute of Public and Environmental Affairs (IPE), these campaigners have made the connection between China's pollution crises and its lack of transparency – and made explicit efforts to change a system characterised by opaque governance. By giving ordinary Chinese people more information about the sources of environmental problems, IPE and its partners have sought to empower and motivate, to help citizens become better supervisors of the polluters poisoning their air and water, and the local officials allowing them to do so.

For people used to reading about the myriad ways in which the Chinese government seeks to control the information citizens have access to – by ploughing vast resources into Internet monitoring, for instance – one of the most striking aspects of this push for open data is that it has been in large part facilitated by the state. Ma's efforts have happened in tandem with the emergence of open government information regulations, finally made law in 2008 after several years of consultation and local pilot projects.

These regulations have been poorly enforced: local government departments, now obliged by law to hand over certain, legally defined details regarding polluting projects, often refuse to do so without using any lawful exemption. But by challenging the system, while making use of it, Ma's efforts can perhaps be seen as those of a 'next-generation' Liang Congjie – the man who teased open the door for China's environmental movement by styling his NGO Friends of Nature as a friend of government too. By establishing himself as both a state ally and an agent of change, Ma has contributed to a sophisticated and effective style of campaigning for twenty-first-century China and scored some notable achievements.

Like so many of the figures who have shaped China's environmental movement, Ma first came to public attention as an investigative journalist (see also Chapter 1). For most of the 1990s, he worked for Hong Kong's *South China Morning Post*, ending up as the newspaper's chief representative in Beijing. Reporting from all over China, Ma learned first-hand how severe pollution and resource degradation were impacting lives and ecosystems.

Ma developed a specific interest in the country's water challenges, from overextraction of groundwater in the arid north to toxicity entering the food chain due to pollution at sea. In 1999, he published his seminal work *China's Water Crisis*, detailing the water shortages, pollution and floods of China's seven key river basins and setting out recommendations for better water governance. Today, the book is often compared to Rachel Carson's 1962 work *Silent Spring*, for its role in spurring the growth of a Chinese domestic environmental movement.

In the same way that Carson's work on the ecological impact of pesticides ignited noisy public debate in the United States, Ma sought to stimulate a citizen voice in China into speaking up for its environmental rights. The severity of the pollution as the country's economic growth gathered an ever more astonishing pace brought home the urgency of the task. By 2006, Ma's research indicated that 70 per cent of rivers were polluted at various levels; 300 million rural residents were drinking unsafe water and a fifth of drinking water sources in major cities were below standard.

In May 2006, Ma founded IPE, and with it an innovative project to map the sources of the country's water pollution problems. In September that year (the same year that he was listed among the world's hundred most influential people by *Time* magazine), Ma explained the thinking behind the project to *chinadialogue*:

> Water pollution is the most serious environmental issue facing China. It has a huge impact on people's health and economic development. That is why we have begun to build this database. To protect water resources, we need to encourage public participation and strengthen law enforcement. In some places, polluting factories and companies are being protected by local governments and officials. The public need to take part in water monitoring and management if the situation is to improve. The first step to get the involvement of the public is to inform them.[23]

Today, IPE runs online maps and databases of both water and air pollution. The aim is both to inform the public and to provide companies and officials with an incentive to comply more diligently with environmental law. IPE collects data on hundreds of environmental violations across China each week – mostly from public sources – with which it continually updates a map illustrating the geographical spread of the country's most polluting firms and municipalities. It is a naming and shaming effort, with a route to redemption for polluters: offenders can get their names removed from their 'blacklist' by passing an independent environmental audit.

By the time Ma picked up the Goldman Environmental Prize in April 2012, the IPE team had documented more than 90,000 air and water violations by both national and multinational companies. The scale of the figure speaks to Ma's argument that too little public pressure is wielded over corporations in China – an argument further bolstered by the government's own statistics on environmental violations. In one revelation in early 2007, SEPA announced it had found eighty-two projects with total investment value of over 112 billion yuan ($18 billion) to be in serious breach of environmental impact assessment law.

Perhaps surprisingly, while highlighting the importance of public pressure on polluters, Ma has avoided gaining a reputation for being 'anti-business'. Rhetorically, his emphasis has always been on positive change, on helping companies to fulfil their duties and in so doing serve their own interests: 'If they take their corporate social responsibilities seriously, they will be able to gain understanding and trust from the communities in which they operate', Ma told *chinadialogue* in his 2006 interview.

Ma has applied the same approach to government, using the language of its interests. In 2007, for instance, he pointed out that the number of mass protests caused by environmental issues had grown by 29 per cent annually for the previous five years. His argument is that not only economic growth but also good environmental governance is crucial to building the 'harmonious society' so prized by China's leadership.[24]

The introduction of open information laws in 2008 – and a decree from the MEP, which specifically focused on disclosure of environmental information – excited great optimism among environmental NGOs. Ma called the measures a 'milestone on the path to guaranteeing the public's right to access environmental information', while a Friends of Nature publication said they were 'extremely significant in promoting public participation in environmental protection'.[25]

China's environmental protection bureaus are now required to proactively release seventeen types of information, including regional environmental quality, amounts of discharge and records of pollution violations, using websites, gazettes and press conferences, as well as newspapers, television and other media that 'make it convenient for the public to be informed'. Citizens can also make direct requests for information, to which departments are obliged to respond in a timely fashion. Under the MEP decree, business also has obligations: enterprises are encouraged to release information such as waste-disposal methods and total annual resource consumption, while those whose emissions have exceeded standards are required to disclose data on their pollution above prescribed limits, construction of environmental protection facilities and emergency plans for sudden pollution accidents. Environmental departments have powers to fine companies that do not comply.

While the measures look robust on paper, transparency campaigners knew from the start that implementation would be a tough challenge. Writing on *chinadialogue* the day the regulations came into force, Ma Jun said: 'It is well-known that there is weak enforcement of laws and regulations in China. As a law that reflects new thinking, the implementation of the measures is expected to be even more challenging.'[26] NGOs – both domestic and international – worked with media and government to promote awareness of the measures, so that 'this historic chance' would not be missed, while IPE distributed to companies a data disclosure form 'to facilitate a more standardised disclosure'.

However, while some companies – such as multinational shirt-maker Esquel Group – immediately stepped up to disclose emissions data, the predictions on poor implementation turned out to be depressingly accurate. Speaking in 2011, Centre for Legal Assistance for Pollution Victims director Wang Canfa explained that an exclusion clause in the regulations was regularly being used to get around the new rules: 'Although the regulations list seventeen types of information that should be disclosed and only one short clause on exemptions, that one short clause has become a catch-all.'[27] The guilty article – Article 8 – states that any data that threatens social stability or national, public or economic security must not be disclosed. In 2010, the State Council weakened the regulations further, ruling that requests could be declined if the information was irrelevant to an applicant's work, life, research or other specific need.

These and other – sometimes unlawful – excuses have been used to avoid handing over data. NGOs attending a 2011 seminar to mark the measures' third anniversary listed a litany of failed attempts to use the laws, as later reported by *chinadialogue*. A Greenpeace request for the pollution record of two companies in Zhuzhou, in Hunan province, was turned down because the firms were 'sensitive' to the release of information; an application by Chen Liwen of Green Beagle for data on a garbage-incineration facility in Jiangsu province was refused on grounds of commercial confidentiality and the fact Green Beagle had no connection to the facility. The list went on.

If these were the experiences of relatively savvy NGOs, what luck were ordinary citizens having when they tried to make use of the regulations? There are a few, inspiring examples: Shanghai resident Xu Taisheng spent three years applying to see the environmental impact assessment for a project of metals giant Baogang Steel in a series of proceedings that eventually led to China's Supreme People's Court. In the end, he got the information he was after and financial compensation. Optimists would add that there is comfort to be drawn from the rising numbers of people seeking to exercise their rights, even if they rarely succeed. According to MEP figures, the ministry received 226 disclosure requests in 2010, a rise of more than 200 per cent on the previous year. In general, however, the last few years have been littered with failed citizen attempts to find out more about the polluters affecting their lives.

Strength in numbers

While official channels for exercising public pressure over polluters have proved unreliable, NGOs have found other ways to exert leverage. One crucial strategy has been to join forces.

Civil-society groups had already proved their ability to unite for greater effect – by jointly signing open letters against the construction of large dams on the Nu River in 2003, for example. But a formal coalition of campaign groups organised by IPE took this a step further and proved an effective force in persuading powerful corporations to restructure their supply chains.

The Green Choice Alliance (GCA), set up in August 2008, comprises forty-one domestic NGOs with a wide geographical spread. From Green Anhui – a sustainable development lobby group in Anhui province, eastern China – to Blue Dalian, an outfit focused on water protection in Dalian city in the north-east, grassroots groups from across the country have linked up to push multinational corporations to operate cleaner manufacturing bases. For China, responsible for almost 20 per cent of global manufacturing output in 2010, issues don't come much bigger.

Transparency has again been at the heart of the campaign. Through IPE's database, corporations can readily access data on the environmental record of potential suppliers – rendering ignorance a feeble excuse for manufacturing goods in a polluting factory, however competitive the price.

Walmart was an early mover. By late 2008, the firm, which has more than 10,000 suppliers in China, was cross-checking its contractor list against IPE's violators database on a monthly basis. Today, a long list of multinationals, including Nike, Unilever and Coca-Cola, collaborate with the GCA initiative, using the database to help monitor their Chinese operations and regulate their supply chains. More than 500 companies have published action plans to clean up their China operations.

In a country where NGOs are small and under-resourced and operate in a restricted field, this kind of partnering is proving important in squaring up to powerful corporate interests. It is also helping to spur an emerging Green consumer movement.

However, one company in particular stood out for its initially cagey and uncooperative approach. The progress campaigners eventually made splintering the tightly closed doors of Apple, the Californian electronics giant – one of the most secretive companies in the world about its supply chain – a mark of how sophisticated China's green campaign machine had become. It elicited comparisons with successful campaigning against the use of child labour by US-based sportswear company Nike in the 1990s.

In an April 2010 report,[28] Ma and colleagues identified twenty-nine leading IT companies whose China supply chains they believed were contributing to regular heavy-metal pollution incidents, including Samsung, HP, Panasonic, IBM, Vodafone and Apple. The previous year, more than 4,000 people – mostly children – had suffered lead poisoning in China, in a spate of scandals involving poorly managed factories (see Chapter 3). Rather than narrowing in on the factories themselves, however, the GCA campaigners followed the goods they were producing. And the trail in many cases led to the world's biggest electronics firms.

One battery manufacturer implicated in a lead-poisoning scandal in the southern Chinese province of Fujian, for instance, turned out to be a major supplier to Narada Power Source – in turn, a supplier to Vodafone, BT and other telecommunications brands.

The GCA wrote to the twenty-nine electronics companies in question, alerting them to the fact their suppliers were contributing to China's pollution and environmental health problems and asking them to be more transparent about their procurement arrangements. Some were quick to respond: Sony, Lucent, Nokia, Seiko and Epson were among the first to talk to the campaigners. In mid-June, Canon said it had already asked the suppliers identified to carry out improvements. IBM pledged to investigate supply-chain pollution and proposed direct dialogue with the NGOs.

But Apple was steadfast in its silence. By the end of June, it was the only American company that had failed to respond. With support from US organisations Pacific Environment and the Business and Human Rights Resource Centre, the campaigners started to mobilise consumers. By mid-July, almost 1,000 angry Americans had written in protest to Apple's then boss Steve Jobs. China's NGOs were no longer using the global community merely to bolster their domestic campaigns, but were actively drawing out the international dimensions of the issues – and tapping into consumer anxieties about the overseas footprint of their everyday products.

The following year, the campaign to crack open Apple stepped up several gears. In January 2011, three NGOs – IPE, Friends of Nature and Green Beagle – released a report criticising the firm's 'culture of secrecy' and listing ten incidents that allegedly showed Apple's suppliers had violated commitments on health, safety and the environment.[29] Among these were the now infamous suicides of twelve employees at a Foxconn factory in Shenzhen and the n-hexane poisoning of 137 workers while cleaning iPhone touch-screens at United Win Technology (the poisoned workers had written to Steve Jobs asking Apple to investigate but received no reply). The report graded the twenty-nine technology companies for their transparency: Apple was in last place.

Apple didn't respond directly to the investigation, but when the firm published its progress report on supplier responsibility the following month it publicly admitted for the first time that United Win Technology was one of its suppliers. This was progress, but it was far from enough to satisfy the NGOs. In August, they published another report, this time claiming to have found problems at twenty-seven suspected Apple suppliers, with impacts including communities blighted by foul-smelling gases and water sources turned milky-white. An explosion at a Foxconn factory in Chengdu, western China, had killed three workers and injured fifteen.

This time, there was a breakthrough. In the face of the sustained pressure, Apple finally broke its silence and agreed to meet with the campaign coalition. On 15 November five Chinese NGOs visited Apple's Beijing office, where they heard that the firm had launched investigations into fifteen suppliers suspected of pollution. The campaigners later told Chinese newspaper *21st Century Business Herald* (16 November 2011) that they were pleased with the more open attitude, but the two sides continued to disagree on the desired extent of corporate transparency. The NGOs would continue to monitor Apple's supply chain, they said.

Notably, China's IT pollution campaign received the tacit backing of the Chinese government. The report that kick-started it all in April 2010 was launched at a seminar organised by a magazine affiliated with the environment ministry. Meanwhile, state media including CCTV and the *People's Daily* have covered its progress. Online environmental portal the Asia Water Project drew two conclusions from this: 'First, that the government recognises the issue's urgency;

and second, that it will require support from a variety of stakeholders to resolve it.'[30] The increasingly well-oiled NGO machine has made it clear it is one such stakeholder.

BOX 2.2   Living with Foxconn

MENG SI IS a Beijing-based freelance reporter. In early 2012, she went to Taiyuan, in Shanxi, to meet a group of residents unhappy with a factory operated by Foxconn, suppliers to Apple.

Yang Xiuduan would love to have an iPhone – on one condition. 'I'll buy it just as soon as we chase Apple out of here', he said, pointing at the Foxconn factory that stands 200 metres from his home.

Thirty-eight-year-old Yang, a mid-ranking employee at a state institution in Taiyuan, and other residents in Hengda Luzhou Apartments started to notice a strange smell shortly after moving into the new housing complex a little over a year ago. First, they blamed a sewer outside. Then, they wondered if it could be the furnishings in their newly decorated apartments. Finally, their eyes turned over the road to the factory that manufactures parts for Apple's high-tech gadgets.

By the summer of last year, residents here were finding the stench unbearable and complaining of coughs, headaches and stomach problems. And they were pointing the finger squarely at the Foxconn factory.

Taiwanese-owned Foxconn is one of Apple's key suppliers. The company shot to global fame in 2010 following a spate of worker suicides at its factory in Shenzhen, a wealthy manufacturing city in south China. And it has stayed in the news since, largely thanks to a high-profile campaign by Beijing-based green NGOs to get Apple to clean up pollution in its supply chain.

But while Foxconn's Shenzhen plant has generated plenty of coverage in the global media, other parts of its operations have been under-reported. That is not for lack of tension: here in Taiyuan, a northern Chinese city best known not for manufacturing but coal-mining, a storm has been brewing between the electronics plant and local residents, who say the factory is blighting their lives.

It's a story playing out all over China, as the industrial boom that started on the east coast spreads across the country. Breakneck expansion has brought jobs and opportunities, but it has also invaded the space between homes and factories, leaving people living side by side with manufacturers and their communities plagued by noxious gases. The supply chain behind Apple's flashy gadgets offers a window into the complexities and costs of China's manufacturing rise.

Five hundred kilometres from Yang Xiuduan's home, environmental groups in Beijing have spent more than a year working to expose pollution violations by Apple's suppliers. This coalition of NGOs, led by transparency campaigner Ma Jun, started monitoring Apple's manufacturers in 2010 and went on to publish two reports revealing serious pollution violations, including in Taiyuan.

Although Apple does not directly manufacture any products itself, the Green activists argued that the firm still has responsibility for the problems they uncovered. As a large and powerful client, the multinational corporation should be demanding better environmental performance from its suppliers, they said.

The Taiyuan residents hoped that the campaign against Apple would pressure both the factory and the government to act, breaking the deadlock and eradicating the stench once and for all. They were worried about their health and the homes they had channelled all their savings into.

These residents believe that Apple's weak environmental regime has led to the chemical odours – which they say they can smell even with the windows closed – and already visible health problems. From breathing difficulties to stomach irritations, people living in this community suffer a range of illnesses that they suspect are linked to the factory's activities, though as is so often the case in the field of environmental health they cannot confirm a causal relationship.

Standing in Yang's apartment complex during my visit, I

too caught whiffs of something strange – a smell close to paint fumes. It wasn't too strong and it came and went with the wind. The residents described the smell in all sorts of ways to me: like sulphur, like burning and even as sickly sweet.

A Taiyuan Foxconn manager, speaking by phone, said that there is an odour problem at the plant and that Apple had come 'two or three times to inspect the facility and audit its emissions data'. However, at the end of February, an Apple spokesperson told *chinadialogue* the audits had detected no pollution problem at the Taiyuan plant.

A zoning problem?

The problems suffered by the residents of Hengda Luzhou Apartments are linked to the way development here was originally planned. According to Shanxi's environmental protection office, the housing complex is '200 metres from Foxconn Technology Industrial Zone'. At that distance, the odours are obvious in the eight buildings closest to the Foxconn factory when there is an easterly wind. They can also be detected in another eight buildings slightly further away.

Liu Xiang of China's Centre for Legal Assistance to Pollution Victims (CLAPV) explained that Chinese law sets different size buffer zones for different types of factory, but that regulations have not yet been determined for certain categories. To know what should have been done in this instance the residents would have to look at the recommendations made in the development's environmental impact assessment – a document that has not been made available to the public – he said.

Liu Xiaowen, chief of the local environmental protection bureau (EPB), admitted that the distance between the residential area and the facility is inadequate, but said that his hands are tied. 'The factory is already there. All we can do is to try our best to find a compromise. We have got duties both to the locals and to the 100,000 Foxconn employees.'

At full capacity, the Hengda Luzhou apartment complex can house 12,000 families, or around 30,000 residents, making it the largest in Shanxi province. Another housing development is under construction to the south of the factory.

The residents have made countless phone calls to environmental authorities at local, city, provincial and national levels, both polite and angry. On 6 August 2011, they stepped their protest up a gear: more than 100 residents blocked the road with their cars, attracting the attention of the provincial government. The locals, the authorities and Foxconn had a meeting, and the residents made four visits to the factory.

Their efforts weren't entirely smooth – locals bearing a letter from the provincial petition office were prevented from entering the city petition office by the police, for example – but progress was made. The meeting opened up lines of communication between the residents and the factory, and from this point Foxconn began to upgrade the equipment at its plant.

The residents' complaints have not stopped, however. Yang and others continue to publish information on Foxconn's pollution online, discuss the problems on microblogs and complain to the environmental authorities. Offline, they organise petitions and factory visits, make phone calls to the local government and factory staff, and use their inside contacts to dig for information.

Chief among their demands is more information. The authorities have come to test the air four times, and the residents want to know precisely what they found out: what gases were present and were they above permitted levels? But they have only received vague answers.

A 2010 investigation into complaints about Foxconn, carried out by the provincial environmental protection bureau, concluded that the odours were coming from the coating workshop and from oil mist created by equipment in the machinery workshop. In 2011, the city-level environmental protection bureau expanded the list: the offensive smells, they said, were caused by fumes from the coating workshop, odours from the waste-water treatment equipment, dust from the recycling workshop and oil mist from the machinery workshop.

The most detailed publically available data can be found in a document from the Shanxi Party Committee's Social Circumstances and Public Opinion Office: 'Monitoring data indicates that levels of seven of the fifty non-methane hydrocarbons (NMHCs) that were tested for are too high.' When levels of NMHCs reach a certain level, they are directly harmful to human health, and under certain conditions can form a photochemical smog, endangering both the environment and people.

But which actual tests did the factory fail? What are the emissions made up of? What dangers do they pose? This is the information residents like Yang want to find out. Meanwhile, they have resorted to buying air purifiers – now stocked in two shops in their complex – and traditional Chinese medicinal remedies. Mr Wei, a resident who has given up his outdoor morning exercises because of the pollution, advises neighbours to take lily bulbs boiled in water as a detoxicant.

What are we breathing?

The failure of the residents to establish exactly what problems they face is not for lack of trying. Last year, Yang decided to apply to the provincial government to see the environmental impact assessment (EIA) for the construction of Foxconn's factory, plus the past three years of environmental monitoring data.

When he arrived at the provincial environmental protection bureau to file his freedom-of-information request, a young civil servant told him he was in the wrong place. Yang followed directions to another floor, where he received an even less welcoming reception. Finally, he managed to lodge his application, but was later telephoned by the bureau: since Yang hadn't explained why he wanted the information, he would have to reapply, they informed him. He filled in the forms again.

Twenty-four days later, Yang received a reply: full pollution monitoring data was not yet available. Once available, it would be released by the company itself. The EIA would not be made public. He could see the document approving the EIA, but would not be allowed to copy or photograph it.

Yang had been hoping to get evidence for a court case against Foxconn, but accepted this was 'a dead end'. His experience is a common one. In May 2008, China introduced a set of regulations intended to enshrine in law the public right to data about polluting projects – the trial 'measures on open environmental information'. But enforcement of this ground-breaking legislation has been challenging, and in the four years since it came into effect many people around the country have found their requests for data repeatedly rejected.

China's advancing cities

Similarly, the continuing friction in Taiyuan is far from an isolated case. Across China, rapidly expanding cities are advancing into the countryside, bringing with them new and complicated dynamics.

At first, the villagers closest to the cities sell their land to developers facing saturated urban markets. Most of the young villagers move to the city to work, while those who stay behind sell their land or rent out their homes. Local governments are keen to attract factories to boost the local economy, while the companies themselves enjoy cheaper land prices than in the city, better infrastructure than in rural areas and preferential treatment from local government.

In Taiyuan, development has followed the route of the Dayun expressway, which links the city to surrounding rural areas. Along the road, villages and fields have one by one turned into mazes of apartment complexes.

Foxconn's facility pre-dates that process. The manufacturer built its facility here in 2005, and work started on the Hengda Luzhou Apartments two years later. Once the surrounding fields were replaced with apartment buildings, Foxconn's days of peace were over. Who allowed the apartments to be built so close to the factory? As is so often the case in China, the answer is lost to history.

At the end of last year, the China Association for Science and Technology announced that local governments were behind 80 per cent of all breaches of land law in the country. A National Development and Reform Commission official has warned that local government's enthusiasm for development zones is leading to 'scattered development, which neither farmland nor energy resources can support'.

Benefits too?

Not everyone is angry, however. For the Hengda Luzhou homeowners, Foxconn means pollution. But for the residents of Chengxi, a village to the north of the apartments and diagonally opposite the factory, it is a source of prosperity.

Mr He, a Chengxi shopkeeper, described how the village had got richer since Foxconn arrived. Locals have been able to sell land to property developers and almost every household here rents rooms to Foxconn employees.

Mrs Gao's husband works at Foxconn. They rent a 30-square-metre, two-room apartment on the third floor of a private dormitory. The building can accommodate seven families on each floor. When they first arrived in 2009, she said, the rent was 200 yuan per month. Now it is 450 yuan.

Many of the homes in the village have signs advertising rooms and there are plenty of restaurants, hotels, clinics and launderettes.

Nobody in Chengxi seemed to know much about the pollution nearby. Liu said 'very few' villagers here had complained about the smells in the past. A woman from Hebei who sells dried foods said that there are strange odours in summer, but they aren't necessarily caused by Foxconn: they could come from burning coal or the sewerage ditch at the front of the village.

The villagers of Chengxi may not care about the odours too much, but that doesn't mean they suffer no impact. In fact, they have lived with the plant for longer than Hengda Luzhou's residents, and Dr Li, a local physician who used to work in a hospital here, believes environmental health issues need attention.

Although there is no quantified data, Li said that the incidence of respiratory problems and congenital disorders among villagers is high. Between 2006 and 2011, the rate of cleft palates, cleft lips, hydrocephaly and spinal problems increased significantly, she said, estimating they may now account for 70 to 80 per cent of all illnesses.

Benzene, an organic pollutant often used in the cleaning and coating of electronic components, is a carcinogen. High degrees of benzene exposure can cause reproductive abnormalities and leukaemia. Dr Li added that respiratory problems are often linked to harmful substances in the air.

According to a source with access to authoritative data, who wished to remain anonymous, between 2006 and the end of 2011 the rate of stillbirths, miscarriages, congential disorders and respiratory problems in the villages around the Foxconn factory – Xicheng, Nanheiyao, Xiaodian, Nanpan and Yangzhuang – was markedly higher than in the period from 2002 to 2006.

Official in the middle

Saddled with the unenviable task of balancing this host of competing priorities – health, growth, stability, jobs and living standards – is local EPB chief Liu Xiaowen, in a case symptomatic of the complex relationship between people and officialdom in boomtown China.

Almost everyone here has Liu's mobile number – and he is feeling the pressure. The 57-year-old visits the factory whenever a complaint comes in, even if it's at the crack of dawn. On 31 December 2011 he even invited Yang Xiuduan and several other residents to dinner (though he asked Yang not to bring anyone who had been abusive when lodging complaints). Making a rather unlikely New Year's Eve party, Liu and his deputy sat down to eat with around a dozen residents' representatives.

'No matter what, we've known each other for a year and they have helped our work', Liu said of the residents. But he explained that it's difficult for him to do anything about the smell: as the Foxconn facility was approved at provincial level, the local environmental protection bureau only has powers to monitor the problem.

He also believes that, as a local official, his duty is to keep his area stable. 'We've got a staff of 10, and we've spent most of our time this year on Foxconn,' he said. 'The public can talk in extreme terms – they don't have any legal responsibilities. But we represent the government and it would be wrong for us to do the same.'

A more stable future?

Do the Foxconn factory's upgrades – made in response to residents' complaints – offer hope for more 'stability'? The early signs are mixed. 'Little' Yang, who lives on the tenth floor of a Hengda Luzhou block, has no faith in the new environmental equipment or monitoring systems. He and many other locals still insist the only answer is for Foxconn to leave.

Yang Xiuduan, meanwhile, believes that public campaigning has had an effect and that the problem is less severe now than in the past. But the residents are struggling to regain trust and a sense of security. Even with the new equipment, they say the smells still come.

And they have learned not to take soothing official words at face value. An article on the provincial government's website on Taiyuan's 'modern circular economy' claims that emissions from the Foxconn facility are entirely controlled. In effect, it says, the factory produces no emissions at all, as all fumes go through a treatment process that renders them harmless. In 2006, Foxconn suddenly became a 'Taiyuan Model Environmental Firm' and a 'Shanxi Green Firm' and senior officials from the State Environmental Protection Agency (now the Ministry of Environmental Protection) visited and praised the plant on a number of occasions.

After months of constant complaining, Yang's wife Jia Sumei has given up: 'Let's move in the summer. I don't want to go through it all again.' But Yang is more confident: 'Don't worry, I believe things will get better', he said.

A new front opens: animal welfare

However, not all of China's campaigns have taken such a consensual approach as the supply-chain activists. One of the arenas of Chinese activism readiest to embrace conflict is also one of its newest: the emerging field of animal welfare.

While species conservation and habitat preservation have been key concerns of China's Green NGO community from the outset, recent years have seen the arrival of a different form of animal-focused lobbying, centred around middle-class, urban consumers. Campaigns with the explicit goal of protecting the welfare, or rights, of animals have taken off in line with the growing wealth of the country's cities and a marked rise in pet ownership. And, from protesters picketing a restaurant serving shark fin to activists blockading 'dog-meat' trucks on highways, this field is no stranger to direct action.

Sometimes, the activism is explicitly environmental: concerns about biodiversity loss merge with anxieties about cruelty. The most prominent example is the fight against shark-fin consumption, where campaigners focus on both the threat to shark numbers and the pain the sharks are put through to supply the trade. Often, however, there are no explicit conservation goals – cats and dogs, the two species that receive probably the greatest amount of attention, are far from endangered. There are nonetheless reasons why it is useful to treat this group of campaigns together, as a single movement. First, they pose a common question about the nature of humans' relationship with other living creatures (in that sense, they are all environmental) and the experience of individual animals, as distinct from their survival as a group. But, even more, these city-centred, consumer-focused stories provide an insight into the shape, direction and complexities of a particular section of Chinese civil society: one powered by the surging, urban middle classes, in love with their ever more numerous pets and ready to question their country's medicinal and culinary traditions.

China is not a country known for its sentimental attitude towards animals. From zoo visitors paying to dangle live chickens into tiger enclosures, to doctors grinding tiger bones into a health tonic, or restaurants serving up feline platters, paws and all, Western newspapers love to recount tales of China's callous approach to other living creatures. But that stereotype is being undermined.

Led by NGOs, or looser volunteer coalitions, and bolstered by an army of vocal citizens online, the emerging animal-welfare movement campaigns to outlaw cruelty, from abusive farming practices to use of animals in circus performances, to drawing bile from live bears for traditional Chinese medicine. Globally, of course, animal welfare is an established campaign ground inhabited by well-funded, international lobby groups. And so the entry of a 'Western' style animal-welfare agenda into Chinese society is perhaps unsurprising. But the manner in which it is panning out provides a window into the unique dynamics and conflicts of a stratified and changing China.

There are many narratives on offer. In one, animal protection campaigners are the true traditionalists, embodying Buddhist and Daoist reverence for the living world in a fight against a brutal, get-rich-quick modernity. In another, wealthy urbanites are pitted against animal traders and transporters who are simply trying to feed their families; or doctors, chefs and community leaders guarding centuries-old traditions. Hao Xiaomao, a lorry driver barricaded by activists on an expressway near Beijing while driving 500 dogs to the slaughterhouse in spring 2011, summed up this side of the argument when he told journalists that the activists who stopped his truck 'think dogs are more important than people'.[31]

Nationalism has worked its way in there too. Some advocates of traditional Chinese medicine have gone so far as to claim activists are involved in a foreign conspiracy to undermine the competitiveness of their industry, while foreign-focused protests – against the hunt of Canadian seals, for example – have proved some of the easiest to get off the ground.

Surging wealth and enduring poverty, modernity and tradition, xenophobia and international collaboration – these are some of the friction points of a country transforming. Some of China's animals are now caught up in the mix.

Dogs and cats have held centre stage. The Harbin expressway stand-off is just one of many roadside rescues to have taken place in recent years. Around 2,000 dogs are thought to have been liberated this way between 2011 and 2012 alone. But these events were not the first battles in the war on dog meat; the earliest blasts of that crusade on the Chinese mainland came from the Chinese Animal Protection Network (CAPN), launched in 2004.

Isolated animal welfare organisations were already working to rescue strays by then, but consumption of dogs and cats hadn't made it onto their agenda. Indeed, these groups were unconvinced that stopping people from eating one or two particular species was anything but an exercise in arbitrary morality, as CAPN later pointed out:

> It is not uncommon to find pro-eating voices from those animal groups. People think eating cats or dogs and protecting them are things in different dimensions. They believe there is no fundamental difference between cattle/pig and cat/dog, therefore eating cats and dogs should be seen as personal choice and culture. This statement is partly true.[32]

So CAPN sought to reframe the debate as one about cruelty rather than taste. 'We want to make more groups aware [that] reducing [the] consumer market is the fundamental solution for related cruelty issues', the group said in a 2008 review of its work.

Supported by international groups including the RSPCA and World Society for the Protection of Animals, CAPN has worked to link animal-lovers across China and to educate the public on the facts of the trade. That many of the 10,000 cats consumed daily in winter in Guangdong province (where the meat is considered a warming food) are stolen from other provinces features heavily in the literature, for instance. In early 2007, the group launched an online 'signing event' which asked people to pledge to avoid cat and dog meat in future. In the following five months, it collected 21,000 signatures. By the spring of 2008, CAPN had forty-eight member groups, two branches and more than 10,000 individual supporters.

The fight for China's 'companion animals' has grown in prominence since. Before the 2008 Olympics, Beijing officials ordered dog meat off the menu at official Games restaurants. Then, in July 2010, Shanghai film-maker and animal-rights campaigner Guo Ke released a headline-hitting documentary about China's cat-meat industry, called San Hua – or 'Three Flowers' – after his pet cat. Shanghai-based magazine *Bund Pictorial*, 19 August 2010, carried a description of one of its scenes:

> At Fa's Cat Restaurant in Guangzhou's Kaiping district, the cook throws cats – too exhausted to struggle – into an iron bucket and beats them with a wooden stick. Five minutes later, the already-stiffening cats are tipped out of the bucket into a cylindrical fur-removing machine. The machine screeches into action and shortly the bloodied corpses are removed and taken to the kitchen for boiling. The cook explains: 'The worse you treat them the better they taste. It makes sure the blood gets into the meat and it tastes delicious.

As awareness of these practices has grown, so has pressure on government. Perhaps the biggest victory for the activists came at the end of 2011, when officials cancelled a 600-year-old dog-meat festival in eastern China's Zhejiang province thanks to a public outcry online. As well as demonstrating the growing power of the animal protection lobby, the event highlighted the knottier impacts of its actions, as locals mourned the passing of an ancient tradition. A provincial government official was quoted in local media as saying 'some villagers argued that they had emotional attachments to the festival, as it had been passed from generation to generation, while some said it should be listed as the city's cultural heritage.'

Similarly, consumption of shark fin has become a controversial issue in Chinese public discourse in recent years. On one side, activists – initially led by foreign NGOs, but increasingly including domestic campaigners – are fighting for legislation to end what they say is a barbaric practice that threatens marine life globally. On the other, a multimillion-dollar industry is protecting its interests, in part by hitting back at perceived attacks on tradition.

San Francisco-based conservation group WildAid estimates that up to 73 million sharks are killed each year in this industry, thrown back into the water to bleed to death after their fins are sliced off. The fins, though tasteless, are valued for their texture, and boiled in a chicken broth to produce a staggeringly expensive Chinese delicacy, shark-fin soup. The impact on shark populations has been devastating: some are estimated to have dropped by as much as 90 per cent in recent decades. Almost all fins that are consumed, 95 per cent in fact, are eaten in Hong Kong, Taiwan and the Chinese mainland.

China's wealthy classes, responsible for driving the trade as well as fighting it, play a more complicated role in this story than in the tale of cats and dogs. Shark-fin soup is a status symbol and demand to have it on the banquet table has soared in line with the numbers able to afford it. But increased interest in animal protection among the Chinese middle class has also stoked campaigns against consumption of the delicacy, and paved the way for symbolic victories: at the end of 2011, upmarket chain Peninsula Hotels announced it was taking shark fin off the menu, followed two months later by the Shangri-La chain.

External pressure has been vital in the campaign to stop this destruction. WildAid can be credited with getting shark fin off the ground as an issue in China. In 2004, it opened a Beijing office and launched a savvy publicity operation, adopting the slogan 'When the buying stops, the killing can too' and bringing in a crucial ingredient: celebrity. Stars, including film actor Jackie Chan and basketball player Yao Ming, have fronted the campaign, boosting its mainstream appeal. In one 2009 advert, a solemn Yao speaks the WildAid slogan to the camera from a seat at a restaurant table; in the background, a de-finned and bloodied shark floats in a fish tank.

Though the initial impetus came from abroad, domestic groups have taken an increasing interest in the fin fight. In March 2009, environmental outfit Green Eyes made national headlines when it petitioned a restaurant in Guangzhou, south China, to release a 200-kilogram nurse shark it had bought for US$3,000. Volunteers protested outside with placards. Eventually the publicity generated forced the provincial fishery authorities to get involved and a home was found for the shark in Guangzhou Ocean Park. Meanwhile, Beijing-based Green Beagle has campaigned for changes to the criteria used to assess the city's 'Green restaurants' – an accolade awarded to supposedly environmentally friendly establishments – to include rejection of shark fin.

There has also been a push for legislation to ban or reduce the sale of shark fin. The latest attempt is an illustrative vignette of Chinese activism, and the unusual nature of an emerging 'civil' space. During China's 2012 parliamentary session, a joint proposal to ban shark fin from government banquets – on grounds that it wastes public resources – was put forward by Ding Liguo, a deputy of the National People's Congress, and publishing tycoon Wan Jie. Wan is also director of the Alxa SEE Ecological Association, an alliance founded by eighty business figures 'committed to ecological protection in China'.

Since 2010, Alxa has run a 'think-tank' with environmental NGOs to educate its members, many of whom are also deputies to or members of one or other of China's parliamentary bodies. The upshot was an opportunity for these NGOs to influence parliamentary proposals. With the shark-fin submission – which was heavily influenced by figures including Zhang Xingsheng, director general of the north Asian arm of the Nature Conservancy – they succeeded. In the words of *China Environmental News*: 'This represents a new way in which green civil society is playing a role in government decision-making.'

But, the Alxa example notwithstanding, business in China is more often the perceived enemy of animal activists than their ally. Campaigning in 2011 and 2012 to stop pharmaceuticals firm and bear-farm operator Guizhentang from listing on Hong Kong's alternative stock exchange is an apt example.

Milking live bears for their bile through a permanent hole in their gall bladder is still legal in China. The bile, believed by a large body of traditional Chinese medicine adherents to help detoxify the body, cleanse the liver and boost vision, is turned into a powder and used as an ingredient in a range of expensive medicines. Some parts of the traditional-medicine establishment question the efficacy of the drug, while others have argued it can be replaced with an artificial product or herbs. But bear bile is still in widespread circulation: Guizhentang says the powder is used in 123 different traditional remedies.

It's a practice long opposed by anti-cruelty campaigners, most notably Hong Kong-based Animals Asia Foundation, which was founded in 1998 and has made bear farming the target of one of its three flagship programmes. In 2000, it achieved the first accord between the Chinese government and a foreign animal welfare NGO, when two state agencies agreed to free 500 bears in Sichuan and to work to end bear farming.

In early 2011, reports that Guizhentang, one of China's largest manufacturers of bear-bile products, was planning an initial public offering provoked fierce opposition. Protesters rallied online and a string of open letters were published. One from Internet portal Tencent, newspaper *Southern Weekend* and sixty-two animal protection organisations asserted that 90 per cent of respondents to online opinion polls supported the elimination of bear farming. Under intense public pressure, the listing was shelved. But a year later, Guizhentang's name again appeared on a list of companies seeking approval to float, published by the China Securities Regulatory Commission (CSRC). The news provoked even more ire than the first time round, and the response gained international media attention.

Animals Asia led the protest with an open letter urging CSRC to kill the application, while angry microbloggers – famous names among them – came out in force. Television presenter Zhang Quanling wrote on her Sina microblog:

If Guizhentang ... is listed publicly, the number of tortured bears will increase from 400 to 1,200. Guizhentang says its tubeless bile-extraction methods don't cause the bears pain. But, heavens, can it really be painless to be confined in such a narrow space every day? Is it really painless having an open wound that never heals? We have long been able to artificially make the active ingredient in bear bile or to replace it with herbal medicines, such as rhubarb. Why do we have to hurt the bears?

The post was forwarded more than 38,000 times and garnered almost 8,000 comments.

The listing was delayed again, while Guizhentang's founder Qiu Shuhua made a tearful appearance on CCTV show *Seeing* (*Kanjian* 看见), in which she defended her firm but expressed regret at ever trying to list. Meanwhile, Guizhentang launched a public relations campaign – even inviting journalists to look around a bear farm – making it clear just how rattled it had been by the onslaught from animal-lovers, NGOs, celebrities and media.

If this looks like a simple story of conflict between the public and a single corporation, however, it has an appendix that reveals more complex dynamics. In the wake of the Guizhentang uproar, traditional-medicine lobbyists launched a counter-attack, relying largely on appeals to nationalism.

While many traditional Chinese medicine doctors have come out to support the use of alternative ingredients to bear bile, a core lobby around the China Association of Traditional Chinese Medicine has adopted a combative position. Animals Asia Foundation – which was founded by British-born Jill Robinson – has been its prime target. In early 2012, the association released a statement directly attacking the charity, which it said was a foreign-backed organisation with a commercial agenda. The charity's goals, the statement said, include 'weakening the competitiveness of the Chinese medicine industry and helping Western interest groups corner the Chinese market in liver- and bile-based drugs.' In the spring, Li Lianda, a senior consultant to the association, called on the Chinese government to expel Animals Asia Foundation for committing anti-Chinese activities.

The bear-bile example is not a one-off. Similar arguments about cruelty, tradition and the efficacy – or not – of substitutes have ranged around other animal products, most famously tiger-bone wine, which is said to boost circulation and energy levels, and which, though illegal to trade in China, still drives a healthy underground industry.

The sensitivities around animal-welfare issues – both commercial and cultural – may also help to explain why one of China's most successful animal-welfare campaigns to date was directed against an industry outside its borders. The North American seal hunt, which each year clubs to death hundreds of thousands of harp seals and grey seals for their fur, meat and oil, was the focus of a campaign urging the Chinese public to 'say NO to Canadian seal products'. The activists used microblogs as well as more formal methods, such as meeting officials and making parliamentary recommendations, in an effective and organised effort. In November 2011, the government postponed plans to finalise a seal-meat trade deal with Canada. As China is one of the industry's key remaining markets, many argue its animal welfare activists could kill the hunt altogether.

Conclusion

The prominence of Internet campaigning on behalf of China's bears and Canada's seals brings this chapter full circle, with a tale of citizens attempting to exercise power online. But behind these neat stories lies the tangle of Chinese civil society, a web of campaigns and alliances, outspoken activists, concerned citizens and networked NGOs. So what, if anything, should we conclude about China today from the history of campaigning outlined in this chapter – from the registering of the first independent NGO, to the stalling of a thirteen-strong dam cascade, to today's occasionally triumphant expressions of public concern on social media networks?

One thing that's certain is that progress isn't linear. The failure to halt construction of a new dam which could wipe out rare fish species on the Yangtze tells us that. It's also clear that each of the scattered successes of recent decades had its unique set of circumstances and players. Often campaigns have been powered by one or two charismatic and brave individuals – no less important for it, but not necessarily readily reproduced. Given all this, and in the context of a country opaquely and erratically governed, it would be rash to make too confident a prediction about the rise of a Chinese 'third sector' as a reliable and effective check on state power.

But it would also be rash to ignore the evidence of a shifting 'civil' space these stories provide, in which citizens and NGOs, as well as state and business actors, contribute to decision-making. Just fifteen years ago, campaigns to protect monkeys and antelopes were considered bold; now, activists attack corporate power and government secrecy. And they have seen their actions change policy.

A key question is whether this evidence is changing or will change public self-perceptions. In 2007, the China Environmental Culture Promotion Association (then part of SEPA) produced a 'People's Livelihood Index'. The survey indicated that, of nine different social issues, pollution was the public's second priority concern, after only commodity prices. But almost half of respondents said that they, as members of the public, were 'not very important' or 'not at all important' in environmental protection. From the fight over Beijing's air to the protection of black bears, there is a growing list of incidents to show this isn't the case; that the public voice does matter. Chinese citizens are becoming players in an effort to build a greener, cleaner and more open society.

Notes

1. *Sina Weibo*, 5 December 2011, www.weibo.com/chengyunnancy.
2. See Zhan Jiang, 'Environmental Journalism in China', in Susan Shirk, ed., *Changing Media, Changing China*, Oxford: Oxford University Press, 2011.

3. Namju Lee, 'The Development of Environmental NGOs in China: A Road to Civil Society?', *China Brief*, vol. 6, no. 23, 2006.

4. Editor-in-chief of *China Development Brief* Fu Tao also makes this point in *Green China: Chinese Insights on Environment and Development*, ed. James Keeley and Zheng Yisheng, London: IIED and Chinese Academy of Social Sciences, 2012.

5. Yu Nan, 'Photographer on Journey to Save King of Swingers', *China Daily*, 10–11 November 2001.

6. Elizabeth Economy, *The River Runs Black*, Ithaca and London: Cornell University Press, 2004, p. 151.

7. Martin Williams, 'The Year of the Monkey', *BBC Wildlife*, vol. 18, no. 1, January 2000.

8. Bao Jiannu, 'Bloody Shawls Exterminating Chiru', *China Daily*, 14 January 1999.

9. For a full account of the Poyang Lake case, see Yang Xiaohong, 'Swan Song at Poyang Lake', an article from *Southern Metropolis Daily* translated and published on chinadialogue.net on 16 March 2012.

10. Jonathan Watts, *When a Billion Chinese Jump*, London: Faber & Faber, 2010, pp. 81–2.

11. Wang Yongchen, 'Farewell to the Baiji', *chinadialogue*, 10 January 2007.

12. Judith Shapiro, *Mao's War Against Nature*, Cambridge: Cambridge University Press, 2001, pp. 62–4.

13. *China Youth Daily*, 29 July 2004. Sam Geall writes in detail about the notion of the activist/journalist as a professional identity, as well as the 'advocate professional', to describe Zhang Kejia and similar characters operating in the Chinese civil sphere. Read more in Chapter 1.

14. Liu Jianqiang, 'Nu River Lessons', *chinadialogue*, 28 March 2007.

15. Dai Qing, ed., *Yangtze! Yangtze!*, Guizhou: People's Publishing House, 1989.

16. Michael Sheridan and Richard Jones, 'Three Gorges Dam Causes Quakes and Landslides', *The Times*, 30 May 2010.

17. Sam Geall, 'China's Search for Greener Values', *chinadialogue*, 21 July 2010.

18. Andrew Mertha, *China's Water Warriors: Citizen Action and Policy Change*, Ithaca NY: Cornell University Press, 2008, p. 119.

19. *Nanfang Chuang*, 6 June 2004, trans. Three Gorges Probe, www.cwwg. org/tgp04.25.06.html.

20. See Mertha, *China's Water Warrior*, for more on what he terms Yu Xiaogang's 'guerrilla theater'.

21. Kristen Nicole McDonald, 'Damming China's Grand Canyon: Pluralization without Democratization in the Nu River Valley' (Ph.D. thesis, University of California, Berkeley, 2007), provides a detailed history and analysis of the attempt to dam the Nu and the campaign to stop it.

22. Han Ziyu, 'Razing the Last Refuge', *chinadialogue*, 9 February 2011.
23. Naomi Li, 'Tackling China's Water Crisis Online', *chinadialogue*, 21 September 2006.
24. Ma Jun, 'How Participation Can Help China's Ailing Environment', *chinadialogue*, 31 January 2007.
25. Ma Jun, 'The Environment Needs Freedom of Information', *chinadialogue*, 9 May 2007; Friends of Nature, *The Green Book*, Beijing, 2007.
26. Ma Jun, 'Your Right To Know: A Historic Moment', *chinadialogue*, 1 May 2008.
27. Meng Si, 'Access Still Barred', *chinadialogue*, 13 May 2011.
28. '2010 Study of Heavy Metal Pollution by IT Brand Supply Chain', compiled by Friends of Nature, Institute of Public and Environmental Affairs and Green Beagle, 24 April 2010, http://pacificenvironment.org/downloads/GCA%20IT%20Campaign%20Report%20Phase%20One.pdf.
29. Friends of Nature, IPE, Green Beagle, *The Other Side of Apple*, 20 January 2011, www.ipe.org.cn/Upload/Report-IT-V-Apple-I-EN.pdf.
30. Asia Water Project, 'Cleaning up China's IT Industry', 26 July 2010, http://chinawaterrisk.org/interviews/cleaning-up-the-it-industry%E2%80%99s-supply-chain-in-china.
31. Meng Si, 'A Dog Fight in China', *chinadialogue*, 15 July 2011.
32. 'Our Work against Consumption of Cat and Dog Meat in China 2007', August 2008, www.capn-online.info/ACReport2007_en.doc.

Further reading

Ed Grumbine, *Where the Dragon Meets the Angry River: Nature and Power in the People's Republic of China*, Washington DC: Shearwater Books, 2010. (A look at the drivers behind the Nu River dam-building moratorium of 2004 and the future of conservation in south-west China.)

Andrew Mertha, *China's Water Warriors: Citizen Action and Policy Change*, Ithaca and London: Cornell University Press, 2008. (Forensic analysis of China's hydropower policymaking processes and the role played by opponents of large-scale dams.)

Kevin J. O'Brien, ed., *Popular Protest in China*, Cambridge MA: Harvard University Press, 2008. (From student protests to anti-dam campaigns, a look at how social movements have unfolded in authoritarian China.)

Paul Waldau, *Animal Rights: What Everyone Needs to Know*, Oxford: Oxford University Press, 2011. (Not a great deal on China in here, but still a useful introduction to the animal welfare campaign sphere globally.)

Jonathan Watts, *When a Billion Chinese Jump*, London: Faber & Faber, 2010. (Ten years of environmental change in China, told through the experiences of the *Guardian*'s former Asia environment correspondent.)

CHAPTER 3

The Yangzonghai case:
struggling for environmental justice

ADAM MOSER

In China today, the tension between environmental protection and economic growth is more evident than almost anywhere else on the planet. China's government is actively addressing many of the problems that arise. But the ability of citizens to use the law to engage in some of these important issues is still unclear.

Few individual legal cases or events provide a better platform to examine the limitations that face the public in attempting to use law and the judicial system to address issues of environmental governance than the case of *Chongqing Green Volunteers* v. *Guodian Yangzonghai Power Company*, known as the Yangzonghai case. The case involved one of China's largest electricity generating companies and touched on core issues that affect China's domestic energy security – a sensitive political topic, which the courts will often attempt to avoid. The Yangzonghai case is both reflective of and shines a light on the state of environmental law and governance in China.

In many respects, Chinese environmental law has changed rapidly and significantly over the past decade. These changes are especially evident in the areas of policy and legislation, the development of environmental courts and public participation. However, environmental law must operate within the confines of China's broader political, economic, legal and administrative regimes – regimes that have evolved slower or in ways not conducive to the enforcement of environmental law. The most evident of these outside forces has been China's focus on economic development above all else.

China's focus on economic growth has been successful in many respects, such as the enormous reduction in poverty. But like many countries before it, China's policies are often indicative of a 'pollute first, clean up later' paradigm. In addition, internal politics within the Chinese Communist Party regarding the independence of China's judiciary have affected the ability of the courts to enforce environmental law. Many of the largest advances made in written law and policy have struggled to significantly improve environmental law enforcement, specifically because environmental law is captive to China's broader economic and political regimes.

This chapter focuses on how environmental law enforcement operates within China's broader governance system and through the judicial system. The first section introduces the problem of environmental law enforcement through the example of lead emissions in China. The following two sections summarise China's legal system and the challenges it faces. Finally, the chapter ends by exploring the issues of public participation and the judiciary's role in environmental law enforcement through the Yangzonghai case study.

Over the past two decades, China has made progress in addressing important environmental issues, notably in the areas of reforestation, improving energy and water efficiency, and developing cleaner and renewable energy. Law played some role in all of these relative successes, but in most cases market-like mechanisms and bureaucratic management tools that rewarded cadres for meeting targets were equally or more important. This was particularly the case for energy-intensity targets set during China's 11th Five-Year Plan period (from 2006 to 2010). Indeed, examples of judicial enforcement involving the energy intensity goals are very hard to find, which might speak to the limited role of law in general in China.

However, there has undoubtedly also been an increase in the use of the law and judicial enforcement. Ten years ago it was rare for a pollution victim, an environmental protection bureau, or an environmental group to use the courts to enforce compliance or to seek redress. However, this is increasingly becoming the norm. While the final outcome of many of these cases has not changed significantly over the past decade (see Box 3.1), the number of cases brought and the public acceptance of using the judicial system to address environmental problems are growing. This has placed increasing pressure on law and the courts to provide for justice effectively.

BOX 3.1 'China's courts fail the environment'

XIA JUN, a lawyer at Zhongzi law office, who acted on behalf of Chongqing Green Volunteers in the case *Chongqing Green Volunteers v. Guodian Yangzonghai Power Company* (the Yangzonghai case), writes:

As a lawyer with a decade-long involvement in environmental rights, I still remember the sighs of my colleagues when I set out on this path: litigation is hard in China; environmental litigation doubly so.

More than a decade ago, in May 2001, *Beijing Youth Daily* published an article titled 'Why Are Pollution Cases So Hard to Bring?' The report quoted Wang Canfa, an environmental law scholar and expert in environmental litigation. 'At the moment, it is hard to resolve environmental disputes,' said Wang. 'First, polluting firms often pay a lot of money in taxes, and so are protected by local governments. Second, it is difficult for victims to provide evidence. And, third, it is hard to bring a case to court. Environmental lawsuits are usually brought by members of the public against a company, presenting a dilemma for the courts. There is a limit to how many cases a judge can handle, and a tricky case can drag on and on. Naturally, they are reluctant to take those cases on.'

Has anything changed in the last ten years? Given my own experience and the cases I am familiar with, I have to conclude that it is still a difficult time for environmental tort cases in China.

This is true for every stage of the process: lodging a complaint, registering a case, assessing damages, winning the case and executing judgments. Each step is a battle, and no real solution has emerged. Perhaps most depressing is the refusal of courts to hear environmental or administrative lawsuits that are legally entitled to a hearing, often on the basis of flimsy reasoning, where a reason is given at all.

The value of environmental litigation lies not only in its ability to make amends for the victims' losses, but also in its service to society more widely. Pollution sanctions and administrative fines are too low to deter breaches of environmental law, but compensation in civil suits – awarded according to harm incurred – is potentially unlimited. High compensation payouts in a number of lawsuits should cause other polluters to pay attention.

'Relying solely on the power of the environmental authorities to deal with large and powerful companies is inadequate,' said Wang Canfa. 'Victims seeking redress through the law courts will reduce pressure on the environmental authorities, and that's a form of public participation.' In other words, pollution victims protecting their private interests will help to achieve public environmental goals. Environmental litigation not only offers a solution to environmental problems, but also benefits the nation and its citizens.

Enforcement of existing environmental laws is poor, and there is huge room for improvement in both judicial independence and public oversight of the justice system.

A major problem is that most courts are prone to interference from local government, and impartial judgments in environmental disputes are hard to come by. Often, cases are not heard – or not heard fairly – because local government funds the court, as well as hiring and firing its staff.

Local governments' love affair with GDP growth, focus on short-term benefits and narrow view of what it means to maintain stability mean that environmental legislation lacks authority and administrative powers are misused. Against this background, it is hardly surprising that many environmental disputes fail even to make it to court.

To offer a brief illustration of this problem, in 2005 the Chengde Intermediate People's Court accepted a joint case brought by more than 1,500 villagers against a steel company that had polluted local groundwater. It was subsequently criticised for doing so by the local Communist Party committee and local government. Then, in July 2010, fishermen from Dalian in northeast China tried to bring a case at Dalian Maritime Court over an oil leak. The judge said helplessly: 'If we heard the fishermen's case, we would lose our jobs.'

Low awareness of environmental legislation and failings in judicial ethics also combine to thwart the efforts of defenders of environmental rights. Some judges are unaware of the special nature of environmental cases, have no experience in handling these cases and lack the ethical standards necessary to work for the people and uphold the rule of law. As a result, it is common for cases that should be heard to be refused.

In 2010, for example, Beijing resident Yang Zi took the Beijing Environmental Protection Bureau to court in an attempt to obtain monitoring data on a medical-waste incinerator near his home. Haidian People's Court found that as the plaintiff's home was outside the area classed as being affected by the facility, he had no right to request the information and rejected the case.

Even more disappointing, environmental health cases – where compensation is sought for disease or deaths caused by pollution – are often refused, meaning grave damage goes ignored or is even covered up. In 2004, I represented the plaintiffs in a case against a mining company in Shaodong county, Hunan province. I tried for three years to get the case heard, ultimately in vain. The court was worried that the case would result in more claims being brought and so opted to ignore it.

Another reason for the refusal to hear certain environmental cases is the lack of adequate processes for assessing damages.

China's Tort Liability Law rules that the burden of proof in pollution cases lies with the polluter, who must prove that there is no causal relationship between the pollution and the harm suffered. But it is common practice for courts to rely on a report by a third-party specialist body to determine if there is a cause-and-effect relationship, and to set the value of the damage done. This means the judges themselves do not take the risk of making these decisions.

Tools are currently in place for evaluating pollution damage to fisheries, so when the fishing industry sues polluters it has access to credible technical back-up. But where other pollution cases are concerned, mechanisms for assessing harm are chaotic. It is often difficult to find an appropriate third-party assessor or assessment method and an authoritative assessment cannot be obtained. As a result, courts refuse to hear cases so as to avoid the risk of having to carry out that assessment themselves.

In certain respects, the judicial environment has been getting worse: some courts which previously welcomed environmental cases have started to refuse them. This prevents specialist courts from playing to their strengths, reduces the inclination of victims to try to bring cases, and undermines the proper handling of environmental disputes.

For example, maritime courts previously seemed happy to take on lawsuits where pollution at sea had been caused by land-based sources (even though the law is unclear as to which court has jurisdiction in such cases). Recently, however, some maritime courts have started to refuse these cases, instead referring plaintiffs to their local courts.

A range of worrying trends indicate China still has a long way to go to establish the rule of law in the environmental sector. Opening the road to judicial solutions to pollution is crucial for both environmental justice and the sustainable development of society. China must speed up judicial reform, strengthen the mechanisms that support Green litigation and create an environment in which courts can issue fair verdicts in environmental disputes and the construction of an 'ecological civilisation' can advance.

Lead poisoning: a darker side of the e-bike boom

Evidence that environmental law enforcement is weak in China and that there is a critical need to improve it is not hard to find. A spate of high-profile incidents of lead poisoning caused by emissions from lead-acid battery plants, battery recyclers and smelters provide a tragic example of the endemic failures that plague enforcement.

Over the past decade, lead-acid battery production in China has boomed. This is partly attributable to a growth in car ownership, but even more so to an explosion in the numbers of electric bicycles, most of which run on cheap, rechargeable lead-acid batteries. There are currently around 100 million people using e-bikes regularly in China. Although they are a greener form of transportation than cars or motorcycles, e-bikes can also be polluting and resource-intensive. This is partly thanks to the footprint of the electricity generation in charging the batteries, but it is also due to the environmental costs of manufacturing and disposing of batteries, most of which have a lifespan of around two years. In 2010, China used nearly one-third of the world's industrial lead, 83 per cent of which went to lead-acid battery production, according to an industry association. That same year, China was the world's largest producer and the largest market for lead-acid batteries, thanks largely to e-bikes. In 2011, China had between 2,000 to 3,000 battery factories, most of them making rechargeable lead batteries for e-bikes and cars.[1]

Dealing with the rapid expansion of an industry as pollution-intensive as lead-acid battery production would be a challenge for any country. An examination of how China attempted to deal with these pollution issues helps to demonstrate the challenges that its environmental law enforcement system faces. From 2005 to 2011, there were dozens of reported mass lead poisoning incidents in China. Sometimes, villagers rioted to force factory closures. Most of the lead poisoning involved in these cases came from local-level airborne pollution, in the form of both lead oxide dust from battery plants and lead carried in emissions from smelters and battery plants.

Though less direct, lead levels in water sources and in the soil are also serious problems.

Two egregious cases in 2009 brought lead pollution into the national spotlight. In Hunan province, in central China, over 1,300 children who attended schools less than 500 metres from a manganese smelter were found to have elevated blood lead levels. Children are particularly vulnerable to lead poisoning, which can affect mental and physical development. The smelter had been operating in the town for just over a year. In Shaanxi province, also in central China, 613 of 731 children tested had dangerously high blood lead levels.[2] In both cases, parents of affected children rioted and destroyed property at the polluting plants. In Hekou village, in the eastern province of Jiangsu, of 110 children tested, 51 had elevated blood lead levels, due to a battery factory located just 100 metres from residents' homes.

Authorities in China are not without legal tools to control lead pollution. Lead oxide, the toxic material most associated with lead poisoning from lead-battery fabrication, is classified as toxic in China's National Registry of Hazardous Waste. One of the earliest and least costly of regulations that specifically addresses lead is the 'Health Protection Zone Standard for Lead Battery Plants' issued by the Ministry of Health in 1989. This standard requires that lead battery plants not be built within 500 to 800 metres from residential communities, depending on the size of the plant and other factors. However, it is estimated that over 95 per cent of China's lead battery plants do not meet the 500-metre standard.

The challenge to China's environmental laws

The passing of China's Environmental Impact Assessment (EIA) Law in 2002 is often cited as a milestone in China's efforts to comprehensively address environmental pollution. The written law includes many global best practices and codifies one of the basic tools in Chinese environmental law, the 'simultaneous system', which requires that pollution control be considered in the design process; the construction process; and in the operation of the facility.

The EIA Law applies to almost every construction project and major renovation. Appropriately, requirements for compliance vary depending on the size of the project. Most small projects that will have a minimal impact on the environment will only need to fill out a form. But projects with the potential to significantly impact the environment need to complete a full environmental assessment report. According to implementing regulations issued by the Ministry of Environmental Protection (MEP), lead-battery plants are categorised as having a high potential to impact the environment and must complete a full environmental assessment report. The finished EIA report must then be submitted to the local, or sometimes provincial, Environmental Protection Bureau (EPB) for approval.

Before approving an EIA, the EPB must ensure that the proposed project will be able to meet all relevant pollution emission standards. This should require testing of the installed pollution control equipment. In addition, a factory must list all of its pollution emissions in accordance with the Declaration and Registration Form for Discharging Pollutants and file the information with the local authorities.

These laws and regulations, if adequately enforced, could significantly limit the environmental and public health damage coming from the lead-battery industry. However, it is estimated that around 60 per cent of the lead-battery factories in China are not officially registered. If plants are not registered, it is unlikely that they have undergone the resource-intensive process of conducting a thorough EIA report. Furthermore, even if a factory has completed its EIA report and has been approved, there is still little reason to assume that its emissions are meeting the relevant standards. Ensuring that an EIA is implemented and standards are met requires diligent oversight by regulators. But, unfortunately, a significant cause for weak environmental law enforcement is the inability or the unwillingness of China's environmental regulators to enforce the law consistently.

The ground level of environmental law enforcement in China is the nearly 3,000 EPBs at the county and city levels. These local-level EPBs report to the provincial-level EPBs, which report to the national level Ministry of Environmental Protection. In theory, all sub-national level EPBs are under the control and direction of the MEP. However, here there is a large discrepancy between theory and practice.

There are several reasons why the MEP's centralised authority is diluted in practice. Since the economic reforms that began in the 1980s, local governments have had far greater de facto autonomy from China's central government. A contributing reason for this autonomy is that local governments are largely responsible for collecting local taxes to fund most local initiatives and local government projects. Importantly, this means that the local governments have more discretion over how to spend their money. For environmental protection, this means that local governments control the bulk of funding that goes to local EPBs and most personnel decisions. In addition, China's primary management system for government officials is skewed towards rewarding officials for increasing GDP growth, which systematically encourages short-term growth over environmental protection.

Most local governments choose to invest in projects that are likely to provide a higher and more immediate return on investment than investments in environmental protection. Sometimes this means that local governments are directly invested in the same polluting industries that are supposed to be regulated by an underfunded EPB. Even if a local government is not directly invested in a local industry, the local government likely relies on the taxes that the industry pays. The smaller a town is, the larger the likelihood that a single factory makes up a significant portion of the town's revenue. In a high-profile incident in 2010, city officials in Guzhen, in the eastern Chinese province of Anhui, fired several EPB officers for their continued attempts to enforce pollution standards on a factory that clearly enjoyed protection from the city government.

Pollution from the lead-battery industry provides a tragic example of the extent that local protectionism of polluters is engrained in China's broader governance regime. Not only have EPBs been unwilling or unable to enforce relevant environmental laws to control pollution, but also local governments have gone so far as to obstruct and even deny blood lead level tests to the children of concerned parents. In March 2012, China's state media reported that parents in Chenzhou, a city of 4.5 million people and 1,000 smelting plants in Hunan in central China were denied access to blood lead level tests. 'The doctors said their equipment was not working and no one knew when it would be fixed,' one mother was quoted as saying. 'They said the child should just drink more milk and eat more lean pork.'[3]

Underfunding of EPBs and local government protection of polluting industries for short-term profit are important examples of how certain aspects of China's broader governance regime work against the strict enforcement of environmental law.

In the case of sulphur dioxide (SO_2) pollution, which is discussed in the Yangzonghai case below, despite the existence of a pollution levy on SO_2 emissions in China since 1982 and numerous regulations issued by the MEP and China's top economic planning agency, the National Development and Reform Commission (NDRC), China struggled until recently to control a rapid rise in these emissions. Only during the period of the 11th Five-Year Plan, from 2006 to 2010, was China able to control and reduce SO_2 emissions, primarily through increased executive enforcement, mainly bureaucratic management tools like the cadre evaluation system, as well as the deployment of SO_2 scrubbers – flue-gas desuphurisation technologies that remove SO_2 from emissions – at coal-fired power plants.[4]

From 2006 to 2009, SO_2 scrubbers were installed on 422 GW of coal-fired power plants. This increased the share of coal plants with scrubbers from 10 per cent in 2005 to 71 per cent in 2010: a massive deployment of hardware in a very short period of time.[5] Though the operation and oversight of scrubbers are improving, technical problems and enforcement gaps remain.

The extent to which China's civil society can help to fill enforcement gaps and ensure compliance remains an open question, in part because of a complicated mix of 'laws', 'regulations', 'policies' and 'goals', which vary greatly in their effectiveness. China's constitution establishes the China's National People's Congress (NPC) as the supreme legislature for the country. While technically only legislation passed by China's national legislature, the National People's Congress, or its standing committee is 'law' (*falu* 法律), in practice the NPC relies heavily on other government organs to determine the detail of the laws it passes.

Many of the laws passed by the NPC are brief and read more like specific policy statements than actionable laws. These laws often call on the State Council, a highly influential executive body chaired by the premier, or an undesignated administrative body, to draft implementing regulations that define the obligations of regulated entities. When these administrative measures are approved by the State Council, they have the status of 'administrative regulations' (*xingzheng fagui* 行政法规) which can have binding legal effect. Moreover, ministries and other government agencies can formulate 'departmental rules' (*bumen guizhang* 部门规章) without formal State Council approval.

As well as passing laws, the NPC also approves policies (*zhengce* 政策) and goals (*mubiao* 目标): measures that are often related to China's Five-Year Plans, the nation's principal economic and social planning framework. The NDRC primarily drafts the plan, with input from ministries, and it is then approved by the NPC. The plan is in one sense law, because it is approved by the NPC. However, it is unlike law because it is generally not enforceable through the judiciary.

This distinction between laws, policies and goals – and between executive enforcement and judicial or legal enforcement – is an important element to consider in analysing recent environmental cases. Executive enforcement refers to the Chinese central government's efforts to motivate local executive officials to support and enforce national policies, usually by linking national policy goals to the Communist Party's cadre evaluation system, which assesses the job performance of local government officials. Judicial or legal enforcement, on the other hand, refers to how laws and regulations are applied and enforced by courts or other legal actors, including the EPBs.

National goals, such as those established in China's Five-Year Plans, are often allocated to provinces and below, to the level of individual cadre evaluations. They can be used to send clear signals to local leaders as to the central government's priorities.[6] In the 11th Five-Year Plan, SO_2 reduction goals were directly linked to the promotion or removal of local leaders.[7] This incentivised local officials to respond with programmes to reduce SO_2 emissions. However, many of these local programmes to control emissions were undertaken independently of existing laws and regulations aimed at SO_2 emissions – the same laws and regulations that are inconsistently enforced primarily due to China's de facto decentralisation of authority.

Professor Yuan Xu, an expert on China's SO_2 regulation, says that the 'relationship between goals and policies partly reflects [the country's] insufficient rule of law. Policies are written and enforced by executives and their enforcement heavily relies on the willingness of these executives.'[8] Xu adds that there are advantages to this relationship, most notably the ability of executives to act to address an issue when the political will is present. The downside, of course, is that when political will weakens, the enforcement of policies and goals suffers. A move towards a regulatory system based on the rule of law 'could provide the necessary continuous pressure and liberate the Chinese top leaders', he says.[9] Additionally, because the government and the Party almost exclusively handle the Plan's enforcement internally, it is removed from the judicial system and in many ways existing law, and thus it is far less conducive to encouraging public participation in enforcement.

It is hard to say definitively that linking SO_2 mitigation to cadre evaluations was alone responsible for emissions reduction during the

11th Five-Year Plan, because numerous other regulatory and policy changes were made during the period. However, it is clear that there was renewed political will to control SO_2 pollution and that the implementation and enforcement of these policies were primarily driven by the executive at both the national and the local level.

The coexistence of overlapping regulatory regimes, enforced by different governmental actors – as is the case with SO_2 regulation – is not necessarily a bad thing. But in China, where the executive is significantly stronger than the judiciary, such dual systems of enforcement can erode the supremacy of law, especially the case when the alternative enforcement system is proven to be more successful. The existence of alternative enforcement channels reduces the burden of responsibility that might otherwise fall on the courts and judges to provide justice.

This duality of enforcement is not the only barrier to judicial enforcement or greater public participation. Generally, laws and regulations that are independent of goals, such as the Environmental Protection Law, the Air Pollution Control Law and the Open Government Information Regulations, provide the legal basis for judicial enforcement.[10] Arguably, their enforcement is in line with developing a rule of law system through increased law-based enforcement. However, many of the enforcement and penalty provisions in these laws are too limited to be effective.

In China, the question of how legal and executive enforcement can coexist still needs resolution – and this is the case in many areas of governance. Overall, the linking of environmental goals to the career advancement of local officials has been effective in reducing targeted pollutants. In this way, the cadre evaluation system and existing law are supportive of each other. But there is little evidence that executive enforcement alone will help develop the capacity for a robust and sophisticated energy and environmental governance system. In practice, cadres tend to do whatever is required to meet their hard targets with little regard for existing law. The 11th Five Year Plan set hard targets for SO_2 emissions and chemical oxygen demand – a measure of water quality – and those targets were met. However, meeting these two targets did little to improve the overall ability of EPBs or the courts to enforce environmental laws and regulations more broadly.[11]

In late 2010, as the 11th Five-Year Plan drew to a close, some local governments haphazardly cut power to factories, hospitals and homes in a rush to meet energy conservation targets. Paradoxically, these cuts resulted in many affected users shifting to less efficient and dirtier diesel generators. These unintended consequences illustrated the risks inherent in emphasising executive enforcement above the law. Shortly after the rush to generators occurred, a senior official with the NDRC commented that what was needed was to 'gradually shift from persuasion and encouragement-based energy conservation to compulsory energy conservation according to the laws.'[12] As will be seen through the discussion of the Yangzonghai Power Company case below, while legal enforcement is weak in comparison to executive enforcement, there are signs that the central government is trying to improve the cohesion between executive enforcement and the legal system.

The next section will begin to examine the role of China's judicial system in environmental law enforcement, and provide insight into the challenges that both pollution victims and judges face in the pursuit of justice.

Struggling for justice

Increasingly, citizens rely on China's judicial system to address breaches of environmental law. The number of administrative and civil environmental law cases rose rapidly from 1995 through 2010. Cases seeking redress for pollution-related damages to health or property have increased at an even faster rate over the same period. Because of the relatively young nature of China's courts and the specialised nature of such cases, it is understandable that the courts continue to struggle with environmental cases. However, like local

EPBs, China's judiciary is not independent from China's broader political and governance regimes.

According to China's constitution, China is a socialist country ruled by law. Article 5 of the constitution states that all state organs, the military, political parties and all enterprises must abide by the law. All violations of the law must be investigated and no organisation or individual is above the law. Article 126 of the constitution states that the courts act independently and are not subject to interference from any administrative or public organisation. But in reality, China's courts are beholden to local governments and the political will of local politicians.

The cornerstone of China's environmental law framework is the 1989 Environmental Protection Law. The law also provides the basis for public engagement in the enforcement of environmental protection. Article 6 states that 'All units and individuals shall have the obligation to protect the environment and shall have the right to report on or file charges against units or individuals that cause pollution or damage to the environment.' Over the past decade, laws and policies were made to promote public participation and grant public access to government information. There was a growing recognition that China's environmental situation could no longer be ignored. New environmental tribunals sprang up around China as a pragmatic attempt to address rampant environmental pollution. Several of the courts which host an environmental tribunal crafted unique provisions that permit legally recognised groups to bring public-interest claims.

In 1997, the State Environmental Protection Agency (SEPA, since upgraded to the Ministry of Environmental Protection in 2008) began to encourage and require some EPBs to operate hotlines for accepting citizen complaints about pollution. By 2001, a national hotline was established. Now local EPBs are required to accept hotline complaints twenty-four hours a day. In many regards, the pollution-reporting hotlines are a success. The number of complaints lodged with the call centres increased steadily from around 300,000 complaints in 2000 to over 700,000 in 2010.

In December 2005, the State Council issued the 'Decision of the State Council on the Implementation of the Scientific Development Concept and the Strengthening of Environmental Protection'. This document highlighted the severity of China's environmental problems and the importance that the central government attaches to environmental protection. It strongly urged civil-society groups to play a larger role in encouraging environmental enforcement and detecting illegal behaviour. It even promoted environmental public-interest lawsuits. Following the State Council's notice, the promotion of public participation in environmental matters increased rapidly.

The largest move to date in promoting public participation was the introduction of Open Government Information (OGI) regulations, which became effective in 2008. China's OGI regulations require government agencies to disclose certain information on their own initiative and to respond to requests for information from the public within fifteen business days. The regulations came after more than eight years of local-level experimentation with OGI initiatives.

The MEP has been one of the most assertive ministries in promoting the OGI regulations. In 2007, SEPA drafted its own Measures on Open Environmental Information (OEI Measures). The measures provide details on how environmental protection bureaus nationwide should implement the OGI regulation and go so far as to state that its purpose is to 'promote the public's involvement in environmental protection'.[13]

Justifiably, Chinese civil-society groups were excited about the potential for these regulations to enhance the public's role in government decision-making, to ensure accountability and environmental protection.[14] Since the OGI regulations became effective in 2008 there have been numerous lawsuits targeting government agencies for failing to disclose information; and the Supreme People's Court issued specific guidance for lower courts on how to handle OGI cases. In addition, several studies specific to environmental information disclosure have been undertaken to compare implementation and effectiveness across different Chinese cities.

In 2007 and 2008, environmental tribunals in China began to multiply, many as a reaction to high-profile water pollution incidents in their respective jurisdictions. At the end of 2011, there were over seventy environmental tribunals at the basic and or intermediate level in at least thirteen of China's thirty-one provinces. In June 2010, the Supreme People's Court (SPC), the highest court in China, issued a circular that included a paragraph expressly permitting courts with a relatively high number of environmental cases to establish environmental tribunals.

The most legally controversial measure taken by some of the environmental tribunal jurisdictions are provisions that ostensibly grant legal standing to legally recognised groups to sue in the name of the public interest. This is controversial, because China's Civil Procedure Law requires that the plaintiff have a 'direct interest' in the case, and the Administrative Procedure Law requires a similar interest related to a specific or concrete action. The SPC has not yet issued a formal statement as to the status of these public-interest standing provisions, but nor has the SPC directly condemned the provisions. The judges to whom the author spoke, from courts that permit public-interest standing, believe that they have informal approval from the SPC. But this issue will not be fully resolved unless the relevant civil and administrative procedure laws are modified.

The jurisdictions that pursued public-interest standing measures did so explicitly to encourage public participation and promote civil enforcement suits. The environmental tribunals justify their existence on the need to adjudicate numerous environmental cases, but there have been few civil enforcement cases brought to the tribunals.

In May 2010, a case brought against the Guodian Yangzonghai coal-fired power plant in south-west China tested the robustness of the newly bestowed rights of the public to participate in environmental decision-making and the ability of China's weak judiciary to uphold these rights.

BOX 3.2   Eight cases that mattered

From a successful challenge to Beijing's planning authorities to damages for mass tadpole deaths, the 2000s were full of turning points for Green law in China. *chinadialogue* compiled its picks of the decade, with advice from ZHANG JINGJING of the Global Network for Public Interest Law; LIU XIANG of the Centre for Legal Assistance to Pollution Victims; ALEX WANG of the University of California, Berkeley School of Law; WANG JIN, professor at Peking University School of Law; ZHU XIAO, professor at Renmin University School of Law; and QIN TIANBAO of Wuhan University School of Law.

The Pinghu tadpoles

Yu Mingda of Pinghu in Zhejiang v. five factories,
including Buyun Dyes and Buyun Chemicals

This case took fourteen years to play out and involved four levels of courts, appeals from three levels of procurators, and four occasions on which representatives from the National People's Congress exercised supervisory duties over the Supreme Court. Lawyers say it 'exhausted all means of judicial redress' and reflects China's struggle between environmental protection and local business interests.

Starting in 1989, Yu Mingda of Pinghu in Zhejiang province, east China, leased land from Pinghu Normal College, where he farmed American river frogs. But over a period from late 1993 to early 1994, his stock of 2.7 million tadpoles all died.

Yu contacted Pinghu Environmental Bureau, which confirmed that the water near the farm had been polluted and told him the pollution had come from five factories, including Buyun Dyes Factory and Buyun Chemicals, located further upstream. These were village enterprises run by Buyun village, which neighboured Yu's farm. The environmental authorities found that the five plants were dumping untreated effluents directly into the river. But the factories denied any link with the dead tadpoles. In December 1995, Yu sued them, demanding 483,000 yuan (US$75,000) in compensation.

In response to a request by the Pinghu Court, the Ministry of Justice's Institute of Forensic Science carried out an assessment and found that the death of the tadpoles was directly and undeniably linked to water pollution from Buyun Dyes. But the court did not accept the finding. On 27 July 1997, one and a half years after accepting the case, Pinghu Court dismissed Yu's claim.

When asked about the decision during an interview with a Zhejiang reporter, the deputy head of Pinghu Intermediate Court said: 'Maybe the pollution was caused by the factories, but that year virtually all the fish and frogs around here died. If we had found in favour of the plaintiff, then many others would have asked for compensation too. Who's going to pay for all those losses?'

In 1998, Shaoxing Intermediate Court upheld the original decision, and in 2001 Zhejiang Higher People's Court did the same. In 2006, the Supreme People's Court accepted the case for review and eventually overturned these decisions in 2009, ordering the five plants to pay Yu 483,000 yuan (US$75,000) in compensation – plus 100,000 yuan (US$15,500) in interest.

Shandong reservoir pollution

Ninety-seven farmers from Lianyungang v. *Jinyimeng Paper and Linshu Chemical Plant*

This case resulted in a huge compensation payout for losses caused by water pollution. The court that handled it was not in the plaintiffs' home town, and did not consider the financial conditions of the companies in question when setting the compensation level. As a result, the amount received by the plaintiffs was equivalent to their estimated losses.

In this case, the government paid compensation in advance and then asked for reimbursement from the companies, not only demonstrating its obligation to protect the environment, but also giving a boost to the lawsuit. Whether or not this practice will be followed by other local governments depends on their willingness.

In the year between June 1999 and June 2000, fish in the Shiliang River Reservoir – at the intersection of the counties of Donghai and Ganyu in Jiangsu province and Linshu county in Shandong province, eastern China – were killed off by major pollution incidents, resulting in severe losses for ninety-seven fish-farming families. The reservoir is the biggest artificial reservoir in Jiangsu and a reserve source of water for the city of Lianyungang.

After each case, the farmers complained to the Shandong provincial government and the State Environmental Protection Agency (now the Ministry of Environmental Protection) as well as visiting Linshu county government to demand compensation – but no solution was offered. In 2007, the ninety-seven affected families brought a lawsuit against the two defendants, requesting that they be ordered to pay 5.6 million yuan (US$866,000) in compensation for loss of fish, and 480,000 yuan (US$74,000) in other costs, including those for investigations, and to prevent further occurrences.

The defendants denied any pollution or causal link, but evidence found during the court's investigation showed that the first defendant was releasing 10,000 tonnes or more of polluted water daily, while the second was releasing about 1,000 tonnes daily – and that water was flowing into the Shiliang River Reservoir. Lianyungang Intermediate People's Court found that the defendants had been releasing pollution and that this was the cause of the plaintiff's losses, and ordered compensation to be paid. An appeal by the defendants to Jiangsu Higher People's Court was rejected. At the end of 2003, the farmers received 5.6 million yuan in compensation.

The Tasman Sea spill

Tianjin Oceanic Bureau v. Infinity Shipping and the London Protection and Indemnity Club

This was China's first international marine ecology civil compensation case. Although the damages awarded were less than hoped for, it was still a landmark case: it made the maritime authorities aware of the possibilities of claiming damages through the courts, laid a foundation for judicial and administrative bodies to better handle these cases, and provided essential experience for public-interest environmental compensation lawsuits.

At 4 a.m. on 23 November 2002, the Maltese-registered tanker *Tasman Sea* collided with the Chinese *Shunkai No. 1*, 23 nautical miles east of the Tianjin Dagu Anchorage, triggering an oil spill. Investigations by the North China Sea Monitoring Centre found that 359.6 square kilometres of ocean were affected, with oil content in sediment reaching 8.1 times normal values. The spill badly damaged the ecology of the Bohai Gulf, an important spawning and feeding ground for ocean fisheries.

After the incident, various parties brought claims in the Tianjin Maritime Court against Infinity Shipping, the tanker's owner, and the London Protection and Indemnity Club (a mutual insurer in the shipping industry). The State Oceanic Administration authorised its Tianjin branch to sue for marine ecological damages of over 98.3 million yuan (US$15 million) on behalf of the state; Tianjin Fisheries and Harbours Office sued for losses to the fishing industry of 18.3 million yuan (US$2.8 million); while Tianjin Tanggu District Dagu Fishing Association, Hebei Luannan County Fishing Association, Tianjin Tanggu District Beitang Fishing Association and Dagu Fishing Association sued for 62.28 million yuan (US$9.6 million) in fishing and fish-farming losses to thousands of fishermen and fish farmers.

On 24 December 2004, decisions were made on the eight separate cases brought against the two defendants in Tianjin Maritime Court. Damages of more than 17 million yuan (US$2.6 million) were awarded to 1,490 fishermen and fish farmers in Luannan, Hangu, Beitang and Dagu for the impact on catches and equipment. On 30 December the court awarded around 10 million yuan (US$1.5 million) in compensation to Tianjin Oceanic Bureau for losses to marine environmental capacity and costs incurred in investigation and assessment; and 15 million yuan (US$2.3 million) to Tianjin Fisheries and Harbours Office for loss of fishery resources and investigation costs.

This case involved ten different legal parties, affected more than 1,500 people, and included requests for compensation of 170 million yuan (US$26.3 million). This was also the first time China had sued an overseas shipping insurer for losses under the terms of the 1992 International Convention on Civil Liability for Oil Pollution Damage since becoming party to the Convention.

The Panjiayuan animal-testing laboratory

Residents of Buildings 4 and 6 at Panjiayuan Nanli, Beijing v. the Beijing Planning Commission

In this case – one of very few successful challenges to the Beijing Planning Commission – one reason given by the court for cancelling the project's planning permission was that an environmental impact assessment should have been carried out but was not, rendering the decision unsound.

Lawsuits over impacts of urban planning on people's lives are actually not uncommon; this particular case is significant because the court accepted it, and the challenge was ultimately successful. Attempts to take planning commissions to court in China frequently collapse because residents fail to secure recognition as valid plaintiffs. In this case, having considered the public interest, the court decided to accept the Panjiayuan residents as plaintiffs. Their success was mainly because the project design violated certain rules set by the state, while media attention was also a contributing factor.

Residents of Panjiayuan Nanli in Beijing say that in 1984 an animal-testing laboratory was built across the road from their homes and, although measures were taken to reduce the odours from the facility, bad smells have affected their quality of life since. In May 2002, the residents learned that another, even bigger, animal laboratory in the same location had received planning permission.

The residents believed the approval process for the facility was illegal and requested that Beijing Planning Commission re-examine its decision; but the commission maintained that its actions were above board. Finally, 182 residents took the commission to court, requesting that the planning permission certificate awarded to the new project be withdrawn.

Wang Canfa, director of the Center for Legal Assistance to Pollution Victims and professor at China University of Political Science and Law, represented the residents. He found that the design of the project fell short of national standards: the laboratories were only 19.6 metres away from residential buildings – well below the required distance of 50 metres – and there was no 20-metre isolation zone, as required by health regulations. Wang also believed the laboratories would affect the local environment – and that, therefore, an environmental impact assessment was needed.

In June 2003, Beijing Xicheng District People's Court issued the first judgment on the case, ordering the Beijing Planning Commission to cancel approval of the new laboratory. The commission did so, but also appealed against the judgment. Finally, the initial judgment was upheld and the Planning Commission dropped the appeal. This case was included in the 2003 Bulletin of the Supreme People's Court.

The Xiping chemical plant

More than 1,700 villagers from Pingnan in Fujian
v. Fujian Rongping Chemicals

This case involved more plaintiffs than any other reported in the Chinese media to date and is representative of group lawsuits in China. While the main factor determining the outcome of a case is not the number of plaintiffs but the evidence, when a lawsuit involves so many claimants the judge may be more careful in making the final decision, on the basis that an unfair judgment could bring adverse impacts to society.

In 1992, the south-east coastal province of Fujian implemented a 'Mountain-Coast Cooperation' policy, with the aim that richer coastal regions would help boost the development of poor mountainous areas. In March that year, Asia's biggest chlorate producer, Rongping United Chemicals – now Fujian (Pingnan) Rongping Chemicals – started construction of a plant in the village of Xiping.

The Rongping factory grew to account for one-third of county government income, but along with economic development came environmental degradation and rising cancer rates. In the nine years from 1995 (the second year the plant was in operation) to 2004, not a single Xiping youth who signed up for military service passed the medical inspection.

In 1995, the factory owners made a one-off payment for loss of crops. But no further compensation was awarded. Then, in 1998, the second phase of the facility went into operation, further damaging local vegetation.

On 7 November 2002, a civil suit was brought against the factory at Ningde Intermediate People's Court, by the residents of Xiping, Houlong and Xiadi villages, led by Zhang Changjian. The villagers asked that the company be ordered to close its facility, clean up the site and nearby mountainside, and pay compensation of 13.5 million yuan (US$2.1 million) for damages to crops and emotional health. The number of villagers participating in the lawsuit reached a new record: 1,721.

The court found that the company had caused losses through environmental pollution and ordered it immediately to stop infringing the plaintiffs' rights, to pay compensation of 250,000 yuan (US$39,000) for damage to timber, fruit trees, bamboo and fields, and to clean up industrial waste on site and nearby. Both parties appealed against this judgment. In 2005 the Higher Court's final judgment rejected the defendant's appeal, and ordered the factory to pay compensation of about 680,000 yuan (US$105,000).

The plaintiffs' lawyer described this decision as the court's 'balancing trick': 'More than ten million yuan would have been considered a heavy fine, while tens of thousands would have been light. The court didn't verify the actual losses sustained, and just gave the villagers a token amount.'

Pollution of the Shiliugang River
Guangzhou Haizhu District Procuratorate
v. Xinzhongxing textile treatment plant.

This was the first example of a procuratorate bringing an environmental public-interest case in China and established a significant model for the rest of the province: in its wake, further instances have occurred in Guangdong, though a similar case is yet to be seen elsewhere in the country.

The Shiliugang River in Guangdong province, south China, once ran clear, but after September 2007 its clean waters turned dark and foul – to the distress of local residents. As a result of complaints, Haizhu Environmental Bureau inspected local companies and found that the Xinzhongxing textile treatment plant was in severe breach of pollution regulations. Washing powder, enzymes and oxalic acid, mixed up with dyes from clothes, were being dumped untreated into the river. In the eight months after the facility opened, it discharged an average of 40 tonnes of waste each day – a total of 9,600 tonnes over the period.

In July 2008, Haizhu Procuratorate sued factory boss Chen Zhongming at Guangzhou Maritime Court for causing water pollution and demanded compensation for losses and costs. In November, the court formed a panel of judges to hear the case and, in December, ruled that Chen was liable for the environmental losses caused by the pollution. Chen was ordered to pay 117,289.20 yuan (US$18,200) in compensation.

This was the first environmental public-interest case brought by a Chinese procuratorate. Haizhu People's Court found that, in accordance with Article 3 of the Water Law, and the Article 73 of the General Principles of Civil Law, Shiliugang River is a national resource, and, as the state's organ of legal supervision, the procuratorate had the right to sue over losses caused within its jurisdiction.

Public interests in Jiangyin

The All-China Environment Federation
v. Jiangyin Port Container Company

This was China's first environmental public-interest case brought by a mass organisation and came to determine the conditions that need to be met to bring a claim of this sort. The All-China Environment Federation has gone on to file several public-interest lawsuits in local environmental courts in Yunnan, Guizhou and other regions. However, this has not resulted in any visible impact on other community organisations. Regional environmental groups are not eligible to bring lawsuits in other parts of the country.

In May 2009, the All-China Environment Federation received a complaint from residents of Jiangyin in Jiangsu, on China's east coast, that Jiangyin Port Container Company was creating air, water and noise pollution during the process of unloading, washing and transporting iron ore, severely impacting their quality of life. After on-site investigations and evidence-gathering, the federation brought an environmental public-interest case in Wuxi Intermediate People's Court, requesting that the company be ordered to stop encroaching on public environmental interests, and remove the risks to sources of drinking water for Jiangyin and Wuxi cities. The court accepted the case.

On 22 September 2009, the case was resolved through mediation and the defendant was required to correct its environmental violations.

The Dingpa Paper Mill

The All-China Environment Federation and Guiyang Public
Environmental Education Centre v. Dingpa Paper Mill

This was the first public-interest case where a non-profit foundation helped to cover litigation costs. This financial support had a remarkable effect, as it allows us to rethink the role of foundations in environmental protection.

But there are two problems: first, as mentioned above, there are regional restrictions when it comes to Green NGOs acting as plaintiffs; second, it is up to the foundation in question to decide whether or not to support lawsuits financially.

The All-China Environment Federation and the Guiyang Public Environmental Education Centre sued the Dingpa paper mill in Wudang district, Guiyang, over the discharge of effluent into the Nanming River and Wu River, an important Yangtze tributary. In 2010, Qingzhen Environmental Court held a public hearing in Wudang district and ordered the Dingpa facility to stop the release of effluent, remove any risks to the Nanming River, and pay reasonable costs to the plaintiffs to cover evidence-gathering, analysis and litigation.

The case was heard by Guiyang Qingzhen People's Environmental Court – the court's fourth public-interest case since it was established. The defendant was ordered to halt pollution immediately and take prompt measures to reduce environmental risks.

With the permission of the court, the plaintiffs applied to the 'Two Lakes and a Reservoir' protection fund – an organisation that campaigns for the conservation of water resources in Guiyang, funded by the Guiyang government – to pay the costs of preparing the case.

The case also used expert testimony. The experts stated that the defendant's factory included effluent storage and settling ponds, and therefore without comprehensive water treatment it would be unable to avoid pollution. The only way to enforce the court's order that the defendant immediately halt pollution would be to close the plant, they said. This expert testimony became court evidence, and will be an important basis for enforcement of the judgment.

The Yangzonghai case

The promotion of public participation and newly established environmental courts emboldened senior environmentalists and public-interest environmental lawyers in China. One such group is the Chongqing Green Volunteers Union, an environmental NGO founded in 1995 by Wu Dengming, a People's Liberation Army veteran and a professor at Chongqing University, who has been actively campaigning on environmental issues since the 1980s.

The story of the the Chongqing Green Volunteers' involvement in the Yangzonghai case began with the establishment of the Kunming environmental tribunal. Kunming is the capital and largest city in Yunnan province, in China's south-west. The impetus for establishing the Kunming environmental tribunal came from a major pollution incident in Yangzong Lake, otherwise known as Yangzonghai. Yangzonghai is located 36 kilometres south-east of Kunming's city centre and is under the environmental supervision of the Chengjiang county EPB and the Kunming city EPB. The 12-kilometre-long lake is something of a scenic spot and a major source of drinking water for tens of thousands of people in the surrounding area. When, in summer 2008, arsenic levels in the lake were found to be ten times higher than the national standard, the incident made national and international headlines as a story indicative of China's environmental enforcement challenges. In response, in December 2008, the Kunming environmental tribunal was established.

The aspiration of the Kunming environmental tribunal was to attract public-interest cases, and the largest difficulty with environmental public-interest suits was the lack of claimants.[15] Indeed, the Kunming Court went to significant lengths to encourage public-interest suits. Not only was public-interest standing permitted by the Kunming environmental tribunal, but also the city created a special fund to provide financial assistance for court fees, lawyer fees and investigative fees to public-interest claimants.

In 2009, shortly after the Kunming environmental tribunal's inception, judges from the tribunal attended workshops and round-tables on environmental law. These workshops, hosted by environmental and public-interest law NGOs, focused on the unique challenges that environmental law cases present to courts and encouraged dialogue on these issues among judges, lawyers and civil society. It was clear from these workshops and discussions that the environmental tribunals were looking to encourage public-interest lawsuits and that the lack of such suits was a concern for the courts.

At one of these workshops, Chongqing Green Volunteers and environmental lawyers discussed with judges from the Kunming environmental tribunal the potential for bringing a public-interest lawsuit. According to the Chongqing Green Volunteers, discussions at the workshop helped clarify not only the type of case that the court would accept, but also a case that could likely win. For example, someone raised the prospect of bringing a case against a large hydropower project, but the judges did not respond positively. It was apparently only after discussing the case of the Guodian Yangzonghai coal-fired power plant with judges – and receiving positive feedback – that the Chongqing Green Volunteers decided to file the case.

So, in May 2010, the Chongqing Green Volunteers filed a public-interest action with the Kunming Intermediate Court's environmental tribunal against the Guodian Yangzonghai Power Company. The case was premised on documented failures of the plant to operate SO_2 scrubbers, resulting in excess emissions of the pollutant, which is a poisonous gas that causes acid rain and can affect human health. Chongqing Green Volunteers claimed that these failures were intentional. Moreover, the case raised the failure of the plant to monitor its carbon dioxide emissions – a move that raised the political sensitivity of the case by touching on the issue of China's global carbon footprint.

Significantly, the case came at a time of heightened energy security concerns in Yunnan province. China's south-west suffered a severe drought from late 2009 until May 2010. From September 2009 until March 2010, hydropower generation in the province fell to nearly half that of the previous year.[16] In neighbouring Guangxi province, hydropower output was reduced by nearly 90 per cent. To meet power demand, Yunnan's coal-fired power generators increased production by 22 per cent from September 2009 through March 2010 and had to rely on high-sulphur coal, due to coal supply constraints. By the first quarter of 2010, Yunnan's SO_2 emissions were up 78 per cent from a year earlier.[17]

The sensitivity of the claims brought meant that the case would be a significant test of the effectiveness of both China's laws aimed at promoting public participation in environmental issues and the newly established environmental courts.

The defendant, the Guodian Yangzonghai Power Company, is a subsidiary of the state-owned China Guodian Corporation, one of China's five largest electricity generating companies. Guodian's Yangzonghai plant is located at the north end of the lake. At present, the plant has a generation capacity of 1,000 MW: two 200 MW units built in 1997 and 1998, and two 300 MW units completed in 2007, which have wet flue gas desulphurisation scrubbers.

According to the complaint from Chongqing Green Volunteers, the power plant failed to obtain the required EIA approval before beginning construction on the two 300 MW units in 2005 and 2006; since 2005, the plant seriously violated national environmental protection laws and policies; consistently failed to control SO_2 emissions; 'fraudulently' reported on its emission control projects; and, without cause, postponed repairs to its scrubbers after being ordered to do so. The complaint also said that the power plant 'maliciously' refused to cooperate with enforcement actions from environmental protection authorities and 'wantonly' evaded paying pollution fees.

Without increased public disclosure of environmental pollution information, Chongqing Green Volunteers would not have been able to obtain the evidence of violations that it relied upon to support its case. The Chongqing Green Volunteers' claims relied heavily on information that was disclosed by the Yunnan provincial EPB and the MEP on their respective websites.

For example, the complaint cites a 2008 report from the investigative team at the Yunnan EPB, which confirms that in 2007 the third unit was put into trial production without proper approval and failed to operate its desulphurisation equipment. The same report alleges that the fourth unit also began trial production without approval and that its smokestack monitoring system was not connected to the Yunnan EPB's network.

Another report cited in the complaint was published in September 2009 by China's Ministry of Environmental Protection. This concluded that the Yangzonghai plant was in violation of the law for the irregular operation of its scrubbers. The complaint also notes that an October 2009 report on pollution reduction and progress from the Yunnan EPB stated that 'a few industries are using high-tech methods to conduct fraud', and that this had affected the province's efforts to reduce pollution. The same report alleged that the Yangzonghai plant was under an obligation to complete repairs to its desulphurisation equipment for its third and fourth units by January 2009, but had failed to do so. The report also claimed that emission concentrations were bypassing the scrubber unit because of the need to repair a component part; that the coal had higher sulphur content than the equipment was designed for; that the operation of the scrubber was abnormal; and that the plant was addressing the issue. The Yunnan EPB's 2010 work plan stated that the power plant's fourth unit should complete repairs to its scrubber system by 30 April 2010.

The complaint cited laws and policies that support its arguments, including the Air Pollution Law, the 11th Five-Year Plan, the Clean Production Law and the 'Decision of the State Council on the Implementation of the Scientific Development Concept and the Strengthening of Environmental Protection'. The Chongqing Green Volunteers' requested remedies that were relatively unique for a civil case in China, but consistent with the public-interest nature of the lawsuit. The requested legal remedies were as follows:

1. Order the Guodian Yangzonghai Power Company to ensure the proper use of its desulphurisation equipment and ensure that sulphur emissions meet all relevant emission standards. Without delay, the defendant should publicly disclose the aforementioned corrections and emission reductions and allow supervision by the claimant, the court and the public.
2. Order the power company to follow the Law on the Promotion of Clean Production with respect to reductions in SO_2 and implement mandatory clean production audits; and immediately and thoroughly disclose clean production audit reports and implementation to the public and permit supervision by the claimant, the court and the public.
3. Order the power company to provide plans for controlling nitrogen oxide and carbon dioxide emissions within three months after the court's decision. The defendant should publicly disclose its implementation of the plan and allow supervision by the claimant, the court and the public.
4. Order the power company to pay 3 million yuan (US$470,000) compensation for environmental damages related to the period that it did not adequately use its desulphurisation equipment and failed consistently to meet SO_2 emission standards.
5. Order the power company to bear the burden of all litigation costs, including the claimant's costs associated with litigation and enforcement, not limited to: case acceptance fee, evaluation and assessment fee, travel and lawyer fees.

In May 2010 the complaint was delivered to the Kunming Court by Wu Dengming. That same day, judges from the environmental court treated Wu to lunch and responded positively to the complaint. The following month, Wu received a call from the Kunming Court informing him that the case would be accepted. But Wu never received any formal, written documents regarding the court's acceptance of the case. In July, he learned that the Kunming environmental tribunal would hear a public-interest case brought by the Kunming EPB, but not against the Guodian Yangzonghai Power Company. Instead, it was against a pig-farm operation for local water pollution. In the following months, Chongqing Green Volunteers' lawyer, Xia Jun, and another experienced environmental lawyer, Zhang Jingjing, travelled to Kunming to try to find out the status of the case. But both were unable to get additional information about the case, and even received conflicting information from different offices within the Kunming court.

In September 2010 a reporter from one of China's leading investigative newspapers, the Guangzhou-based *Southern Weekend*, travelled to Kunming to research the case and determine why the environmental tribunal had accepted the pig-farm case over the case against the power plant. The report concluded that the environmental tribunal chose the pig farm case because it would be much easier for the court to enforce a ruling against a smaller, less powerful defendant than against one of China's largest power generators. The title of the piece was: 'Wielding a Big Bat to Hit a Mosquito'.[18] The metaphor implied, of course, that the pig farm was a weak target for the environmental tribunal, which was intended to be a powerful weapon against polluters. The article helped to spur discussion among the environmental community in China about what was intended to be the first public-interest case brought by an independent NGO in China.

Chongqing Green Volunteers' lawyers tried to meet with the environmental tribunal again in January 2011, but its judges were unavailable. Finally, in March 2012, the Kunming court informed the Chongqing Green Volunteers that the case against Yangzonghai Power Company would not be accepted.

The Yangzonghai case never, in fact, became a case.

Squashing the mosquito

Article 112 of China's Civil Procedure Law requires that a court respond to a complaint within seven days, by accepting it and notifying the parties, or by issuing an order as to why the complaint does not meet the requirements for acceptance. If the claimant is unsatisfied, the claimant can appeal. It is relatively common in China for courts to refuse to accept certain cases, and there is little to compel courts to issue an order explaining their non-acceptance.

China's judiciary is weak when it comes to protecting the environment for two main reasons. First, judges are often unfamiliar with how to apply environmental laws and particularly with the issues of causation and evidence specific to environmental cases. Second, a lack of independence means that courts often favour the short-term economic concerns of local governments over the application of law or legitimate environmental concerns.

Several of the Kunming environmental tribunal judges and some Chinese environmental law scholars have commented that the complaint filed in the Yangzonghai case failed to state a specific claim and that the remedies requested were unorthodox and would have been too difficult for the court to enforce.

In many ways, the pig-farm case was similar to traditional civil tort cases that Chinese courts are used to dealing with, with the exception that the case was classified as a public-interest standing case. In contrast, the Chongqing Green Volunteers' case against Yangzonghai Power Company was intentionally designed by the plaintiff to be different from a regular tort case. For example, the case against Yangzonghai Power relies almost solely on the power plant's violation of laws and policies, not on direct damages suffered by a specific group. Similarly, the compensation requested is not for specified victims, but rather environmental damage generally. Everything, from the complaint's alleged harms to the remedies requested, could only have a realistic expectation of being considered by a court under the new and uncharted public-interest standing provisions, with which the Kunming environmental tribunal and other environmental tribunals across China are still experimenting.

Despite efforts and forums designed to share information regarding what would make a good public-interest case, there was likely miscommunication between the court and civil-society groups as to just how public in nature a public-interest case should be. It is likely that in the Yangzonghai case, Chongqing Green Volunteers and the public-interest lawyers had unreasonable expectations, considering the lack of clarity and controversy about the recognition of public-interest standing, for what the environmental tribunal could reasonably achieve. Comparing the Yangzonghai case to the pig-farm case accepted by the Kunming court helps to illustrate this predicament.

The claimant in the pig-farm case was the Kunming EPB. Arguably, the Kunming EPB does not need to bring a public-interest case, because it can bring an administrative enforcement case against the pig farm. Moreover, the Kunming EPB, as a government regulator in charge of regulating the pig farm – and having had its previous orders to the pig farm ignored, could claim to have a 'direct interest' in the case.

China's civil law clearly allows for victims who suffer direct loss as the result of a legal breach by others to bring a claim against the culprit. Therefore, in the pig farm case, another potential claimant could have been the pollution victims, who were directly impacted by the pig farm's pollution. The local water supply for some people in the area was harmed and a local small business suffered heavy losses because of the farm's pollution. Arguably, these victims have direct losses related to the pig farm's discharges and can bring a case for damages on their own behalf.

The Kunming EPB, in charge of protecting the environment for the benefit of society at large, has an interest in getting compensation for the victims. This factor helped make the complaint and the remedies requested in the pig-farm pollution case more conventional and familiar to cases that the court would have handled previously. Significantly, the Kunming environmental tribunal refers to the fine imposed on the pig farm as 'compensation', of which a large portion went to remedy harm to the pollution victims. This is consistent with conventional remedies to civil tort cases, such as the award of damages which are intended to address the harm caused by the defendant and compensate those affected by that harm. Characterising the fine as 'compensation' helped lessen the legal gap between China's civil law on the books, which requires a case to be brought by a person with 'direct interest' in the case, with the legal uncertainty that surrounds 'pure' public-interest standing, which the EPB relied on in the pig-farm case.

More influential may be the role that the Kunming People's Procuratorate – the government prosecutor, a powerful government entity – played in the case. In the pig-farm case, the procuratorate was supportive of the EPB from the start and sat with the EPB at trial as a sign of support. Some public-interest advocates worry that if a precedent for procuratorate support is set in public-interest standing cases, then courts will be reluctant to accept cases or rule in favour of plaintiffs if the procuratorate is not directly supporting their case.

Conclusion

China's energy and environmental governance challenges are daunting. Recent efforts to include energy efficiency and environmental targets in the cadre evaluation system and efforts to promote public participation and open government information illustrate that China takes addressing energy and environmental issues seriously. As is the case with any rapidly developing system, there are growing pains. China's energy and environmental governance systems are still trying to find the right balance between the need to achieve immediate results with demands to develop a deeper and more robust system of accountability based on law and conducive to public engagement.

The case of *Chongqing Green Volunteers Union* v. *Guodian Yangzonghai Power Company* provides a detailed example of how the many elements of government action, law and the public's expectations interact within the current system. China's judiciary remains weak; if it is to play an active role in promoting public participation and enforcing laws, the enforcement and penalty provisions included in laws and regulations must be strengthened. Efforts to link the cadre evaluation system's targets to the enhanced enforcement of existing laws and the broader capacity-building of regulators generally should be promoted. China's National People's Congress or its standing committee should pass law that clarifies the right of citizens to sue in the public interest or provide for public-interest standing in amendments to specific laws.

The monitoring of emissions from coal-fired power plants is improving, but there remains room for additional improvement. Considering the ostensible promotion of public participation within China's environmental governance framework, it is not implausible that the public could play a larger role in ensuring the veracity of emissions data if given the chance. However, SO_2 regulation in China now straddles two enforcement systems: one based in law and reliant on judicial enforcement; the other reliant on executive enforcement, and based in the internal cadre evaluation system of China's Communist Party. So long as executive enforcement remains removed from the law on the books, and from judicial oversight, the opportunity for public participation will likely be limited in comparison to a system based on law and judicial enforcement.

Notes

1. The uncertainty in these numbers comes from the fact that the majority of these factories are very small and up to 60 per cent of battery factories in China are not registered with the relevant authorities.
2. Jonathan Watts, www.guardian.co.uk/environment/2009/aug/17/china-lead-factory-protest.
3. Xinhua, 'Blood Lead Level Testing Resumed amid Public Outcry', 29 March 2012, www.china.org.cn/china/2012-03/29/content_25019214.htm.
4. Yuan Xu, 'The Use of a Goal for SO_2 Mitigation Planning and Management in China's 11th Five-Year Plan', *Journal of Environmental Planning and Management*, vol. 54, no. 6, July 2011, pp. 769–83.

5. Yuan Xu, 'Improvements in the Operation of SO_2 Scrubbers in China's Coal Power Plants', *Environmental Science & Technology* 45, 2011, pp. 380–85.

6. Xu, 'The Use of a Goal for SO_2 Mitigation Planning and Management', p. 779.

7. Ibid., p. 778.

8. Ibid., p. 780.

9. Ibid., p. 781.

10. It is not uncommon for executive orders and regulations to rely on enforcement of penalty provisions in laws passed by NPC. For example, 'Order 28 Management Methods for Automatic Emissions Monitoring of Polluting Sources', 2005, cites the APCL Article 46 for general penalties regarding the failure to use pollution control and monitoring systems.

11. For example, hard targets were not set for lead and other heavy metal emissions during the 11th Five Year Plan and their overall emissions increased rapidly and contributed to major social unrest.

12. 'China to Prioritize Compulsory Energy Conservation', *People's Daily* online, 30 November 2010, http://english.people.com.cn/90001/90778/90 862/7216129.html; Adam Moser, 'Insights into the Role of Law and Plan in China', *China Environmental Governance* blog, http://chinaenvironmentalgovernance.com/2010/12/07/insights-into-the-role-of-law-and-plan.

13. Article 11 of the OEI Measures sets forth the information that environmental protection bureaus are required to disclose and how: including the breakdown of total emission quotas for major pollutants as they relate to emission permits, and information regarding violations by polluters. Like the OGI Regulation, Article 12 of the OEI Measures states that information that regards state secrets or proprietary information of a private party is not to be disclosed. Neither the OGI Regulation nor the OEI Measurers clearly defines what qualifies as a state secret or a proprietary trade secret and this failure is considered a weakness in both of the rules.

14. Ma Jun, 'The Environment Needs Freedom of Information', 9 May 2007, www.chinadialogue.net/article/show/single/en/990-The-environment-needs-freedom-of-information.

15. Meng Dengliao (孟登科), 'Wielding a Big Bat to Hit a Mosquito: The Inside Story of Yunnan's First Environmental Public Interest Case' (抡起大棒打蚊子——云南环境公益诉讼第一案出台内情), *Southern Weekly*, 1 October 2010, www.infzm.com/content/5078.

16. Ministry of Environmental Protection, Hanzai zhishi 'liangwu' xiaojian fandan ('旱灾致使两污消减反弹' Drought results in 'extra-polluting' cuts), 16 April, 2010 www.zhb.gov.cn/zhxx/gzdt/201004/t20100416_188275.htm 16 April, 2010.

17. Ministry of Environmental Protection, Yanzhong ganhan daozhi eryanghualiu paifang liang fandan ('严重干旱导致二氧化硫排放量反弹' 'Severe

drought leads to rebound in sulphur dioxide emissions') 22 April 2010 www.zhb.gov.cn/zhxx/hjyw/201004/t20100422_188549.htm.
18. Meng Dengliao, 'Wielding a Big Bat to Hit a Mosquito'.

Further reading

Dan Guttman, 'Different Operating Systems', *Environmental Forum*, vol. 25, no. 6, 2008, p. 27, www.epa.gov/ogc/china/guttman.pdf. (A short explanation of the difference between laws and plans in China, and how this difference is viewed outside China.)

Jingjing Liu, 'Overview of the Chinese Legal System', *Environmental Law Reporter News and Analysis*, vol. 41, no. 10, 2011. (A short introduction to China's legal system, with attention paid to China's environmental governance.)

Adam Moser and Tseming Yang (2011) 'Environmental Tort Litigation in China', *Environmental Law Reporter News and Analysis*, vol. 41, no. 10, 2011. (An overview of environmental tort litigation and tort law in China.)

Randall Peerenboom, *China's Long March toward Rule of Law*, Cambridge: Cambridge University Press, 2002. (This book provides an in-depth and historical look into the development of China's legal system and the rule of law.)

Benjamin Van Rooij (2010) 'People v. Pollution: Understanding Citizen Action Against Pollution in China', *Journal of Contemporary China*, vol. 19, no. 63.

Xuehua Zhang, 'Green Bounty Hunters, Engaging Chinese Citizens in Local Environmental Enforcement', *China Environment*, Series 11, 2010, pp. 137–53, www.wilsoncenter.org/sites/default/files/CES%2011%20Inside%20Cover,%20F oreword%20and%20Table%20of%20Contents_0.pdf.

CHAPTER 4

Alchemy of a protest:
the case of Xiamen PX

JONATHAN ANSFIELD

One week before Christmas in 2007, en route to San Francisco for a holiday with his wife and girls, Chen Yu-hao stopped in Beijing for a secret meeting with government intermediaries. Pressure was mounting to resolve his ordeal down in Xiamen, a breezy island port opposite his native Taiwan. There he faced a popular insurgency against his trophy project. At stake was a plan to build a US$1.4 billion addition to a chemical plant in a fast-changing area just across a bridge from the city centre. Once completed it would yield projected annual revenues of $10.8 billion, equivalent to three-fifths of Xiamen's GDP that year. The key ingredient was paraxylene, an upstream petrochemical in everything from polyester apparel to plastic bottles. While not the most toxic chemical to produce, politically it had grown quite hazardous. By now it was known around China by its fear-inducing shorthand 'PX'.

Chen, then 67, was nearly as infamous as the chemical he coveted. He was also elusive: at no other point during the dispute, or since, would he be seen or heard. Slight in build and slow of step, he was the founder and overlord of petrochemicals and property conglomerate Xianglu, the biggest single taxpayer in Xiamen. He presided at board meetings, and even slept inside the company's administrative headquarters, in a third-floor suite. When we met, however, he denied having any title or stake in the company. Executives and state bureaucrats knew to address him as Adviser Chen rather than Boss, his erstwhile moniker. Chen had severed formal ties from the firm years earlier, after his multibillion-dollar empire in Taiwan crumbled in a heap of debt and lawsuits, and he was placed on Taiwan's most-wanted list for ducking trial. Now, the industrialist charged, he was being 'demonised' and 'politically persecuted' on this side of the Strait as well. He was in Beijing to ply the backchannels, in a bid to save his reputation and his project. Chen's suite at the Jianguo Garden Hotel was dimly lit, the curtains drawn. 'This affair', he sulked, 'has made me very depressed.'

An unprecedented sequence of events that year had thrust the project from the political backrooms into the public spotlight. It unfurled in the spring, when a decorated group of scientists used the legislative sessions in Beijing to lobby against Chen's project, prophesying a slew of safety hazards. Tensions peaked in the summer, after an alarmist mobile-phone message from a mystery sender called on Xiameners to 'stroll' against Chen Yu-hao and his 'atomic time bomb'. The threat of street marches forced officials to freeze construction pending a broad new environmental impact assessment. When the report was submitted for public review earlier that December, Xiameners seethed once more. 'Xiamen people gave him the opportunity to start a new home,' wrote the columnist Lian Yue, a blogger and arch-critic of the project, in the Guangzhou-based newspaper *Southern Metropolis Daily* on 6 December 2007. 'How could he repay good with evil?'

Now top local officials were about to pass judgement, but in Communist Party newspapers mixed signals were being emitted from on high. Chen Yu-hao did not appear rattled. In fact he had been on the counter-attack for months. Quietly he was pressing his case with national leaders, central ministries and local courts. His company also was beginning to speak out. On 13 December 2007, Tenglong Aromatics, Xianglu's PX subsidiary, managed to publish an open letter in the influential newspaper *Southern Weekend*. And Chen had summoned this American reporter to an interview, excerpts of which were later published online by *Newsweek*.

Chen cast himself, along with his project, as the victim of slanderous distortions at the hands of political and media foes. 'You can't have people twist it,' he told me. 'But here people have twisted it.' Notwithstanding his personal agenda – to build his factory – he posed some intriguing questions. 'This so-called popular opinion, is it real, or is it instigated?' he asked. If his PX plant had to move, what about those abutting other cities in China? 'Do they all have to move as well?' He also wondered why 'the Xiamen government are not so friendly toward us anymore'. Yet nothing had been finalised, he insisted; the future of his project lay ultimately with the same central leaders who had approved it in the first place. 'The government must speak as one voice – central, province and city.'

Chen's arguments seemed a rehearsal for his meeting later that same morning. After agreeing to finish the interview the next day, he and an associate disappeared into a black Buick sedan. Their car cut west down Chang'an Avenue, then snaked northward around the Party leadership fortress of Zhongnanhai, into Xicheng District, the ministerial quarter of the old city. It finally pulled up at the Jintai Hotel. The Jintai is a relic of the early 1990s, an unassuming bathroom-tiled edifice with a bowling alley, where top leaders and ministers have been known to share banquets with tycoons, overseas Chinese in particular. Chen Yu-hao shuffled in.

Birth of a movement

The result of the showdown in Xiamen is well known by now: Chen's PX project eventually was forced to relocate down the coast of Fujian province. The outcome was a catharsis for urban environmentalism, and an alpha moment for the not-in-my-backyard cause in the People's Republic: the first time, it was thought, that a city had shot down a centrally mandated petrochemical project. Numerous media outlets characterised the case as a 'people's victory' and a breakthrough for civil society. It has spurred a legacy of knock-on protests in other cities, against proposed PX and other projects. Officials, experts and activists in China have since drawn from it critical lessons for environmental advocacy as well as government response. The very word 'PX' has remained a potential trigger for public outrage.

But to this day, many of the facts regarding the planning, legality and safety risks of the project remain highly disputable and distorted in the public domain. The same could also be said for a heady mix of shifting motives, interests and political machinations at play behind the scenes. Some would call the Xiamen PX saga a backlash against the abuse of power and lack of public accountability in the city planning process. Others would term it more of a battle between vested-interest groups over the future of a neighbourhood. In the most Machiavellian analysis, it could be a read as an allegory for the adaptive capacity of China's single-party apparatus.

On a broader level, the case demonstrated the tension between economic and political development in China over the past thirty years. China's cities and manufacturing hubs have come very far, very fast during that period. It would not have happened, however, with the kind of zoning strictures and community oversight observed in more developed countries. Just a few decades ago, the pillar of Chinese urban life was the factory commune, incorporating smokestacks and tenements in dangerously close range. This union disintegrated as the planned economy and welfare state waned and markets and private investment took root. A new contest for space and resources emerged. Governments began plotting downtown commercial centres, development zones, industrial parks and massive public works. State and private corporations rushed in and built factories, refineries and power stations. Developers threw up high-rise compounds and gated villa communities. A new urban bourgeoisie started buying their own homes, upping their needs for power, water, transport, waste disposal, telecommunications and other daily conveniences. Among the citizenry, economic progress spurred new civic demands. 'People started to think, I've spent all of this money myself to buy this home,' said Zhang Jingjing, an environmental lawyer, when we spoke in early 2012. 'What are the dangers around me?'

Laws and regulators, however, lagged far behind. Developers in China typically have had seventy- to ninety-year leases, while home buyers possess 'land use rights'. City land remains state-owned, city planning and zoning a rigidly top-down, bureaucratic concern, and the government the dominant authority to alter the landscape in the name of the 'public interest'. That said, local officials also could be easily swayed by the prospect of bribes to line their pockets, GDP figures to boost performance ratings, land sales crucial to their balance sheets, and networks of rent-seeking contractors and regulators who preyed off this grey economy. Newly reassigned leaders arrived on the scene and routinely tweaked planning blueprints, championing their own pet projects, in violation of existing plans. 'Planning is not as fast as change', goes one Chinese saying often heard within the political beltway. In Chinese cities and villages, plans always change.

Public input remained an afterthought. The Environmental Impact Assessment (EIA) Law, passed in 2002 and effective the following year, as well as the Administrative Licensing Law (ALL), provided the legal underpinnings for public participation in China's environmental regime. But the provisions of EIA and ALL, like most Chinese laws, were open-ended and hard to enforce. Article 11 of the EIA law, for instance, required that expert and public opinion be solicited and taken into careful consideration, whether through public hearings or other means, in special cases ranging from industry to animal husbandry that 'may cause unfavourable environmental impacts or directly involve the environmental interests of the general public'. There were few clear imperatives. In 2004 and 2006, the State Environmental Protection Administration (SEPA, later upgraded to the Ministry of Environmental Protection) released implementation measures that elaborated on citizens' rights to hearings and placed added stress on information disclosure. Yet in most cases, at best, residents were asked to take part in slipshod surveys which were often trumped up by assessors, who were state-designated and company-hired.

EIA procedures had long been riddled with such loopholes. Most alarmingly, Chinese law does not absolutely require companies to complete the assessment and approval process before moving forward with projects. Instead they could *buban*, or make up the environmental assessment after they had already broken ground. In 2004, after the SEPA vice director Pan Yue famously unfurled a 'storm' of suspensions on around thirty industrial projects that had dodged their EIAs, the companies used the *buban* clause to secure approvals and resume construction, paying a fine no higher than the maximum of just 200,000 yuan. Later the same firms, in the process of completing the approval process, were solicited by SEPA to donate to an environmental culture fund, which was run by an aide-de-camp of Pan named Wang Pangpu. The collusive fundraising tactic later came under scrutiny in a corruption probe that quietly shook the ministry in 2008 and 2009. Wang received a lengthy prison term and Pan, questioned for months, was effectively sidelined for years thereafter, in what was seen as political payback.

A more basic dysfunction was the monopolistic nature of the EIAs themselves. A fixed number of state academic institutions were certified to carry out studies, making the process particularly prone to corruption, abuses and collusion with local environmental protection officials. The investigative business magazine *Caijing*, in a 25 June 2007 spread on the Xiamen PX case, cited Ma Zhong, an EIA expert on a panel connected to SEPA, who estimated that the passage rate of assessments of basic infrastructure projects was 99 per cent. At that rate, Ma reasoned, how could China's pollution problems be so abysmal? Clearly, EIA practices were absurdly flawed.

The proliferation of the Internet and a growing body of laws and regulations nonetheless presented new cudgels for concerned residents to assert themselves. They also had the aid of watchdog media and an alliance of NGOs, intellectuals, lawyers and enterprising environmental officials led by Pan Yue. Infuriated residents and environmentalists, cut out of the loop, deployed EIA-related law to force public hearings in two landmark cases in Beijing. In the most renowned instance, in 2005, Pan and SEPA responded by ordering officials at Yuanmingyuan Park, site of the Old Summer Palace, to remove plastic sheeting laid to prevent seepage into a local lake, without approvals, after opponents charged that it would damage plant and animal species and deplete groundwater levels. The year before, the Beijing community of Baiwang Jiayuan challenged the building of high-voltage towers by the Beijing Electric Power Company, part of a fever of construction preceding the 2008 Olympics. Residents argued that the recommended buffer zone of just 5 metres was unsafe and recommended the power lines be buried instead.

As tempers flared between construction crews and the Baiwang Jiayuan community, predominately migrant workers who had settled in Beijing, SEPA introduced new implementation measures expanding on the Administrative Licensing Law, which effectively compelled the Beijing environmental protection bureau to convene a hearing. It took place on August 2004, the first of its kind in China, in an open forum where rural migrants vented directly before Beijing officials. A crowd of residents peacefully assembled outside the site wearing matching T-shirts under the banner 'Resist Radiation Pollution'. Less than a month later, the Beijing environmental authority announced it would not rescind its earlier approval of the project. Most problematically, perhaps three-quarters of the towers were already built.

Nonetheless, a trend had been established, and these highly publicised incidents had a contagious effect on local citizens. In a 2007 controversy over a waste incineration facility in Beijing, residents across town in the Liulitun neighbourhood consulted veterans of the Baiwang Jiayuan struggle. Environmental campaigners engaged in the Xiamen PX battle likewise consulted the lawyer Zhang Jingjing, who had advised residents in the Beijing cases. 'So already', she said, 'there was a lot of communication between these people about how to deal with companies and officials.'

The Xiamen case exposed and sharpened national awareness of the shortcomings of public participation in China. But long-term institutional progress was another matter. As Pan Yue observed in January 2008, when *Newsweek* bureau chief Melinda Liu and I met him at SEPA offices in Beijing: 'The Xiamen PX Project is not a victory of people's opinion, but manifested a systematic problem. It shows the demands of the middle class on the environment. It shows the relationship between environmental assessment, the middle class and the environment.' The government had become more willing to acknowledge the dire state of the country's ecosystems, but was far less ready to address the dirty business dealings and choking political system. In the environmental clashes that had arisen, civic leaders and citizens were not so much fighting for their lives as for a say in their lives. The battle of Xiamen raised the question of who really won in the end: public will, vested interests or the supra-legal imperative of Communist Party rule in China – stability above all.

Xiamen: seeds of conflict

Xiamen has never really been shaped by the natives. The town is positioned at the mouth of the Nine Dragon River; its name, which came from the Manchus, refers to a gateway. Portuguese and other European traders first visited in the 1500s, pirates plundered the coast, and the Manchus drove out the Ming. Later, the tea trading centre was one of five colonial treaty ports opened in 1842 after the first Opium War, when it was captured by the British in the Battle of Amoy – Xiamen's old English name, derived from its pronunciation in the Min Nan language. During this period, missionaries made inroads along the coast and tens of thousands of southern Fukienese families emigrated and spread Hokkienese culture overseas, to Taiwan, south-east Asia and the Americas.

Europeans and Americans, along with many rich Fukienese returnees, built quaint colonial houses on the camel-backed slopes of Gulangyu island, Xiamen's main tourist attraction, where many of these old homes have been converted into cafés and bed-and-breakfasts in recent years, as gentrification has taken hold.

Communist forces captured Xiamen and Gulangyu island in October 1949, but Nationalist defenders repelled an attack on Jinmen island, just 10 kilometres away, as they fled to Taiwan. In the cross-Strait crises of the 1950s, the two sides shelled one another. For decades under Mao, development in Xiamen and much of the southern Fujian coast was paralysed because of the tensions.

In 1980, Beijing designated Xiamen as one of four Special Economic Zones to lure foreign trade and investment, particularly from overseas Chinese. But Xiamen grew slowly through much of that decade in comparison to the Pearl River Delta, due to a conservative leadership and continuing security concerns. To this day, the richest local businessmen are generally not from Xiamen but from Quanzhou and less prominent cities with storied entrepreneurial traditions. One kingpin from Jinjiang, Lai Changxing, lorded over Xiamen through much of the 1990s, smuggling cars, cigarettes and petrol, until the biggest corruption probe in Communist Party history brought down his Yuanhua Group and some 200 party and military officials. (Lai fled to Canada in 1999, only to be extradited to China in 2011 and sentenced to life in prison in 2012.) Many Xiameners remember Lai fondly for his conquests: undercutting fixed petrol prices; bedding starlets for hundreds of thousands of dollars a night; 1,000-yuan birthday presents to men from his village when they turned 50. His legend underscored the fact that Xiamen, for all its attractions, was always a small business town, prime for the taking by anyone with big dreams.

Only a digital-age controversy could challenge business-as-usual and expose the cosy web of relationships at work in China's increasingly prosperous eastern cities.

The deal that got away

The seeds of the PX conflict were planted nearly two decades earlier, in 1989. With Taiwan democratising and cross-Strait rivalry beginning to mellow, then Chinese premier Li Peng flew in and authorised the establishment of the Xiamen Haicang Taiwanese Investment Zone, on the peninsula south-east of Xiamen island, across an inlet channel from the Xiamen shipping port. The 100-square-kilometre zone, China's largest to this day, sat on a thumbprint of coastal farmland rimmed by hills, jutting into the bay. The area is known as Haicang. In January 1990, with the blessing of paramount leader Deng Xiaoping, a large chunk of the land was anointed a base for petrochemical development. The move was designed with a singular goal: to court Taiwan's most powerful businessman of the era, Wang Yung-ching, chief of Taiwan's monolithic Formosa Plastics.

Wang planned to build an integrated petrochemical facility, spread over 20 square kilometres of dirt-cheap farmland, with an initial investment of US$6 billion to $7.2 billion. Known as Project 901, after its inaugural year and month, it would have employed 10,000 people and pumped out 11 million tonnes of paraxylene and other mid- and down-stream chemicals annually. The project easily would have accounted for the bulk of Xiamen's GDP and tax base at the time. Some farmers and experts were privately concerned, and there was the beginning of a backlash. But no large-scale controversy ever emerged over the Formosa Plastics petrochemical base.

'Back then, we were poor,' said Wang Guangguo, a retired chemistry professor at Xiamen University, who later advised the government in the planning of Haicang, but groused that he never had the ear of decision-makers on larger issues. When we spoke in May 2012, he was serving as chair of the advisory board of Xiamen Green Cross, the city's trailblazing environmental NGO. 'Originally, this plan was a mistake. But the ordinary people at the time were lacking in environmental awareness,' said Wang. He handed me a copy of a thin volume he published at the time on environmental safety standards. He said the book was based entirely on Soviet standards from the Chernobyl era, and noted that standards had not progressed nearly as much as should have been the case since. In 1990, Xiamen academicians did speak up, but in favour of the company. One Academy of Sciences fellow, Cai Qirui, had pronounced Wang Yung-ching's plans free of pollution.

The deal fell apart in the end, due not to environmental hang-ups but to a morass of business and political issues. While China offered generous terms, Wang Yung-ching pushed for a series of added concessions, including tax breaks and an autonomous shipping zone with a Taiwan bank. The shipping zone was a political non-starter, and Zhu Rongji, who exerted influence as vice premier, bristled at the competition it would pose to state-owned firms just beginning to acquire similar capabilities. Taiwan's president Lee Teng-hui also worried that if Wang made a big plunge, a domino effect might ensue, with Taiwanese industrialists crossing the Strait with core technology and investment. He lured Wang back, in part with incentives to build in Mailiao, Taiwan.

To this day, some Xiameners speak of Formosa Plastics as the deal that got away. For better or worse, it forever altered the economic and strategic trajectory of the city, and left an array of government and business interests to vie over how a huge swathe of land would be developed. The episode also skewed local views of Taiwanese industrialists, bound to be sized up against the vaunted Wang Yung-ching. Although Wang backed out, he forfeited his 100 million yuan downpayment on the land, a calculated token of goodwill. This financed the building of the district's Haicang Hospital and Yankui Elementary School. Wang went on to set up over ten production bases in China, in everything from plastics to steel and power, despite being restricted from setting up a fully integrated base by the Taiwan government's China-bound investment regulations.

Chen Yu-hao, by any measure, was no Wang Yung-ching. His uncle had been a famous businessman based in Japan, known in certain circles of the Far East as the 'king of pearls'. Preternaturally ambitious himself, Chen became known in Taiwan for taking the long view, but also for taking big risks with big investments and loans. His scandalous back story would inform the course of the PX affair, both publicly and behind the scenes.

In the 1990s, Chen Yu-hao was still a major player in Taiwan. There he built up the conglomerate Tuntex, with subsidiaries in property development, petrochemicals, textiles, construction, textiles and fuel. Long childless, his wife finally gave birth to twin daughters in the late 1990s, when she was over 50 years old – then thought to be the oldest successful in-vitro fertilisation in Taiwan. Like many Taiwanese businessmen, he also cultivated a tangled web of relationships with politicians, and spread his donations generously across the political spectrum, hedging his bets carefully according to the prevailing political winds. He had staunch ties to Taiwan's Nationalist Party, known as the Kuomingtang or KMT, dating back decades. But back in the 1980s, Chen told me, a prominent young idealistic maritime lawyer had represented his family in a claim over a shipping dispute. The lawyer was Chen Shui-bian, the independence-minded candidate who would go on to lead the upstart Democratic People's Party (DPP) and became Taiwan's president in 2000. The two Chens were both from the southern city of Tainan. Chen Yu-hao would throw some money towards his campaign, too.

In Xiamen, Chen Yu-hao started small. He arrived in the early 1990s, in the wake of the Formosa Plastics bust. He first lay in the shadow of his partner, Liem Sioe Liong, then Indonesia's richest man. Liem, who grew up in Fujian, was the original legal representative of Xianglu. But Chen assumed control after the fall of Indonesia's President Suharto, when Liem's empire nearly crumbled. As the Asian financial crisis rippled through Taiwan in the mid- to late 1990s and real estate entered a prolonged slump, Chen's investments also soured badly. Then in May 2001 a massive blaze ripped through a major high-tech complex built by Tuntex that Chen owned in Taipei, causing some TWD2 billion (US$60 million) in losses. It was described as Taiwan's worst-ever high-rise inferno, and, Taiwanese familiar with Chen said, was the tipping point for his fortunes in Taiwan.

Prosecutors began investigating Chen in 2002 and 2003, after he was unable to pay outstanding debts and began defaulting on loans. In 2002, he was charged with breach of trust on accusations of embezzling TWD4.11 billion (around US$115 million at the time) from his companies in Taiwan. Many published accounts alleged that he diverted funds to his investments in China, though the alleged sums differed widely in those reports. His wife, Lin Fu-mei, was also implicated. All along, Chen protested his innocence. The case was a misunderstanding over borrowed funds, he explained to me in great detail, and presented court documents indicating that the amount he actually owed was US$8 million; but the details were grossly inflated, he contended, in the Taiwanese press. Chen maintained he was being blackballed by Chen Shui-bian, the pro-sovereignty candidate who won the 2000 election, ending five decades of KMT dominance, on account of his extensive business ties to the mainland and historic political ties to KMT party leaders.

Critics in Taiwan told my *Newsweek* colleagues that Chen had been sheltered for too long. An official from the Investigation Bureau at Taiwan's Ministry of Justice, who did not want to be named, said that although Chen's alleged crimes occurred in the mid-1990s, he was not investigated earlier because of his KMT connections. In April 2003, an arrest warrant was issued for Chen and Lin when they failed to show for a hearing on their embezzlement charges. Taiwanese authorities declared them fugitives in May 2003 when they failed to show up to a second hearing. President Chen Shui-bian added insult to injury, putting Chen Yu-hao on Taiwan's most-wanted list, but the couple had already relocated to Xiamen and California, where Chen was getting involved in property development in the San Francisco area. The family never returned to Taiwan after 2002.

Chen's mounting trouble in Taiwan did not stop him from deepening his ties and investments on the mainland. Critics allege that it only spurred him on. In 2001, Xianglu began to pump out purified terephthalic acid (PTA), a downstream chemical from PX used to make a polyester resin and related textiles. The company's PTA project won approval relatively easily, because it was built on a small scale and only involved one small slice of the petrochemical production process. Chen had also started another company focused on property, Dongyao Enterprises, which built Donglian Mansion in central Beijing. The building's first floor was the Beijing branch of the Taiwan Affairs Office. By 2002, during the height of Chen Shui-bian's reign, Chen headed a growing list of Taiwanese tycoons who faced scrutiny from Taiwan's legislative Yuan for shirking debt to state banks in Taiwan while pouring investment into the mainland. Sections of Taiwan's press reported this as a scandal.

The animosities between the two Chens, the tycoon and the president, only deepened. During the bitterly contested 2004 presidential race in Taiwan, Chen Yu-hao printed letters in Taiwanese newspapers suggesting the president was corrupt. He accused Chen Shui-bian and his wife of misreporting campaign donations, starting from his earlier campaigns; the businessman said he knew so because he was the donor. The DPP admitted to receiving TWD10 million (around US$300,000) from Chen Yu-hao during the 2000 presidential campaign. But Chen Yu-hao alleged that the amount donated to the DPP and Chen Shui-bian was higher, and that he personally handed cash to the president's wheelchair-bound wife. The office of the president, who was narrowly re-elected, countered that Beijing had put him up to it. In summer 2006, as the drive to recall president Chen was gathering steam, Chen Yu-hao publicly alleged that he had given another TWD6 million in political donations to Chen Shui-bian's wife in 1994 and 1998 that was never recorded. She denied ever meeting him.

Chen's growing clout on the mainland coincided with an increasingly polarised state of cross-Strait relations. Beijing had courted Taiwan business with increasingly attractive policies. Since Chen Shui-bian took power, the Communist Party had also focused its Taiwan policy tack on 'opposing Taiwan independence', and forged buddy-buddy ties once unthinkable with its Nationalist wartime foes in the KMT.

Chen Yu-hao had begun to pursue the PX project in 2001. Because of his fall from grace in Taiwan, ironically, he was unfettered by protective Taiwan investment regulations – unlike Wang Yung-ching, who never got approval from either side to produce PX in China. By the early 2000s, Chen's company Xianglu had already become the biggest taxpayer in Xiamen on the back of revenues from PTA, chemical fibre and other polymer and plastic spin-offs. But PX, the upstream chemical, was the single ingredient that could help Chen fuse his production line and make him exponentially richer. Gaining approval was no minor feat, though. Of about sixteen PX plants in operation or under construction around China by 2007, all were owned wholly or jointly by the state giants, most by the petrochemical firm Sinopec. Chen was trying to build the first 100 per cent privately invested site. Chen Yu-hao's contretemps with Chen Shui-bian came in the thick of the application process to build the PX facility between 2004 and 2006. Critics widely posited a connection to cross-Strait politics, though later Chen vehemently denied any when we met. He said he was just a Chinese businessman. 'I'm not a politician. I have friends who support Taiwan independence as well as friends who support unification,' he told me. 'All I say is that I am Chinese. Chinese have a saying, "Blood is thicker than water."'

A city at a crossroads

Plans were moving ahead for Chen and Xianglu. The State Council, China's cabinet, had given its preliminary approval to the PX proposal in early 2004. In July 2005, the State Environmental Protection Administration (SEPA) cleared the environmental inspection report. But the report was never made available to the public, in violation of the law. And, just as problematically, the report was not required to take into account the area surrounding the plant. The city government had clearly designated the southern Haicang industrial area for petrochemical production, in its plans for 1995–2010 and for 2005–20. It had been adopted into plans at the provincial level and it was in the national ledger for the industry. Xiamen officials remained under pressure to clear farmland and cultivate industry in the development zone.

Yet, as Xiamen boomed and sprawled, industrialisation and urbanisation were headed on a collision course. In the hole left a decade earlier by Formosa Plastics, Haicang was already developing in another direction. Around 2000, residential properties began cropping up in the south-eastern corner of the peninsula. The building boom was spurred predominately by the city government-controlled Xiamen Haicang Investment Group, known around Xiamen as 'Haitou'. Haicang was then but a rough, craggy and desolate space of land, albeit with a fine perch overlooking the sea. So, under the guidance of the Xiamen government, the Haicang management commission created Haitou to cash in on that land. At the time, the government leaned towards putting up simple properties they could sell easily. They didn't think much beyond developing dormitories for local factories. But then Haitou brought in a famous marketing guru, Ye Maozhong, one of the so-called 'idea kings' who leapt to fame in the early days of the commercial media and private entreneurship, to help market the area. Ye convinced Haitou to think bigger, in terms of luxury real estate. He minted a marketing concept accordingly, to position Haicang up the value chain, and Haitou blanketed the city with advertisements.

Haitou built Future Coast, its first project, around 2000. The name was prophetic: the project and subsequent developments attracted many new settlers, from other parts of Fujian and from distant provinces. In a major policy initiative in 2003, the Xiamen government began offering a local urban *hukou* – the exclusionary residency permits that afford local benefits – to people who bought apartments in Haicang and other areas outside the central island of the city, to bolster the suburban property market. Then in 2005, the Xiamen government began promoting Haicang as a 'second centre' of the city, fundamentally altering Xiamen's strategy of urban planning from an 'island city' to a 'bay city'. Haicang was a launch pad for the overhaul. By June 2007, Haicang had twenty-three different projects under development or up for sale, according to *Caijing* magazine.

Some of the earliest opponents of the PX project were among those lured by the promise of the area. Many had come to Xiamen from poorer provinces to work somewhere that promised a less frenetic, white-collar lifestyle. Some came from as far away as China's north-east, others from Sichuan, in western China, and some from Jiangxi, in the south. In the beginning, property prices were rock bottom – much cheaper than on the main island. In 2006, Xiamen ranked second in a survey of the most liveable cities conducted by the Beijing-based Horizon Group, behind only Dalian. The environment was one key factor taken into account.

When I visited in late 2007, luxury high-rises were shooting up along the shoreline. Many were built or being built in the petrochemical zone, within a few kilometres of Xianglu. House-hunting *xiao zi* ('petty bourgeoisie') plied the boardwalk, which was dotted with coffee houses. But just inland, flatbed trucks stacked with flammable materials rattled down ghostly avenues embellished by transplanted palms. Haicang only stopped auctioning land for property developments in mid-2006, when SEPA launched a new initiative to conduct 'strategic environmental assessments', designed to examine entire areas rather than individual projects. Environmental vice director Pan Yue later described Haicang's schizophrenic development as a case of faulty 'positioning', and said his bureau only discovered the city's planning problem after they approved the project. A conflict was brewing geographically, but few people recognised it.

A pivotal moment came in January 2006. Chinese leader Hu Jintao inspected the Taiwan investment zone in Haicang, where he wholeheartedly endorsed the progress and the sixty-nine Taiwanese ventures there, including petrochemical development. 'Mainland authorities concerned will be dedicated to providing Taiwan compatriots with assistance and services', said Hu. His visit was seldom mentioned after trouble cropped up the next year, but to many officials and business-men alike this was an unmistakable green light to push forward. But the final and most difficult hurdle, approval from the National Development Reform Commission (NDRC), had yet to be cleared.

To get the PX project passed, Xianglu would need patrons in the local government as well. The initiative took root under Zheng Lizhong, the Xiamen party secretary from 2002 to 2005, who had taken up a post in the Taiwan Affairs Office. His replacement was He Lifeng, one of Fujian's most powerful men, who became a PX champion. The Guangdong native studied for his doctorate in the finance department of Xiamen University at the dawn of reforms. He was vice director of the city's finance department in the mid-1980s, when China's leader Xi Jinping was deputy mayor, before serving as a vice mayor himself and then as a leader in two other major cities in the province, Quanzhou and Fuzhou. He was seen as a member of the clique of Party risers in coastal provinces associated with former leader Jiang Zemin and his growth-focused economic prescriptions. Importantly, he had earned a seat on the Party standing committee of the province years earlier.

As Party boss in Fuzhou, He Lifeng built up a reputation for ramming through his 'image projects' and steamrolling those who stood in the way. His power politicking and large-scale, growth-oriented policies won him a collection of nicknames, including *He Fengzi*: Madman He. In one infamous incident, he was instrumental in the smearing and jailing of a renegade county party secretary, Huang Jingao, who published an unusual whistleblowing letter on the *People's Daily* website that alleged the area was so corrupted that he had to wear a bulletproof vest.

He's approach did not change much on arriving in Xiamen. He had been pushing through a controversial and expensive rapid transit network. One of his early personnel moves, Xiamen insiders said, was to place his brother in a commanding post with a primary city-owned contractor. Some referred to him by another nickname, *He Da Chai*: He the Great Demolisher. Like any Party riser in the provinces, He's job description was to spur economic development and safeguard social harmony. He earned a reputation as a bully and a schemer on both fronts. Businessmen and media types around Xiamen widely described him as *badao*, 'domineering'.

He Lifeng vigorously lobbied the central government on behalf of the PX plant, company executives and others recalled. In 2006, he spent an extended period time in the capital to help the project win approval from the NDRC. 'He Lifeng stayed a long time in Beijing', during the period before the project secured approvals, one former Xianglu executive recalled. Finally, that July, the NDRC agreed to grant the licence to produce PX.

By the spring of that year, white-collar migrants who once flocked to Haicang for sea views and sweet breezes had taken to online real-estate forums in anger over the impending addition. They complained over the foul stench of a nearby wastewater treatment plant and the vinegary odour of the neighbouring chemical plant, Xianglu. On these sites they also started crowdsourcing research on the environmental risks of the looming PX project. Huang Qizhong, a 30-year-old home-buyer who nursed visions of 'a big French window' and 'a vast lawn', fired off a post that May, with his name and mobile number, calling on neighbours to band together to 'save ourselves and our fruits, our homes'. His gambit was later reported on an official website. A group of local settlers coalesced into a nexus of propertied petitioners. They wrote to the district government, the mayor's office and the local EPB that May, but got no response. On the Xiamen channel of the Soufun property-search website, one long thread in June 2006 dissected data on the chemical emissions standards for the Xiamen area. People posted to the thread in search of the environmental report that had granted the project passage. No one could find it.

So in July Huang and the others sent letters to SEPA and the NDRC. But by the time the letters arrived – they tracked the deliveries – the NDRC had already issued its approval for the Tenglong Aromatic PX plant. The document also asked the city development and Reform Commission to 'accelerate the project'.

One Xiamener who saw the brewing conflict years earlier was Ma Tiannan, who started out her career as a management consultant for a local firm, at the time the Haicang property market was just starting to sprout. Haitou was a client. It was around the same time, in 1999, that Ma founded Xiamen's first environmental NGO, Green Cross. In summer 2007, they became the first registered environmental grassroots organisation in the city, and as of 2012 remained alone in this regard. Green Cross boomed over the years: it became famous in Xiamen for running an annual event in April called Island Care Day, which mobilised volunteers to plant mangroves and pick up trash along the shore. The core group of volunteers grew from a few dozen to a few hundred. Some years, as many as 30,000 people participated in the clean-up effort.

Ma first encountered Huang's group of eleven or twelve concerned residents of Haicang in May 2006. They complained about problems with a water treatment plant 500 metres away from Future Coast, which had acquired the new nickname 'Stinky Coast'. They griped about the acidic stench permeating from the Xianglu plant – He Lifeng's office had ignored complaints from the homeowners. And they worried about the PX plant they heard Xianglu planned to build. Ma accompanied them to take photos of the water treatment facility.

Ma also sought out Xiamen's Environmental Protection Bureau (EPB) chief, Xie Haisheng, with whom she had forged a strong relationship during his decade in the job. In his office, he pulled out a large map of the area. Xie told her that when property developments had started going up in Haicang, he had registered strong opposition and noted the contradictions in local planning. In October 2005, a magazine under the Xiamen EPB had also published an essay that warned that the clash would only worsen and chronicled complaints from people who blamed deteriorating air quality on the petrochemical development. But local policymakers had failed to take up the challenge. Ma passed on to him the feedback she was hearing from the Haicang resident activists. She recalled Xie's response: 'Haicang is a place that basically just is not suitable for people to live. You should encourage them to move away.'

When Ma relayed the message to the Haicang residents' group, they were 'very depressed', she said. They had come to Xiamen from less prosperous provinces to build better lives. But they were not interested in the long, hard route of a legal challenge or the wide-angle issues of public participation and environmentalism. They just wanted to purge the plants. Ma offered to advise them on publicising their case and filing requests for information and approvals based on existing laws. She tried to lure them to an August 2006 legal conference on changes in the environmental impact assessment law, and on field trips to visit the reservoir and see the sewage treatment plant and power lines that had provoked fears. The Haicang residents wouldn't go. 'The more I listened to them the less hope I had. They felt the law is too slow and can't help them solve problems,' she said. 'They thought, 'If you are environmental group, then you should be able to resolve these things for me.' Instead, it was a chemist with a hand in the law-making process who would become their saviour.

Zhao Yufen was born in Henan province, central China, in 1948, but moved to Taiwan with her parents the following year, as the Communist Party swept to power. Shortly after completing her doctorate in the United States, in 1978, she decided to visit her maternal grandparents on the mainland; in the chill of the time, the Taiwan government would not allow her to return. The next year she took up a research post at the Chinese Academy of Sciences (CAS), and just over a decade later was elected a CAS academician. In 2000, she transferred from Tsinghua University to Xiamen University. Significantly, she also was named a member of the China People's Political Consultative Conference, a political advisory body.

Zhao's involvement in the anti-PX cause was not purely a matter of public concern. Like the new suburbanites concerned about their sea views and property values, Zhao had a competing interest in the site of the Tenglong PX plant, too. Only a sympathetic press made certain that it never became widely known. Under an agreement between Xiamen University and Haicang, Zhao was pursuing a plan at the time to build a biopharmaceuticals plant on a vacant corner of the same lot. In the spring of 2006, she visited the property at the invitation of Haicang party secretary Zhong Xingguo, who courted them to build the project there. She willingly told the Shanghai-based newspaper *China Business News* the story the next year, showing the paper's Fuzhou-based correspondent, Shao Fanqing, blueprints for the project. 'It accorded with the government's newer goals to develop low-carbon, low-emissions projects', Shao, who left the paper in 2012, told me in Fuzhou. But just as they moved to secure the land, they were alerted to the word circulating online about plans for the Tenglong project; their parcel was earmarked as a refuse station for the plant. In one subsequent interview, Zhao explicitly told another Chinese journalist not to mention this connection. No other media outlet ever did.

Zhao and her Xiamen University colleagues 'were conscious of the appearance of a conflict of interest', said Shao, the reporter. But their dealings with Haicang showed that 'clearly sometimes the district and the city were not on the same page'.

Zhao began to take a hard look at the PX project when it broke ground in November 2006. She contacted a junior colleague, Xiamen University environmental scientist Yuan Dongxing, and told her that she and a group of academicians were planning to take up the issue with the city government. Zhao was the straight-talking veteran among the pair, Yuan more oblique and diplomatic. Neither was a specialist in aromatics, the class of chemicals to which PX belongs. But Yuan agreed to help and contacted colleagues at the university and abroad to enlist their support. They soon mounted a simulation to gauge the impact of the project, based on standard emissions from PX and PTA plants and Xiamen's historical weather patterns. The results were startling: the affected areas would vary from season to season, based on the direction of the winds, but the pollution could be serious. A mere breeze, she noted, could provoke neighbourhood complaints about the acidic stench. By the end of

November, a letter from Zhao and five other CAS academicians based in Xiamen landed on the desk of He Lifeng. In December, Zhao wrote directly to Fujian province Party boss Lu Zhangong and governor Huang Xiaojing. She proposed that the project move out of Xiamen to another location in the province and that the province sort out the resultant loss in tax proceeds. Xiamen leaders finally agreed to meet the experts a few weeks later.

They gathered on 6 January 2007, at a Xiamen hotel. Zhao was accompanied by a number of other Xiamen University academicians, including the vice president of the school in charge of science and technology, Zhang Ying. Representing the government were He Lifeng, the executive vice mayor Ding Guoyan, and two other powerful members of the municipal Party committee. The university was emboldened to an extent by that fact that it is a national-level institution, meaning it does not answer directly to the Xiamen government but to the national Ministry of Education. However, the meeting did not go well. He Lifeng arrived more than ten minutes late, according to Shao's account in *China Business News*, by which time Zhao was already winding up her slide presentation. Yuan and the rest spoke in succession, registering their opposition to locating the project in Xiamen. He Lifeng responded coolly. He told them that he had never heard of a PX plant exploding, and this project had secured approval from environmental protection authorities. In addition, he said, his government was only carrying through a project endorsed by Beijing; he could do nothing more than hear them out. Zhao and her colleagues pressed him on the potential safety hazards and pushed for a fresh scientific review of the project. He said that would require central government authorisation. In an hour and a half, the scholars got nowhere.

The meeting helped convince Zhao to take the fight to Beijing, although the campaign against PX might well have petered out there were she not a delegate to the CPPCC, the official advisory body to China's legislature. Comprising mainly non-Communist Party luminaries, such as academics, celebrities, retired officials and businessmen, the conference makes recommendations, not policy. But CPPCC delegates have managed at times to gain traction on certain issues, given a little publicity. During the annual national meeting of the body in the capital that March, Zhao took advantage of the platform. She enlisted 105 top scientists and veteran officials to sign her submission: 'A Proposal Recommending the Relocation of the Xiamen Haicang PX Project'. It was adopted as a top recommendation of the body during the session.

Paraxylene can inflame the eyes, nose and throat – and in cases of overexposure can impair the nerves. Material Safety Data Sheets list its health rating as 'moderate'. In their proposal, the academics appeared to embellish upon the risks. They called it a dangerous chemical that would drive up rates of cancer and birth defects. They argued that international norms recommended a buffer zone of 70 to 100 kilometres between plants and metropolitan areas; even in China, they said, the average was 20 kilometres. Since the site in Haicang was located just 1.5 kilometres from residential areas, and ran the risk of a leak or explosion, they demanded the project be immediately moved. Zhao also stated – inaccurately, but most damagingly – that paraxylene belonged to the same class of carcinogenic chemicals as that at a plant on the banks of the Songhua River in north-eastern China which exploded in late 2005, leaking benzene and causing a water shut-off for millions. (Benzene was a common by-product of PX, and later reports alleged that Tenglong could produce some 238,000 tonnes of it.) Zhao and her co-authors rightly questioned the process by which the PX project passed its original environmental assessment in 2005 and criticised the fact that it had not been released to the public.

A pointed counter-argument from local officials and company executives, throughout the affair, was that Zhao and her colleagues overstated the hazards, prompting citizens and critics to exaggerate further. Zhao herself confided to Shao in April that some of their statements were overly inflammatory. The toxicity of the Xiamen project and other PX sites would become a recurring matter of debate.

But the media and bloggers largely reported the scientists' claims at face value. Zhao was already the leader of a movement. Within a couple days of the close of the legislative meetings in Beijing, the influential *China Youth Daily* and the *China Business Journal,* a modest broadsheet sponsored by the Academy of Social Sciences, interviewed Zhao and brought her proposal national attention online. Central government officials were caught off guard by the initial wave of press coverage. Proposals adopted by the CPPCC are forwarded to relevant government departments to examine and weigh whether to act. But media quoted SEPA's Pan Yue and other officials as noting that the project had already passed inspection. Only the NDRC, the licensor of the project, could do anything about it.

Online mutiny

Among the first in Xiamen to seize on news of Zhao's proposal were homeowners' representatives of Haicang. Re-energised, they fumed on popular local web forums like Xiamen House and Xiamen Fish. On 23 March 2007, Huang Qizhong and eight others left a formal note of complaint on the website of the Fujian environmental protection bureau, titled 'Save Haicang people's right to live, stop the petrochemical project'. They said the chemical smell of the air would assail their nostrils after rains or in the middle of the night, interrupting their sleep, making children cry and striking fear into expectant mothers. They had been complaining for years to police and environmental hotlines. But whereas Xiamen had an air monitoring station, three years later Haicang still did not.

Soon the blogger Lian Yue let fly with shocking effect. Lian, more than any other voice, hit the nerve of a citizenry conscious of its perch on the Taiwan strait. Lian was a prolific contributor to the pioneering Beijing-based forum Bullog (which would be shuttered by authorities two years later), and a freelance columnist for *Southern Weekend* and other newspapers. Late that March, he issued the first of hundreds of screeds on the case. He proceeded to repeat a common distortion, identifying PX as the same chemical that contaminated the Songhua River in 2005. 'Xiamen claims to be the most gentle and fragrant city in China. Maybe later it will become the smokiest city in China', he wrote. 'Under extreme situations, for example war or terror attacks, it would be a gift to opponents and terrorists. If this factory made one slip (forget about the human lives, they are not worth much in any case), it would be a lethal blow to Fujian's economy, and likely an astronomical loss in GDP.'

Lian – whose real name is Zhong Xiaoyong – had been living the writer's life on the sleepy islet of Gulangyu. He was inspired by Zhao's proposal 'to mobilise the force of his columns', he said when we met over coffee later that year. He called his work on the case the interactive product of 'traditional and new media'. He also sensed that his role as a newspaper columnist made him more powerful and protected than most bloggers. 'If you don't first go through the traditional media and go directly through the blog, it can be very troublesome,' he said. Lian avoided getting overly entangled with other local activists on the ground. 'These connections will greatly increase the risks you're taking,' he said. 'Because they' – the authorities – 'can say you're "inciting" or "organising" opposition.' Instead he stuck to writing and aimed to blog about news reports. 'For people in the media, the most important thing is to allow more people to know the news.' Despite the overstatements and inaccuracies that were being spread about the safety of the plant, he felt that a proposal signed by 105 CPPCC delegates, including chemists, oceanographers, environmentalists and officials, was a solid foundation for action. 'If you can't believe them, you can't believe anyone. We're not God. We are not omniscient. That's why everyone's repeating this '105 experts' line. Because it's credible.'

In the immediate vicinity of Xianglu, years of breathing in dubious fumes and vapours did not inspire goodwill or trust. Wencuo village was a shanty-town strip that ran behind the Xianglu compound. There I got to know Mr Wen, long-time neighbour who also did contracting for the company. He claimed Xianglu had skimped on air and water treatment technology for years and, like plants across China, 'only turned the filters on when inspectors came'. What remained of Wencuo would eventually be flattened if the PX project went forward. He and other villagers later told me of how they had often complained to local departments of acrid emissions, unreported leaks and rising cancer rates.

Even those white-collar employees at Xianglu who lived in Haicang had private concerns. Although they defended the company and its environmental record on the whole, they knew there were always risks. They could smell the discharge from the plant, and they feared the hit to their property values like everyone else. 'In my heart of hearts, I didn't want to be living next to chemical factories or processing factories,' the former Xianglu executive acknowledged. 'We wanted to be living by clear skies and blue water.'

Tensions mounted steadily that spring as the local government dug in its heels. Officials stressed that the project had the blessing of the central government and had taken all necessary precautions to pass environmental inspection. Local newspapers and television spots highlighted the financial and technological input to the Xiamen economy.

The company itself, meanwhile, was a spectral figure in the swirl of controversy. The city propaganda department took care of the publicity on its behalf. Asked later about their PR strategy, Chen and other senior executives said they had no choice in the matter. Early on, they sought to convene a public forum with experts to clarify what they considered drastic misconceptions about the project and paraxylene production, but were forced to scrap the idea. Local officials told them 'not to stir up trouble', a Tenglong official said. Such clamps were standard procedure when it came to managing corporate crises in China, where companies view themselves as beholden to the government. The company had anxieties regarding the media from the start, executives acknowledged, given Chen's troubles in Taiwan and the vinegary stench wafting around Haicang. So executives could only pin their faith on their 'parent officials', as the official termed Xiamen leaders. 'Let's put it this way,' he said. 'The publicity work is the work the government should do. As a company, we provide the technical support.'

Leaving it to the government to defend the safety of the project backfired badly, though it is doubtful whether the company could have done much better on its own. So bad was public cynicism that the joke around Xiamen was that Chen Yu-hao was sent by Chen Shui-bian, as part of some toxic plot. While local government media remained supportive or silent, company executives could feel the pressure mounting from the national press and the local buzz online. Not that Chen Yu-hao seemed alarmed. 'Chen was still very confident', said the former company executive. After all, Chen reasoned, the central government had approved the project and enshrined it in long-term plans for the region and the industry.

Central planners did not appear to be on edge either. Just before the May Day holiday, the deputy head of the industrial project office of the NDRC, Li Ningning, led a team including a CPPCC representative to Xiamen and carried out an on-site inspection in the company of a Xiamen vice mayor. On 15 May, Li and Zhao Yufen met in Beijing, but Zhao was disappointed by what she heard, as she told *Oriental Outlook Weekly* magazine on 26 May. Li informed her that the team had determined that a newly built satellite campus of Beijing Normal University was just 3 kilometres from the site of the PX plant, inside a buffer zone originally drawn around it. Other developments had gone up inside the buffer zone as well. Li said the NDRC had already requested that Xiamen carry out a strategic assessment and make adjustments. Yet Li reiterated that the plant had obtained approvals from SEPA in 2005 and the NDRC in 2006; so, other than some technical modifications, not much could be done. Zhao was alarmed enough that she brought forward her return to Xiamen to the next day.

Zhao and her colleagues had been struggling to obtain a copy of the original EIA that passed SEPA in 2005, without much success. The Xiamen EPB had a copy, but the scholars were prevented from seeing it. During the 1 May holiday, on travelling to Beijing for a CPPCC members training seminar, Zhao asked a friend at Beijing Huagong University to help her obtain a copy through an assessment organisation connected to the school. But the report, which should have been made available to the public in the first place, had been marked confidential, she learned. One person responsible told *Oriental Outlook Weekly* that it had been kept secret to protect the project owners. Despite multiple efforts, including appealing to the NDRC official, Zhao failed to obtain a copy of the report. But she would not give up the search, and even raised the possibility of suing the environmental regulator to get the report.

The *Oriental Outlook Weekly* article carried the title, '100 CPPCC Members Have Difficulty Blocking a 10 Billion Yuan Chemical Project'. In the piece, another Xiamen University professor, who was not identified, argued that even under the vague EIA Law of 2003, the project should not have been approved if the level of public participation or voting in the report was too low. The reporter visited the Beijing Normal University auxiliary campus in Haicang and interviewed several teachers there. 'No one knew that such a big project was about to break ground in their midst, and it went without saying that they had not been consulted', he wrote.

Meanwhile, work to clear the land and build was accelerating. Imported equipment was soon to arrive at the port. A contractor from neighbouring Zhejiang province was moving ahead with pilings. The *Southern Weekend* on 27 May detailed how the land had been requisitioned and cleared at record speed for Haicang.

Construction had accelerated that spring at the behest of He Lifeng himself, according to a letter Zhao had received, which she showed the *Oriental Outlook Weekly* reporter, signed by the Haicang district construction, environmental protection and economic development bureaus as well as the villages of Wencuo, Dongyu and Zhongshan, which surrounded the Xianglu plant. It claimed that after Zhao went public at the legislative meetings, party secretary He had convened a meeting of local officials on 18 March and demanded: 'We must unify our thinking. The delegates have said their piece. We shall pay no attention. We must pick up the pace on this.' The Haicang district Party committee convened a meeting two days later to unify their message and push ahead with construction. The letter also alleged that Xiamen was organising delegations to go to Beijing to advance the cause of other chemical plants on its docket.

Repeated in several media exposés in late May, He Lifeng's purported message to ignore the CPPCC delegates went viral. Calls to protest spread in the comment trails of blogs and articles on national news portals, even as local web police were clamping down on forums in Xiamen. 'Protect Home', a blog aggregating updates on the kerfuffle on the popular portal Sina.com, excerpted He Lifeng's reported order to push forward on the morning of 26 May. The post was viewed more than 6,000 times within days and elicited more than 200 comments. A comment thread the same day ran 'Madman He', followed by 'Go to Damned Hell, PX', and then 'He Lifeng, Drop Dead!' Another post that day screamed 'Save Xiamen!' It then referred to the protest call in mobile phone text messages. 'A text from a friend said that on 1 June people would march in protest on the government building to express our will. I am determined to go that day and tie a yellow ribbon. Though our power is limited, yet we still want to fight like Don Quixote.'

By now the outcry had mushroomed, spreading from the web to mobile phones and text-messaging. To sidestep the government's tactics to quash calls for unauthorized protests, messages resorted to calling for *jiti sanbu*, or 'collective strolls', popularizing a new euphemism for organized demonstrations. 'It's like trying to keep a lid on a pressure cooker,' recalled Ma Tiannan. 'The more the government wanted to block this, the more people wanted to speak up.'

In the latter part of May, one particular text message was said to have been forwarded as many as a million times around the city:

Taiwan's Chen Yu-hao and the Xianglu Group have begun construction on a PX chemical project in Haicang. Once this highly toxic chemical goes into production, it will mean that an atomic time bomb has been released on Xiamen island. Xiamen people will have to live their lives with leukemia and with children born with congenital defects. We want life, we want good health! International organizations have determined that this sort of special project should only be developed 100 kilometres or more outside a city, but Xiamen is only 16 kilometres from the project at farthest. For the sake of our future generations, please act!

At the end of the message, there was a call for Xiamen residents to demonstrate in the streets on 1 June, Children's Day.

The sender was anonymous. The contents suggested he or she most likely came from central Xiamen, and was either a parent or a grandparent. But his or her identity would remain an enduring whodunnit. Lian would later call the incendiary message a 'miracle', as though anti-PX protests were immaculately conceived.

As the uproar neared a crescendo in late May, several progressive media outlets attempted to temper the hysteria with a scientific perspective. *Southern Weekend* interviewed a chemical specialist at the Chinese Academy of Sciences, who called paraxylene a 'mild toxic … no different from any ordinary chemical whose risks can be controlled'. He dismissed the rumours that it could lead to deformed babies as 'exaggerated'. On 31 May the paper also published an interview with the Taiwanese general manager of the project, which Xianglu published on its own website, aimed at dispelling a host of claims: he distinguished PX from the benzene and nitrobenzene in the Songhua River crisis, and said that 'its safety indicator is in the same class as gasoline'; he cited examples of PX sites in close proximity to other cities in China and others around the world located within a few kilometres of neighbourhoods; and he introduced environmental technology and emergency plans developed in conjunction with the government, which met 'advanced global standards'. But the paper noted that the paranoia over the unknown dangers in their midst was already driving down the property market. It cited a real-estate analyst who had studied Haicang, who stated that 'as many as 30 per cent of the buyers attempted to back out of their deals'.

Ma Tiannan's group, Green Cross, started receiving phone calls from citizens, including middle school students, asking how they could participate in the protests – although her organization had to be careful not to get directly involved, she said. Likewise, community website Xiamen Fish was forced to administer a self-inflicted wound to protect itself. In late May, Yan Xiao, better known by the handle 'Fish Head', told friends that his staff were deleting posts so feverishly that 'their hands had gone numb'. One or two days before the 1 June protests, they shut down the website, saying it was 'undergoing repairs'. The outside world thought the site had been ordered to shut down, whereas in fact they did it themselves. The Beijing-based bloggers' collective Bullog, whose website remained uncensored, took on greater significance as Xiamen sites fell quiet.

On 28 May, the *Xiamen Evening News* published a long interview with city environmental protection bureau director Xie Haisheng. 'The Haicang PX project is under construction after being approved according to legal state procedures' ran the title. 'This was publicly regarded as the signal that the government is strongly pushing the project forward', *Southern Weekend* observed on 31 May. It was also a stain on the reputation of Xie, who had been seen as a well-intended environmentalist, but was compelled by his superiors to defend the project.

Then, as the call to protest buzzed around the city, the government made an abrupt reversal. On 29 May, Xiamen leaders were summoned to an emergency meeting of the provincial Party committee in Fuzhou to report on the project and the public outcry. Just before nine o'clock the next morning, 30 May, the executive vice mayor Ding Guoyan announced the decision to postpone construction and commission a new and more extensive environmental assessment of the entire petrochemical industrial zone. He gave no further details and no timetable, other than noting that the decision had the support of those higher up.

Xiamen leaders, state media contacts confirmed, had succumbed to pressure from the central authorities, who were plugged into the protest buzz via *neican*, or internal reports, from Xinhua news agency journalists on the ground. Premier Wen Jiabao, they said, had personally ordered the project suspended on the eve of the protests, directing local authorities to handle the situation delicately for the sake of preserving social stability. Vice premier Zeng Peiyan weighed in as well. The internal directives also called for investigating the project for any evidence of problems. Local officials were pressed most of all to keep people off the streets. One central media journalist recalled the message: 'The point was: we don't want to spark turmoil or a large mass incident.'

The day the decision to suspend the plant was announced, the Xiamen media swarmed to the makeshift project headquarters. The subsidiary general manager, Lin Yinzong, was forced to face reporters. Since the government had made this decision, he said, the company had to respect it – it was suspending construction and clearing all the earth movers and other equipment from the site.

Internally, however, company bosses were incensed: they had received no official notice from the government of the suspension, or the freezing of their bank loans (and they never would). Chen had flown to the United States, despite the tensions, to attend to personal business. But at his behest, Xianglu sent an urgent notice pleading their case to the Taiwan Affairs Office of the State Council, a copy of which I later viewed. Although the need to preserve stability was understood, the company wrote, this was 'a disaster we cannot bear'. It also pointed out that the government had not communicated with the company. 'Who will bear the burden of the losses caused by this hasty decision?' the notice asked, calling for the project to 'return to the track of stable construction'.

But, despite high-level intervention, it was too late to head off the 'stroll'. Instead, local govern- ment and police looked to weaken and subdue the demonstration through tried-and-tested methods of crowd control. Originally, the protesters intended to make their way toward the site of the plant on Haicang. So the city closed off the bridge early in the morning of 1 June, meaning no traffic could pass, even public buses. The authorities also feared the involvement of students from Xiamen University, particularly given the approaching anniversary of the military crackdown on student-led protests in Tiananmen Square of 3–4 June 1989. Zhao Yufen was suddenly muzzled by Party authorities at the university. Later in the day, a phalanx of military police barricaded the gates of the school. Another point of sensitivity was the involvement of the residents of Haicang. Over in Wencuo village, police arrived and had village officials stand at the gate to monitor who was going in and out. Villagers were warned not to take part in the 'illegal gathering'. At least half a dozen went anyway, including one young man who showed me footage he took on his mobile phone. It featured him and his buddies from around the village hoisting a banner and hollering 'Protect Xiamen!'

The strolls

Taiwan's democratic transition in the 1980s was underpinned by landmark nimby protests against a number of major corporations and polluting projects, which highlighted the abuses and corruption of a system lacking in public participation. Some Xiameners said it was from Taiwan that they learned something about civil disobedience over the years. Fujian people were tuned into the political soap operas across the Strait – or the pro-Beijing slant on it, anyway – through local state television and the Internet. Many would also hear about Taiwan from relatives and business partners. Perhaps the rhythms of people power had sunk in: the protests in Xiamen were extraordinarily civil and well-orchestrated, especially considering there was no acknowledged organiser.

The stroll took shape slowly. At first somewhere between 300 and 600 people gathered on the pavement by the huge grassy square outside the city government offices. They were forced to double back after finding the bridge to Haicang blocked off, but by midday they coursed through the streets by the thousands in the wilting heat, passing city government offices and chanting 'Serve the people!' – the Party motto emblazoned atop the municipal headquarters. Some called out the city boss by name: 'He Lifeng, take a hike!' The suspension and further assessment of the project were far from enough. Protesters demanded the plant be expelled altogether.

In advance reports to higher authorities, the city had vastly under-anticipated the numbers who would protest. Multitudes of onlookers joined the stroll. Many police, media and plainclothes security agents mixed in as well. Real-estate companies from Haicang passed out bottles of water. Ding Guoyan, the deputy mayor, watched the crowd amass around the square from inside the municipal head-quarters, only slipping out after they passed. 'This was smart,' said the reporter Shao Fanqing, who was also on the scene. 'Otherwise there would have been a conflict.'

Microblogging would only make inroads in China a couple years later, but bloggers and bulletin boards filled the breach despite numerous disruptions. A number of bloggers came to Xiamen by train to broadcast the protests in real time, including the citizen journalist known as Zola, who had shot to fame earlier in the year covering a property stand-off in Chongqing. The logs of two Guangzhou-based bloggers, 'Beifeng' (the pseudonym of Wen Yunchao, a media veteran) and '37' (John Kennedy, a young American China hand) – who sent text messages to their colleagues to put straight online – became instant classics in the canon of Chinese blogging.

> *37*: about 500 Wujing [armed police] are circling around. Old women are yelling: 'reject pollution, protect Xiamen!' A large group of people are gathered at the Xiamen municipal government buildings and want in. A large red banner has been pulled out.

> *Beifeng*: someone at the municipal government gate is holding up a banner which reads: resist PX, protect Egret Island [an alternative name for Xiamen], police are trying to grab it away from him. ...

> There are at least over 10,000 people here, the march is on!

People keep joining in along the way, the procession keeps getting longer.

More and more people can be seen wearing yellow ribbons.

Along the way many people are handing out printouts and yellow ribbons. I've tied one on my bag which reads: people's livelihoods, democracy, people's rights, harmony. Police are filming me now. I'm giving them lots of poses.

There are seventy senior citizens here saying: 'for the next generation, we don't mind settling accounts this late in life, it's worth it!

Few of the protesters had experienced anything like this before, but those who had naturally emerged at the head of the pack. Li Yiqiang, a local leader of a citizen alliance that had mounted anti-Japanese protests over the disputed Diaoyu islands (known as the Senkakus in Japan), was hard to miss during the protests, since he donned a gas mask.

Huang Zhaohui, a smiley man with a shaven pate, also stood out in the crowd that day, having tied a yellow ribbon around his head. Huang paid little attention when he received the sensational text message about the protest on 26 May, and did not send it on. But on 30 May, he read an online bulletin board on the chatroom service QQ and his interest was piqued. Then aged 42 with his own small automation firm, he described himself as environmentally inclined but hardly an idealist of any sort. 'I just want to live a good life', he said frankly. He escorted me around Xiamen in his second-generation Toyota Prius, the economical hybrid car then gaining popularity in suburban America, but not in China, where it was subject to high import duties and no Green subsidies (only 3,700 were sold in China from 2005 to 2009). Huang got his for its good fuel mileage and low emissions, but also out of sheer curiosity. (He spent a year taking it apart and reassembling it, just to study the technology.) He wasn't political either. He was in Nanjing as a university student during 4 June 1989, but as a Communist Youth League member was instilled with the notion not to sacrifice one's future on any activity that ran counter to the government or the Party. 'I still respect the Communist Party', he said. 'If you replaced it with something else, things would not necessarily be better.'

On the morning of 1 June, Huang and colleagues went out to buy materials but the store hadn't opened, so they chose to drop by the protest dressed in their company jumpers. 'This demonstration was different from 4 June,' said Huang, who was moved by the scene. 'There were a lot of old men and old women and government officials as well.' But while he viewed the march as a 'peaceful model' for others to follow, government officials did not respond in kind. He said they were poor crisis managers and showed no confidence. 'They didn't dare engage in dialogue and they didn't think that dialogue was necessary.' With the project already on hold, for one, they had little room to negotiate.

Xiamen Green Cross, already well monitored, found its position even more precarious as Xiameners posted messages and photos from the protests to their website. Calls came from unidentified authorities, warning them they had to 'better manage' their site. Under pressure, Ma Tiannan posted a notice on the website saying that the group neither supported nor opposed the protests, and had not organised them. Because the protests did not get official approval, she reasoned, they could not openly support an illegal activity. But she could support it individually and privately. The scientist Zhao Yufen also issued a protective statement at the behest of the university and the city, saying that she had stopped accepting interviews and imploring students not to join in.

While Chinese netizens could track the protest over blogs and bulletin boards, Chinese leaders were briefed by internal cables far more detailed and frequent than the few bits of information the official news wires gave the public. The pressure for updates from the offices of the party leadership in Beijing surged as protesters shuffled towards the gates of Xiamen University that afternoon, I was told. The Xinhua News Agency's Fuzhou bureau scrambled to reassign a photographer, who was shooting curvaceous sports car models at an auto show, to the scene of the protests outside the locked gates of the university.

Although the protests had unfolded in an impromptu manner, they were the culmination of a long chain of activity. 'All the people who participated – from intellectuals, to CPPCC members, to the traditional media, to the web and finally the city residents – fulfilled their duties,' columnist Lian Yue would later tell me. 'If any of those links had broken, this outcome could not have occurred.' But Lian Yue did not take to the streets himself. The police came to his house a day or two before the protest, explaining that they wanted to check up on a routine matter, but refusing to give any specific reasons. Lian turned them away, saying he was busy and if they wanted to meet they should make an appointment. After ten minutes, they left. But concerned friends advised him to steer clear of the strolls.

The protests continued the next day, 2 June. Blogger Beifeng described the day as blisteringly hot, with more young faces on-hand. The non-violent, good-natured atmosphere continued, according to his SMS updates. But later on, the vibe changed:

> A broadcast has begun declaring this assembly illegal, demanding people leave the scene as soon as possible, telling them not to be taken advantage of by hostile forces:
> 'To the masses of the people: Yesterday and today our city has seen two days of illegal gathering and demonstrating. Gathering now at the city government gate is illegal behavior. The city Public Security Department calls for the crowd of spectators and those with no understanding of the truth to leave quickly. Do not be taken advantage of by those who break the law.'
> The sky is very black, it's about to rain. They're repeating the broadcast now, asking the crowd of spectators to leave quickly.
> The police have begun trying to drive people out but black rainclouds cover the city and people are just ducking under the People's Meeting Hall to get out of the rain.
> People are vastly outnumbered by the police strength and are stuck due to the rain. There could be some danger.
> Police and military police are getting completely soaked.

The protest wound down that evening. There were a few tussles with police and at least four people were injured, according to the updates on Bullog, but most of the demonstrators went home, soaking wet.

After the protests, official police notices went up in communities throughout the city, urging participants to give themselves up. He Lifeng had unleashed a hunt to find the protest organisers. Local online bulletin boards remained censored, or 'harmonised'. As many as two dozen suspected instigators were detained in all, though word spread online and most were set free within days. Xiameners became skittish: one foreign journalist described secretive meetings with organisers on the ferry. They would surreptitiously flash a text message on their phone, then just as quickly hide it away. There were run-ins even among activists too, with Lian Yue and other radicals attacking Ma Tiannan and Xiamen Green Cross for their stated neutrality. Many protests in China died out and devolved in similar ways.

Within days, Huang Zhaohui was collared by plainclothes police. He was accused of helping to incite and orchestrate the protests, allegations he adamantly denied. He was released after three days. 'Even the policeman who grabbed me said they dislike this project', he said. 'Because they are Xiamen citizens too. They have homes here and live here. But they have no choice. Because they have orders from above. That's their rice bowl – that's their job. So they wanted me to understand them.'

A murky review

The police crackdown was coupled with a propaganda surge, as the city stepped up its initiatives to educate the public about the potential project. It issued 250,000 copies of a cartoon-illustrated pamphlet entitled *How Much Do You Know about PX?*, filled with information that had been provided mainly by Xianglu. But it appeared to do little to satisfy the public hunger for real information and participation.

The strolls and suspension had left He Lifeng's government in an awkward limbo. He had bungled the furore and underestimated the threat and scale of the protests in his communications with senior officials. As one Beijing-based official close to SEPA described it, 'his hands were burned'. The central government was watching how Xiamen would handle the public after the unrest. Many of the online attacks were targeted at He Lifeng himself, due to his penchant for massive projects: large landfills, highway flyovers right along the coastline and the rapid transit light rail network – questionable in a city of Xiamen's scale and relatively low density. Prior to the PX affair he had come under scrutiny from Party corruption investigators, said official sources in Xiamen. The fate of the PX project was in the hands of a nexus of higher authorities and outside forces he could not fully control. He was angling for promotion in the autumn, they said, and another bout of upheaval could threaten his job.

Xiamen thus ventured into uncharted territory. It was SEPA's Pan Yue, as much as anyone, who had recommended that Xiamen commission a strategic environmental assessment and public review of the area. According to the account of the Beijing official, He Lifeng and Pan Yue had friendly ties – and He had sought out Pan over the matter at the climax of the protests. To backtrack in this way was tantamount to admitting the impotence and abuse of impact assessment mechanisms in China. But Pan saw a high-profile opportunity to advance his 2006 regulatory initiative to promote the role of area assessments and public review in the planning process. For He it was a means to buy time and present a credible framework for public involvement in the final decision process. Pan made a further announcement about it on 7 June.

But there were early indications that the assessment and review would be politically fraught. Following the marches, the *South China Morning Post* reported on 11 July, a top NDRC official led a delegation to Fuzhou and Xiamen to probe the case. *Caijing* reported on 25 June that a team of SEPA experts carried out a preliminary investigation as well at the time. Yet no authorized outfit would agree to perform the assessment initially, due to the uproar surrounding the case. In July, the Chinese Research Academy of Environmental Sciences (CRAES) in Beijing, a state institute set up under SEPA, was designated to carry out the area assessment. But there were serious questions as to whether the process would be an experimental referendum or an empty promise.

Even though Pan had weighed in, his hands were tied. People close to SEPA said that he had been compromised by the fact that his office had given the green light to the project originally. For several years, progressive-minded journalists at Party outlets and metropolitan tabloids had rallied around the well-connected Pan and his Green initiatives; now a few aimed oblique criticism at his office's dealings. At base, moreover, Pan and his colleagues at SEPA had minimal authority to intervene in individual projects, and practically none over re-zoning entire areas. 'To tell you the truth, I could do nothing about the PX project if the project was going forward,' Pan told us half a year later. 'The reason is that [on paper] all the projects are much more environmentally friendly, more advanced in technology and more standardised compared with all the projects we have done before,' he said. 'But if all the projects were squeezed together in one place, it would be a problem. I have been appealing this problem for two and a half years, but so far nothing has happened.'

Despite a promised reassessment, six months of relative silence fell over Xiamen. Like thousands of flare-ups of mass unrest across China each year, it all appeared to burn out just as quickly. The carrot-and-stick reaction from the government, combined with a pragmatic public, produced an eerie quiet in the interim.

To a large extent, the calm was reinforced by a virtual media blackout. In July, Xiamen authorities went so far as to announce new draft regulations requiring netizens to leave comments on local websites under their actual names, making He's the first local government in China to move ahead with the highly contentious policy of 'real-name registration' on the Internet. One official was quoted in the state press saying that the city sought greater control over web content after the PX protest. Another denied any link. In any case, online commentators and independently minded metropolitans around the country cast suspicion on the move. It triggered national criticism and soon the city quietly shelved the draft rules. Still, more and more Xiamen websites were requiring users to register even to perform simple functions like searches.

Chen Yu-hao lobbied during the interim in the only manner he could: behind the scenes. The outside world continued to see Xiamen and Xianglu as in cahoots to push forward the multi-billion-dollar plant. But relations began to chill precipitously in the aftermath of the suspension and the protests, according to company leaders and members of the state press. 'The two sides grew increasingly hostile towards one another', said the former Xianglu executive. Chen thought the decision against the plant to suspend construction was mainly the work of the local government, but he reckoned that it could be overruled at the central level. He hoped that he could play one off against the other, by going over the head of the local government and writing letter after letter straight to Beijing. 'Boss Chen did not have a lot of tactics,' said the executive. 'He was a letter-writing freak.'

Letters I was shown were addressed to president Hu, premier Wen, the rest of the leadership and many prominent ministers. One was sent to KMT chairman Lian Chan ahead of a meeting with Hu, another to the Ministry of State Security. In every one, Chen highlighted his role as a huge taxpayer in Xiamen and a staunch opponent of Taiwanese independence and advocate of reunification. He presented a two-pronged argument for his project. He contended that the local government had 'opposed the central government' by suspending the plant – a serious offence – and damaged their authority in the process. And he argued that this turn of events was bad for investors, like him, from Taiwan. He was committed to building in the original spot as designated. In a letter of 24 November to Chen Yunlin, head of the Taiwan Affairs Office, he demanded that construction be resumed and wrote emotionally about his 'dreams'.

He dreamt that he would earn US$10 billion annually in revenues, which was considered well within reach, and that once he had made $500 million to $1 billion in post-tax profits, he would establish a 'Cross-Strait Peaceful Development Fund'.

Just how high Chen's patronage ties ran was a central intrigue for media covering the case. It was never fully clear, but speculation was rampant. Despite his delicate position, Chen was in an expansionist mode. At one point circa 2006 he was in discussion with local governments across the country on eight major property development deals, though not one came to fruition, as the PX case sapped his financing, said the former executive. Overseas Chinese media did not fail to note that the CEO of Xianglu at the time, Yu Xinchang, was formerly China CEO of Hewlett Packard, and boss there of Jiang Mianheng, the son of the former leader Jiang Zemin. But Yu did not seem to play a significant role in the dispute, and no letter was ever written from Chen to Jiang Zemin, to the executive's knowledge.

Nor did Chen have any real backers among the central leaders, despite nearly two decades in business in Fujian. Following the leadership reshuffle at the Party Congress that October, three out of nine members of the Politburo Standing Committee had served earlier as high officials in Fujian – Jia Qinglin, He Guoqiang and the future leader of China, Xi Jinping. But Chen was not known to have cozy ties with any of these potentates.

He had, however, cultivated high-placed patrons in the Taiwan Affairs Office, where He Lifeng's predecessor as Xiamen Party chief, Zheng Lizhong, was now the executive deputy director, effectively the second-in-command. Moreover, the Party Central Committee's Leading Small Group on Taiwan Affairs was headed by Hu Jintao, who made reintegration with the self-ruled island a focal point, and was believed to view the push as a cornerstone of his political legacy. Mainland efforts at courting Taiwanese businessmen and rapprochement with the KMT were only intensifying as Taiwan's presidential elections loomed just around the corner, in March 2008. Behind the scenes, the central media journalist on the case told me, the most vigorous proponent of the PX project in the government was without a doubt the Taiwan Affairs Office, and 'they were very assertive'.

It was well known that Chen Yu-hao had appealed to Taiwan Affairs after the project was suspended, using the rationale of safeguarding Taiwanese business interests. But few knew that the body had responded forcefully on Chen's behalf, exerting pressure on the Fujian bureau of state news agency Xinhua, which prompted an internal corruption probe.

The probe stemmed particularly from Xinhua's activities in June, when, immediately following the strolls, the local bureau had compiled a potentially damaging and influential internal report. This showed widespread local aversion among officials and ordinary folk towards the project and hope that it would be relocated. In an internal interview at the time with the Xiamen bureau chief of Xinhua, He Lifeng himself explicitly voiced the opinion that the project should be moved out of Haicang. Xinhua internal reports also indicated that the company's losses due to the suspension were not as heavy as Chen argued. Xianglu had not put up much cash of its own; its subsidiary Tenglong had received a syndicated loan from five different state banks, led by one of China's big four state leviathans, the Agricultural Bank of China. Thus the state had a stake in the project, as well as some degree of leverage. Xinhua's internal survey also registered the widespread hostility of well-heeled citizens and business owners. This bolstered the argument that it would be bad for the local economy in the long term if Xiamen pushed ahead with the now-notorious project, and that it would be very difficult to pacify the people of Xiamen.

While the Xinhua reporters supported a somewhat populist liberal viewpoint, they worked to report objectively and independently, the central media journalist argued. But Chen and his executives learned of the reports and pressed the Taiwan Affairs Office to address their suspicions of corruption and bias. Taiwan Affairs applied pressure, and that eventually prompted the Xinhua discipline inspection body to conduct a probe of the local bureau. The Chinese central bureaucracy is built in silos, meaning a senior leader or leaders likely had to weigh in for one organ to compel an investigation of another. Procedures were officially launched, and top Xinhua officials in Fuzhou and Xiamen were summoned to Beijing for questioning. What followed was unclear. But there were no repercussions said the journalist, who insisted that Xinhua had done no wrong. 'If you want to say we were an interest group, then all Xiamen residents were an interest group.'

At the time of the 17th Party Congress that October, a heady mix of interests were in play. The Taiwan business lobby was but one. The government in June had unveiled its first national policy programme to combat climate change, and president Hu amplified China's stance on the commitments of developing countries to 'sustainable development' and 'environment-friendly society' at the APEC forum in Sydney that September. From his perch among policymakers in Fuzhou, Shao Fanqing later told me that China's diplomatic forays played into official considerations over the PX affair. Hu's policy orientation of social harmony and sustainable growth, dubbed the 'scientific development concept', was also to be enshrined in the Communist Party charter at the Congress, where Hu called for a 'conservation culture' and the Party for the first time devoted a section in the political report – a bedrock of its agenda for the next five years – to the country's environmental policy, including new pollution-reduction goals. But in the Party trenches, the run-up to the Congress would be defined more than anything by the tussle for promotion. (He Lifeng, for one, had an alternate seat on the Party Central Committee waiting for him.) That meant leaders around the country were particularly touchy about unrest on their home turf. In their minds, nothing could take precedence over social stability, especially when job security was at stake.

Among political insiders following the case, a deepening sense of cynicism and conservatism set in, and it was underscored by a shadowy new development that autumn. In October, word spread around Beijing of official written instructions the previous month from Hu Jintao himself, on resolving the impasse over the PX plant in Xiamen. These advised shielding 'social stability' on the one hand and cross-Strait ties on the other. But orders from Party leaders tend to come in the form of general guidelines for lower officials to intuit and implement as circumstances require, and the content and implications of Hu's orders varied, depending on whom I asked.

Hu's instructions, according to the official connected to SEPA, recommended in no uncertain terms that the plant should be built, based on considerations of Taiwanese business interests and cross-Strait relations. At an executive meeting of the State Council at the time, with SEPA representatives present, it was decided to implement the instructions. It would be up to the Xiamen government to carry out the process.

But as the instructions were read on the ground in Xiamen, according to the the central media journalist, 'there was no clear slant'. Rather, Hu's orders delicately balanced the interests of stability with those of Taiwanese business. Hu also called for the Taiwanese losses to be studied and clearly determined, and the 'mass incident' (the protest) to be dealt with appropriately. It would be up to the Xiamen government to find that balance, to handle the process and announce the decision. And therein lay the rub.

The murky politics at play were evident when I travelled to Xiamen that November. Xiamen government departments were waiting for the environmental impact assessment of the area by the Research Academy of Environmental Sciences in Beijing. 'The report is not complete yet', team member Li Xiang said over the phone.

Yet for many weeks, opponents from Lian Yue down to Haicang villagers and developers had been hearing otherwise. Many ordinary Xiameners nodded, with no basis at all, that the 'PX is back on'. Occasionally someone would argue that the work 'never really stopped'. Most admitted they did not know the situation, but simply assumed the worst. Despite hopes that the new assessment would be open and involve the public, to this point the entire process was 'operating in a black box', as some said. Local web forums were muzzled on the matter. The city government-controlled dailies had run only vague briefs on visits by team members.

To understand the evolution of Haicang, you might imagine the building of Las Vegas in the middle of the Nevada Desert in the 1930s and 1940s. Only here, Taiwanese businessmen played the role of Jewish and Italian kingpins, the palm trees were planted for industrial parks instead of casinos, and the gaming commission was the Communist Party. The layout was somewhat typical of development zones around the country. Carving a crescent through Haicang was the auxiliary campus of Beijing Normal University. One autumn Sunday, students were playing a friendly game of football on the pitch nearby the buttery-white main building of the school. The new subdivision appeared as though airdropped in from an American suburb, but for the smokestacks of Xianglu lingering ominously in the background.

A slim strip of an older village remained between the school and the plant. Thousands of 'villages' in China look like it, squeezed by industry on one hand and suburbia on the other – a shanty town, supporting the development around it. I was led into the village by a woman in her twenties who was trying to lose me. When I mentioned the proximity to the PX facility, it set her off. 'Are you doing an investigation?' She said the emissions from the older facility used to be so heavy you could smell it, but now it was better filtered. As for the PX project: 'The pollution will be very severe,' she responded with a chilly tone. But, she said, 'Most people here didn't even know about it before this happened.'

As sensitive and excitable as residents were over the perceived danger in their midst, most of those to whom I spoke expressed similar attitudes of detachment and resignation. A 70-year-old man surnamed Wu, watering a few scattered plants on the side of the road, spoke more openly about the risks of the project but said he himself had no idea of the actual dangers. 'We're still waiting for the assessment,' he said, adding a familiar refrain: 'We can only put our trust in the city government and Party committee to make the right decision.'

A strong sense of powerlessness also pervaded what lay ahead. Industry had been encroaching on agriculture here for two decades, so the stoicism of many peasants seemed only natural. At the edge of the road through the village closest to Xianglu, another man, Chai Yacong, emerged from a shin-deep bog of fertiliser, leaving a rusty discolouration on his trousers, and walked me into a small plot of chives, Japanese rape and a few longan trees. 'The money from farming here is still pretty good. It's just that we don't have land anymore.' Over the past fifteen years, much of his leased plot had been requisitioned for the Xianglu campus, the Haicang government, and a viaduct built to channel sewage from local factories into the sea. Then there was 'the other big problem' facing the village, he said without prompting, 'that PX project'.

His son worked at the existing Xianglu facility loading crates of fibres onto trucks, but even he only learned about the PX project in early 2007 by word of mouth. Now he heard it was back on. 'The state already signed a contract with them. It's already being built. How can it be stopped?'

The 300-acre tract that would be home to the PX plant was a Mars-like depression of reddish earth across the road from Xianglu's main base; it was empty but for temporary offices built of pre-fabricated materials in the low-slung, aircraft hangar style. When I approached, a Xianglu division manager returning from his lunch asserted that the assessment was effectively finished and the project passed. Now, he said, he and other plant engineers were at work finalising blueprints. They had pencilled in a target date to resume land preparations: 1 January, at the earliest. But before Xiamen authorities could give the go-ahead, they 'have to wait to see if city residents make another fuss', said the man, who withheld his name and said he was not authorised to speak. Mr Wen, the garrulous site contractor who lived down an alleyway across the road in Wencuo, had heard the same. 'The government would be sacrificing the small interests of the common people to look after the big interests of Taiwanese businessmen,' he said. 'But if people really protest again, it won't.'

The most sobering outlook seemed to come from Lian Yue over coffee on Gulangyu Island: 'Everybody feels like we've already done all we could with the civilised forces we've got,' he sighed. 'In this society, if you can get to the extent of taking to the streets and marching, you've reached the limit.' But Lian was a deft rhetorician, and he continued to challenge the government to make an enlightened and popular choice: 'The Xiamen affair is a touchstone for the Chinese government: is it really determined to start to change the environment? If this project starts up again, that proves that it isn't yet.'

Fresh from the Party congress, state employees nationwide were studying President Hu's prescribed recipe for 'scientific development': fairer, friendlier, cleaner and greener. But assessing what was or wasn't 'scientific development', in the case of Haicang, was proving to be a decidedly political science. In an interview following an inspection in Xiamen in late November, a Tsinghua University expert advising the government on the process, Jin Yong, stressed that the impact assessment process should not be 'politicised' before it was complete, whether by Taiwanese business and political ties or 'the concerns towards the ordinary people'. Meanwhile some local experts still saw the case through the prism of the March presidential elections in Taiwan. 'Anything related to Taiwan is being considered more carefully and comprehensively right now, in case it may affect the election one way or the other', Zhang Wensheng, a professor at the Taiwan Research Institute at Xiamen University, told me.

Meanwhile, Xianglu was making an unpublicised legal manoeuvre. By November, the Taiwanese company quietly filed suit in a Beijing court against the scientists Zhao Yufen and Yuan Dongxing for defamation, alleging that their statements to the press distorted the facts and misled the public. 'Because we feel that we've been wronged, we hope to use this to clarify the matter', Tenglong Aromatics' top executive told me when we met later that month. (Management finally agreed to speak on condition that individual names not be used.) While Zhao was immune from prosecution over her CPPCC proposal, statements to the press were another matter. 'Our goal is simple,' said the executive, 'to get them to clear up the truth and restore our reputation.' It was the company management's first proper interview since the affair erupted; he and another Taiwanese executive, both US-trained, spent two and a half hours defending the project. They asserted that Chinese regulations only stipulate a separation zone of 700 metres for a facility of this type, and showed Google Earth images of PX plants adjacent to residential neighbourhoods in Japan, the Netherlands, Singapore, Texas and Nanjing.

We were inside the warehouse-like headquarters on an otherwise desolate work site; the present staff of 370 were busy at work at computer cubicles. The ongoing preparations displayed their confidence in pressing forward, the executives said. They acknowledged that 'Adviser Chen' was valued because of 'his experience in dealing with the government', but denied any suggestions of tinkering behind the scenes. 'The key is having an investment environment ruled by law,' said the top executive. 'We very much hope and anticipate that the government will resolve the current predicament speedily and appropriately.'

The man in the gas mask during the strolls, Li Yiqiang, framed the challenge facing the local government as well as anyone. A well-known anti-Japan agitator in Xiamen and a rare veteran in the craft of direct action, he became a lead marcher in June by default. Li was only paroled after spending fifty-five days in custody, the longest known detention of any of the protesters at the time. When we met over tea in late November, he had just been questioned a second time and told he could easily be imprisoned for illegally demonstrating – a scare tactic. His view was that some Xiameners, including himself, would look to march again if they sensed the government 'covertly manipulated' the assessment, but not if they went about it openly according to 'standard, legal procedure'. It was a lot to ask.

The spoken road

At the turn of December, the six-month suspension period was finally up. On 5 December, with little forewarning, the Xiamen government released the long-promised environmental impact assessment for the project and the Haicang area from the China Research Academy of Environmental Sciences. Airing the full text of the report in official city media, embattled city authorities exhorted Xiameners to take the 'spoken road of public opinion', as the *Xiamen Evening News* put it – in other words, stay off the streets. In the eighteen-minute official press conference that morning, local journalists there said, the term 'PX' was not even mentioned. There were no questions taken. But the development quickly made national news. The item was held from the front page of the mainstream web portal Sina, but was slotted third on the domestic news page.

The assessment report was viewed in hindsight as balanced and independent on the whole, though it was based largely on information provided by the local government. It primarily faulted local planning – implicitly, the work of administrations preceding He Lifeng's – for spawning 'contradictions' with the development of the new residential centre after petrochemicals did not take off as originally planned. 'It is not possible to keep away air pollution with only about a 300-metre forest segregation belt between the two areas,' read the report. 'The more development there is, the more contradictions there will be.'

To many readers, the report clearly indicated that construction of the new chemical facilities could move forward, provided the plant took precautions and the city made adjustments. It suggested moving out two schools on either side of the commercial property zone and the 4,690 remaining villagers housed within the segregation belt, who had yet to be relocated as planned, and boosting water treatment and other pollution controls. At the same time, the report implicated Xianglu and other firms for past instances of emissions and inspection violations. 'Some of them started production before they received permission from the environmental protection bureau. This has brought about air pollution and had a negative impact on the living conditions of the residents there.' But, ultimately, the report was open-ended and conditional as to the future direction of development:

> We suggest the government make a clear development orientation between building an industrial area and constructing a second-ary city centre in Haicang. If it chooses the area for industrial development, it should adjust and limit the population numbers there and leave more space for a segregation belt. It should ensure sufficient supervision and controls over pollution. Otherwise, it should not allow industrial development as the main leading force in the area.

Most crucially, the release of the report marked the start of a ten-day period of 'public participation' to collect feedback, which would be included as an addendum to the completed report. People were invited to submit their views by email, post or telephone to the city government or the Beijing-based research academy. The final decision rested at least nominally with the city government, which reserved the right to designate the primary use of Haicang District on the city's master plan.

Unsurprisingly, most Xiameners were profoundly sceptical at first. On the main city government-backed web portal Xiamen Net, 700 comments poured in within a few hours. A representative trail of comments on 5 December ran thus:

> PX is still being built; quick, turn on your [pollution] gauges.
>
> If PX does not go, we will go.
>
> Get out!!!

Can't the people's government think about the people!!!

The day PX comes on-line is the day I leave Xiamen.

A Xianglu spokesman whom I rang that day commented: 'It seems to me that it favours us.' Company officials were privately fuming at the accusations of shirking inspections earlier in the decade, which they would later characterise as fabrication. But he made no mention of this. 'It talks about villages moving, but not us', he said.

Yet the report was non-committal, consciously leaving the door ajar for folks in Xiamen to weigh in: property or petrochemicals? For most there was no question.

Soon after the report was released, Xiamen Net started a poll on the project, with the approval of local authorities. Of more than 58,000 votes cast, 55,000 were against the project and 3,000 for it. But the poll was mysteriously aborted after less than two days. The website explained that it had neglected to screen for multiple votes cast from the same IP address, rendering the lopsided results invalid. But officials also had been reminded of standing orders from the Party's central propaganda department not to conduct referendum-style votes on sensitive public issues.

Thus for all its euphoria and openness, the public participation period was also channelled and constrained, stage-managed on the go. The government sought to lend it legitimacy without losing control.

The review stage culminated in two days of public hearings on 13–14 December. The participants included some 80 representatives of the municipal People's Congress and Political Consultative Conference and 107 members of the general public. The members of the public were selected by a televised lottery pick from the 624 people who registered online, although journalists said that not all of the participants were randomly selected. Yuan Dongxing and Lian Yue were among those invited to attend and speak, as were individual employees of Xianglu. Many of the most prominent constituencies were represented among the cast of characters.

The two-day session ran for eight hours in total. Outside of Xinhua, the main Party newspapers and city-owned press, the media were shut out of the proceedings. When a China Central Television news magazine programme asked for clips of the forum that week, the Xiamen propaganda office said it could only provide video, not audio, a director of the programme told me. Yet as the hearing unfolded a senior Xiamen propaganda official who presided, Lin Congming, tried to set a tone of fair debate, borrowing the line on freedom of speech commonly misattributed to Voltaire: 'I disapprove of what you say, but I will defend to the death your right to say it', Lin commented.

Of the 107 public representatives, 91 opposed the project, 15 voiced support and 1 left without speaking, Xinhua reported. 'If you were going to pick two apples to eat, knowing that one of them was poisonous and the other was not, then who would dare make the choice?' said a male doctor that Xinhua quoted, identified as 'Representative No. 31'. Among 80 local lawmakers and political advisers, 15 addressed the forum and 14 spoke against the plan to build the PX plant. Zeng Huaqun, a local lawmaker and also a law professor at Xiamen University, said: 'It's not whether the city should build it or not, it's that the project must be stopped immediately. It's time to make a decision now.' But a local CPPCC member, Lu Shaofeng, said: 'Xiamen cannot just rely on tourism for development or on scenery for attracting talented people.' While the company was only allowed to release a statement online, several Tenglong employees spoke. They were seen as puppets, drawing jeers of suspicion when they failed to state their company affiliation up-front.

State media, including some of the country's more respected and discerning market-liberal outlets, gushed over the ten-day exercise in public participation. They declared it a success for 'democratic decision-making' and pronounced a 'popular victory' practically fait accompli. But it was *People's Daily*, the Party flagship, that put the handling of the case in strategic perspective: 'In terms of respecting city residents' right to know, the Xiamen city government put on a make-up class,' the paper intoned, pointing to past lapses. 'In terms of opening up channels and listening to the will of the people, the Xiamen city government went from a passive position to taking the initiative.'

The city's shift in strategy was telling. In fact, numerous inside sources believed that the local government and some central officials were already determined to move the plant. The conflict between petrochemicals and property had come to a head; the local government did not want further unrest or scrutiny of its planning decisions; and He Lifeng didn't want his 'madman' image to haunt his career. City leaders would trade future GDP figures for immediate popularity points. But they needed to demonstrate a clear public mandate to forge a broader consensus at the central levels and push through a decision. Xiameners could obviously be counted on to register their opposition. 'They could play it hands-off and let things go, because they knew very clearly what the outcome would be,' the central media journalist reflected years later. 'In China, if the government is really permitting openness and transparency, it's because the government wants openness and transparency to get what it wants.'

On 16 December, city and province leaders met in private in Fuzhou and decided that they should make an internal recommendation to halt the PX project in Xiamen. Instead they would push for it to relocate to a little-developed strip on the Gulei peninsula in Zhangzhou, around 100 kilometres down the coast. Rumours of this possible scenario had been floating around Xiamen in the intervening months. It meant the province would keep the project, making it a 'win–win' solution, as Fujian leaders put it. News of the recommendation to move the plant was first leaked in the *Ta Kung Pao* on 18 December, one of three pro-Beijing papers in Hong Kong with close Party ties. But the newspaper's correspondent in Fuzhou, who witnessed part of the meeting, had jumped the gun. Nothing was official yet, and the Hong Kong-based rival paper *Wen Wei Po* the same day refuted the report. Both it and Xinhua quoted a Fujian government spokesperson who said the matter was still being deliberated. But the next day *Southern Weekend* echoed *Ta Kung Pao*, noting that local officials had to wait for Beijing to confirm their recommendation. The narrative of a people's victory over PX was taking shape in the press, though it would take many months to formalise.

It was in the midst of this denouement that I met Chen Yu-hao in Beijing. The morning after his meeting at the Jintai Hotel, we were back at his darkened hotel suite before he flew off for the Christmas holiday. He had the television tuned to a Chinese symphony orchestra performance, and strains of the Smetana symphonic poem *Má vlast* underscored his tone of hopeful defiance. Chen would not discuss his meeting the day before. (By that point, the company had grown reliant on the state-operated China International Engineering Consulting Cooperation as its go-between with the government.) But Chen smarted at how the company had been muzzled throughout. 'I feel that you can clarify things abroad, but not in China', he said. I asked if he had had any meetings with He Lifeng of late. 'Not too many. The Xiamen city government has always hoped we would move.' All along? I asked. 'From late May, when [the suspension] was decided, they've been enlisting people all along to ask us to propose ourselves that we relocate.' What have they been saying? 'They said that now there's the will of the people, they have already demonstrated and so forth, so they don't want the headache. I said if you want us to move, the government has to order us to move. It's not we who want to move. Legally, it's different.'

Chen, like his managers, argued Xianglu's case logically in terms of China's existing legal procedures. At base, he noted, they obtained all the necessary licences to build in an area that had been zoned for them in the first place. But that occurred under the old regime of local planning and governance, dominated by cadres and investors. The new rules of the game incorporated the citizens of Xiamen, local property owners and businesses, intellectuals, bloggers and national media. The uproar had nudged the government somewhat closer towards its nominal but uncomfortable role as regulator.

Chen and his opponents did agree on one thing: that all parties would benefit, officials included, if the approval process were publicised and incorporated citizen input from the start. 'But whether or not to make it public it is not up to us,' Chen said. 'It's the government's process. If it's going to be made public, the government must make it public, like in the United States... If that's the way it really was, I'd prefer it. If they'd told us back then we couldn't do it here, we'd pull out, and we wouldn't lose anything.'

But did the Xiamen case signal a positive trend of nimby empowerment? Chen saw it differently. 'The Cultural Revolution was not right, but wasn't it the popular will?' he steamed. 'I think China is in a learning stage. In that learning stage, sometimes things will happen that are rather irregular... This environmental assessment, we all believe, is a social responsibility and should be done. And there should be responsibility toward the common folk. But in the process, when everyone's trying to be more open, there are misunderstandings of democracy and different ways of executing it.'

A few days later that December, Xiamen leaders called a meeting of local officials from government departments and media outlets. Around 1,000 people were there in total. The purpose, according to one Xiamen-based journalist who was there, was to 'unify minds' as authorities girded themselves for a definitive announcement. He Lifeng presided. While 'he kept things rather vague', according to the journalist, he made clear that the city would be relocating the project. The move would be a 'win–win' for Xiamen, He told his comrades: even if the PX plant was built there, Xianglu's future expansion would be hindered in Haicang district; thus it would be better off elsewhere, and he singled out the Gulei peninsula as a possibility. But for now, the city boss warned, Xiamen was still waiting for central government to sign off on the recommendation, so in the meantime it was particularly critical for officials and media to help maintain social stability. He said he hoped the PX case would no longer be 'a focus of the media', so as to avoid any 'unnecessary interference' before a decision was announced.

The aftermath – and a mystery solved

Xiamen's climbdown helped the city government repair its public image, and netted He Lifeng political points for resolving the dispute (in 2009, he became vice party secretary of Tianjin, overseeing the Binhai New Area – a plum post). Pan Yue and other reformists with the State Environmental Protection Administration (SEPA), which within months was promoted to full ministerial status as the Ministry of Environmental Protection, also hoped to capitalise by further institutionalising the assessment and review mechanisms. But within weeks, provincial leaders and planners elsewhere were groaning over the outcome. 'They are complaining that Fujian [province] went too "soft",' said one official source. 'They believe the Xiamen way of dealing with things set a very bad precedent.'

Before the coup over PX in Xiamen was even complete, echoes sounded in nimby-style protests against a Maglev train line extension in Shanghai, a transformer station in Beijing and an oil and ethylene refinery outside Chengdu. And in Nanjing, residents were clamouring over a PX operation that a Sinopec subsidiary was building in a similarly fraught location: within a few kilometres of a satellite campus of Nanjing University in a local suburb. There, too, the local government went ahead and threw up sprawling new residential developments and school complexes after the area was already zoned for the petrochemical project. Led by veteran teachers living on the campus, people had sent letters to premier Wen Jiabao and other officials and stormed the web forums. But Nanjing managed to keep the hubbub out of the papers. The fact that plant belonged to a state-owned petrochemical giant, not a private Taiwanese firm, and that it was nearly ready to go on-line, helped keep the plant on track.

Nonetheless, as civic resistance hopscotched from city to city, it became much trickier for the central government to close out the Xiamen case. 'They don't want to provide an example that would set off a chain reaction,' said the central media journalist in Xiamen. 'But it seems a chain reaction's already under way.' Another small demonstration was the direct by-product of the suspension in Xiamen. In late January, dozens of Tenglong PX engineers and technical staff descended on city headquarters in defiance of Xiamen's moves to expel the project, incited by a company proposal to lay off about 100 of the 375 staff due to the prolonged delay. The next day over lunch in the canteen of Xianglu headquarters, the top plant executive told me the company had lost many millions of dollars in outlays and $1 billion in potential revenues. 'We don't know for sure if we will move or not, but meantime the idea for the cuts has come up because of the delay', he said.

Xiamen PX fast became a misnomer in the spring of 2008, as Fujian officials quietly negotiated to jettison it from Xiamen and relocate down the shore on the Gulei peninsula, in the city of Zhangzhou, a strip of fishing villages far less populous and developed. Central government planners remained hesitant to commit to such a move, however. It would require a new round of approvals and feasibility studies; the construction of new port, power and water facilities; and a financial package of fresh concessions and compensation.

The prospective move was further complicated when thousands of villagers blocked traffic in a sit-in against the relocation plans in Dongshan, one county over from the proposed site up the peninsula. That spiralled into several days of protests and bloody clashes with baton-toting police early that March; a dozen were hospitalised and fifteen arrested. 'You hear the news? Now they're strolling on Gulei peninsula!' a journalist friend from Xiamen told me over the phone. Much as in Xiamen, local propaganda officials tried at first to convince the public that the PX factory would not pose a risk and would bolster the local economy. This only further inflamed public tempers. To quell the protests, county officials assured people that the move had yet to be settled and the central government would decide.

One year after Zhao Yufen and her colleagues raised a ruckus at the March meetings in Beijing, the leadership from Xiamen, Fujian and Zhangzhou faced a barrage of questions from the press over the PX project at the National People's Congress. It was the only time throughout the ordeal that they would be forced to address the media directly. The violence in Zhangzhou days before only sharpened the tensions. 'Because right now this PX project is rather sensitive, so we have not said it's going to land in Zhangzhou', mayor Li Jianguo told me outside the provincial meeting chamber. He had slipped out midway through an open deliberations session to relieve himself. 'There's only this intention, an intention is all,' he said. 'The main problem is that, because the masses basically do not get what PX is, and are unclear about it, and we've had relatively little contact with this sort of thing, correct guidance is needed on these moves. Because if you look overseas, there are a lot of PX [plants]. Like in Singapore, there is only a little over 600 metres between the plant equipment and [city areas].'

When I asked the relevant leaders for an update on the project during the press conference, their long monologues showed that they remained snagged in a political bind, between external pressures to allay public fears and internal pressure to stem the rash of knock-on protests over projects there and elsewhere. As such, they hedged conservatively and airbrushed the controversy. They claimed it was only self-evident that while the plant was 'a good project', it was no longer fit in Xiamen as the city developed into a modern, scenic tourist hub of logistics, shipping and high-tech industries. They glossed over the property development in Haicang and other past sins in planning that sparked the issue. They made it seem instead as though the city simply ran out of space and hit a fork in the road. 'For example, this project could be placed there [in Haicang],' said the Fujian Party chief, Lu Zhangong. 'But to turn this project into a petrochemical district, a petrochemical base, would be difficult. There's no leftover land to develop further. So Xiamen people were correct to have complaints.'

Lu announced that Fujian province agreed with Xiamen's opinion not to proceed with the PX project, 'because this place Xiamen is too small'. But he added: 'Before the move is set, first the national government must agree to you relocating. Second, the company's choice must be respected.' But public opinion was no longer an obstacle, according to Lu. 'So now there basically aren't any clear-cut problems, but because of various factors some of the masses are still reacting with accusations. The place where they're reacting in Zhangzhou, Dongshan... huh, this has even less to do with Dongshan.'

In the end, the decision-making came full circle. The final resting point of the PX project was once again a matter for high government officials and company bosses to decide. Beginning in early 2008, Xiamen and Xianglu held negotiations for compensation to complete the move down the coast. Xianglu eventually demanded 3 billion yuan. The city government counter-offered with 1 billion-plus, and not in cash but in construction and engineering fees to rebuild, which figured to benefit local state contractors. The city government insisted it could not draw from local finances and could only barter instead. At one meeting on 18 March, according to a transcript I was later shown, city leaders knuckled down and made it known there was no room to negotiate. 'And remember, you still have business in Xiamen', city vice mayor Pei Jinjia was quoted as saying.

As late as the end of 2008, his fate effectively sealed, Chen Yu-hao was still writing letters to Chinese leaders crying foul and inveighing against the local government. In November 2008 he wrote directly to Hu Jintao. 'I am Chen Yu-hao from Taiwan', he opened humbly enough, before proceeding to allege that the case had disrupted the 'normal development of the country' and weakened the country's competitiveness. If his grievances could spur central authorities to correct the mistakes of Xiamen and other local governments, he wrote, 'then the country can rapidly develop and march down the strong and healthy road, and be among the top countries in the world', he mused grandiosely. 'Only then ... will the opportunity costs I have paid be worthwhile.' In a final flourish, Chen placed his own struggle on a par with that over Taiwan's sovereignty: he hoped in his lifetime to see the reunification of the country, he wrote, and a fair resolution to the company's ordeal.

The record of major urban environmental protests in the wake of Xiamen gave many observers the sinking feeling that the impact was more psychological and political than procedural or institutional. Knock-on uprisings against petrochemical projects had simmered in Nanjing, Sichuan and Fujian in 2008, but to little avail. In the meantime, the 2008 Olympics and the political and economic upheaval that book-ended it led the Communist Party to intensify its all-encompassing focus on 'stability maintenance'. A turning point was the protest against an ethylene plant in spring 2008 in Pengzhou, outside the Sichuan capital of Chengdu. Authorities arrested and later sentenced the dissident writer Tan Zuoren for subversion. Some Chinese environmentalists contend that a chilling effect set in during the course of repeated crackdowns on dissent that followed, marked by a drop-off in landmark cases.

But as China has embraced social media, nimbyism has heated up, and 'anti-PX' has proven to be an enduring and consequential meme in public life. In August 2011, typhoon Meihua penetrated a dyke protecting the country's largest PX plant, 20 kilometres outside of Dalian, another prideful port that often tips Xiamen in surveys of China's most liveable cities. Public mistrust had been brewing there ever since the site quietly came on-stream in 2009. Fanned by messages on Chinese microblogging services, and fears ingrained that spring by the fallout at the Fukushima nuclear facilities across the Yellow Sea in Japan, an estimated 10,000 citizens stormed the square in front of the municipal government building one Sunday, demanding the PX plant be moved and the risks be fully disclosed.

That was the end of the uproar, however. The government did not dare to drag out the issue via a process of public debate or discussion, let alone a new strategic assessment of the region, as in Xiamen. What followed was a national news blackout and internal deliberations. Most Dalianers seemingly moved on. At the time of writing, the future of that project was unclear. The *Economic Observer* reported in December 2011 that Dalian officials had retracted their pledge to move the plant to an industrial park on a remote island and authorised the resumption of operations. But the city government denied that and subsequent reports, and maintained it was proceeding with relocation plans on a 'legal, scientific and orderly' basis. In a *chinadialogue* article on 6 September 2011, Professor Tang Hao, of South China Normal University, astutely judged Dalian PX the latest instance of 'interaction without rules' in China. The phenomenon, he wrote, comprised three stages:

> [F]irst, local interest groups and local governments push ahead with a polluting project in violation of environmental regulations. Second, local people spontaneously organise mass protests against the project in question, an activity supported by neither law nor policy. And third, in response to the threat to social stability created by the protests, local government halts the project – again, breaching laws. At every stage, the existing rules are lightly cast aside by all participants.

In the summer of 2012, young marchers packed the streets in violent revolt against a metals refinery in Shifang, Sichuan province, and a waste discharge pipeline to a Japanese paper factory in Qidong on the Jiangsu coast. The local governments promptly suppressed the protests and scrapped both projects. Again, this was the safest expediency. The fact that both were private concerns only eased the decision-making process. In October, thousands demonstrated against a plan to expand into paraxylene at a base outside of Ningbo. Armed police clashed with protesters, arresting dozens. The local government quickly announced it would block the addition to the facility, pending further assessment. During the 18th Party Congress in November, China's environmental protection minister Zhou Shengxian announced that the government had mandated 'social risk assessments' on all major industrial projects. But it was uncertain what the mechanism entailed.

The Xiamen PX saga fell under the rubric of rash political interventionism too, both a one-off political crisis and a harbinger of things to come. 'It was a climax for the environmental movement,' Zhang Jingjing told me in March 2012, five years after the issue first hit the Chinese press. 'But it also gave governments a kind of teaching material for the future. When these protests break out, they know how to control this.'

Five years after Xiamen 'strolled' in outrage, the crater where the PX plant would have stood was partly a dump site of concrete slabs. Behind it stretched a shiny sea of plastic-covered polytunnels, where the village of Qunyao was growing a significant percentage of the leafy greens that Xiameners eat. The area remained a patchwork of agriculture, shanty housing, car dealerships and processing factories; of guarded residential compounds, gleaming new office buildings, and the pre-existing petrochemical base of Xianglu. It was a hotchpotch born of shifting master plans and stages of development. The coast was filling in with high-rises, though the place was a graveyard at night. Billboards for luxury developments such as 'Grand Coast' soared over the bridge back to the main island, where the clouds over the sea separate like clotted cream. The Haicang government was pushing to accelerate its shift to the service industry, but the going was slow. Xiamen's new cutting edge, a sleek sprawl of software parks and convention facilities, had risen on the opposite end of town near the airport, not here in Haicang.

Around Future Coast and the blocks nearby Xianglu, the glue-like reek of the chemical refineries was somehow undetectable to the nose – either the effect of the wind or added filtering of the emissions, or both, depending on whom you asked. Xianglu had slipped into crisis by the end of 2008, as the stalled projects froze the group's liquidity under a pit of bank debt and the global recession squeezed orders. Several hundred workers were furloughed and hundreds blocked the gates of the company in protest. The government bequeathed emergency assistance to help big companies pull through, and the group posted record profits on PTA production in 2011. The new facility on Gulei peninsula was due to come online in 2013, slated to produce 800,000 tonnes of PX a year and an additional 2 million tonnes of PTA, a feedstock to the polymer industry, which would make Xianglu China's second biggest producer of PTA. But Chinese news reports revealed that the environmental ministry had blocked a move by the firm to produce an added raw material, while displaced fisherman and farmers were still agitating for better compensation.

The news circulating by early 2012 was that Xianglu might relocate its entire production line to Gulei, and turn its old base in Haicang into a huge new mixed-use property development, the Xianglu Cultural and Industry Park. It would be a multibillion-dollar development designed to attract tourists: another big project from Boss Chen. A Xianglu executive told me: 'We are just cooperating with the government's overall plans.'

The change in course was ironic but rational. Over a lunch of steamed Hakka cuisine in Haicang one day, the former Xianglu executive summed up the whole kerfuffle in stark terms. 'The interests of the PX plant were up against the interests of the property developers, and the property developers won out,' he told me. 'In reality, the genuine interests of the common people were not at the front of the officials' minds.' My central media colleague was no more sanguine, reflecting on the Darwinian adaptability of Party rule. 'Generally, as with the PX affair, only when the interests at the highest levels are allied with the interests at the lowest level can it lead to, on the surface, a 'civil society' incident,' the journalist said. 'And the interests at the highest levels line up with the interests at the lowest levels at certain points when the emphasis on social stability and stability overrides all else... This is the Party's ability to self-correct.'

The halcyon days of Zhao Yufen and Yuan Dongxing as activist intellectuals were typically short-lived. They still haven't talked to the media since the time of the protests. Some five years after she and her Xiamen University colleagues launched their proposal at the two congresses, Zhao declined to discuss the affair despite repeated requests, even in private. 'It's in the past,' she told me. 'There's no real use in discussing it. So can we just let it be?'

But the case is far from forgotten. In Fuzhou, Shao Fanqing recalled that a professor and friend of his at the Central Party School in Beijing had approached him a few years earlier to write a case study of the PX uprising. It would be used to train rising cadres who cycle through mid-career. The professor wanted to know how the insurrection arose and what was the latest progress, Shao said. 'He wanted to use this affair to teach officials how to govern a city.' But Shao declined, calculating that his nervous editors would not be pleased. To him the anti-PX insurrection, no matter the machinations of its resolution, was still a monumental breakthrough in the mindset of the people. 'Citizen awareness was really woken up,' he said. 'Only five years on, we can't fully judge the impact.'

While visiting Xiamen that May, I came to learn of a 50-something-year-old woman who was viewed in certain circles as a martyr of the affair. She was a senior official whom the police took into custody a few days after the strolls. On the orders of city leaders, she was detained in secret for well over a year. She was finally let go, but was stripped of her post and all her benefits as a civil servant. She never sought retribution thereafter, it was said, and she had no interest in discussing the case or the unsung role she had played. She had a daughter studying in Australia and simply wanted to move on. But there were stories, said Green Cross pioneer Ma Tiannan, of mere strangers spotting her at restaurants around town and picking up her tab, simply to convey their appreciation.

The woman's name was Zhang Hong, and she had been a top prosecutor in Xiamen until the peak of the PX upheaval. Sketchy rumours had spread five years earlier, but had gone unconfirmed. Until now. It was Zhang Hong, in fact, who transmitted the viral text message – the one that branded the PX project an 'atomic bomb' that would spawn leukaemia and congenital defects, the one that galvanised the 1–2 June strolls. Or at least she had taken responsibility for it. 'We can say that her text message was far too inflammatory and unscientific, but it really did mobilise the entire city', said Ma Tiannan.

Zhang Hong's younger brother, Zhang Huan, happened to be the owner of one of Xiamen's oldest and most popular bars, Sky Word, a grungy late-1990s' affair with a crowd of middle-aged Chinese regulars sprinkled with expats; they played billiards, chugged bottled beer and heard live bands on weekends. Zhang Huan was a veteran of the 1989 student protests who had spent a few years hanging out in Austria. He was the dilettante of a family of local officials. Zhang Hong was the achiever.

Over a bottle of gin one early morning at Sky Word, Zhang Huan told his story of how the explosive text message materialised. His sister did not write it, he explained. She could be idealistic and naive but also cool-headed and perspicacious – not one to do something so rash. Instead the instigator was her neighbour: a far younger, pregnant woman who lived in her building in central Xiamen. Neither owned any property in Haicang or had any link to the Haicang Investment Group, as had been alleged. The two women barely knew each other. But during the height of the uprising, they encountered each other one day on their way out. The woman asked if she could borrow Zhang Hong's phone to send an anti-PX message, ostensibly thinking that it might sound more legitimate and create more of an impact coming from Zhang. In the heat of the moment, Zhang consented. It was a conscious decision, but not a fully considered one. The message went out to Zhang's entire list of contacts. Later, security authorities easily tracked down the source.

Zhang Hong was detained a few days after the strolls. She had not taken part herself (her brother had). But because she was a high official, she was treated harshly and in a covert manner. The fact that the 30-year veteran prosecutor headed the economic corruption division at the time did not help her cause. Though she was considered an upstanding official, she naturally had made enemies as well. The person who had ordered her detention, and was responsible for the handling of her case, was He Lifeng. The pregnant neighbour was detained too at the time, for urging protests on local web forums, but was let go within days at Zhang Hong's behest. She, unlike any protester, bore the consequences. 'When you think back, Xiamen PX is already past,' said her brother. 'But 100 years from now, it may be regarded as a crucial turning point. We don't know.'

CHAPTER 5

Defending Tiger Leaping Gorge

LIU JIANQIANG

Even if you had enough gold to fill the Jinsha River Valley, it wouldn't be enough to buy up this free-spirited river, nor would it be enough to buy up our homeland.

Xiao Liangzhong

The story that follows, of the campaign to stop the damming of Tiger Leaping Gorge, is of one of the most important victories for China's environmental movement over the past decade. Its success showed that a group of stakeholders joining forces to defend their rights – with the support of the media, civil society and the public – can defeat a formidable alliance between government and big business.

But since 2011, China's big hydropower companies have broken free again, like wild beasts caged for too long. Now they will engulf China's rivers, section by section. Their sights are fixed on the Jinsha River, in China's south-western provinces of Yunnan and Sichuan.

The Jinsha River is a tributary of Asia's longest river, the Yangtze. This surging, raging river is now being sectioned up in a plan to divide it into slices of tamed water, separated by a cascade of twenty-five dams. It won't be long before there is a reservoir every

100 kilometres or less along the river: the largest group of reservoirs in the world. The total installed capacity will be equivalent to four Three Gorges Dams.

Since global dam building has centred on China, whose hydro development has focused on the south-west, the Jinsha River has arguably become the epicentre of world hydropower development.

China aims to increase its installed hydropower capacity by 140 gigawatts between 2011 and 2015, spurring a Great Leap Forward in the country's south-west.[1] Apart from the Jinanqiao hydropower plant, which is owned by a private holding company, the remaining twenty-four dams would all be controlled by one of the five state-owned hydropower giants: the Three Gorges Corporation, China Resources, Datang, Huadian and Huaneng. Like warlords, they are plotting to carve up the Jinsha River between them.

Over the past eight years, the strong momentum driving the development of China's hydropower sector has been kept in check by fierce public opposition. Chinese NGOs, the media and people displaced by dams have also played a major role. But as China's demand for energy grows, the sector's strength is on the rebound. Hydropower projects are highly sought after by banks, because their operating costs are low and they promise quick and high returns. Every major state-owned power company wants to seize its piece of the pie.

Ironically, it is under a Green banner that China has unleashed the hydropower sector, as part of 'energy conservation and emissions reduction'. A favourite slogan of Chinese hydropower companies now is that they are 'addressing climate change'. Particularly when they can combine 'addressing climate change' with the conversion of river resources into big money.

In the run-up to the Chinese Communist Party's 18th Party Congress in 2012, China's top economic planner, the National Development and Reform Commission (NDRC), as well as the Ministry of Environmental Protection (MEP), began to relax their controls on hydropower. Many suspect that they do not want to create any friction between themselves and the big state enterprises and provinces eager to develop hydropower projects, friction which might affect officials' chances of future promotion. The dam projects on the Jinsha River have so far not only been environmentally destructive and infringed on the rights of those people being resettled, they have also been unlawful. In 2005, two mega-projects on the Jinsha River – the Xiangjiaba Dam and the Xiluodu Dam – were forced to halt work as a penalty for starting construction before approval had been granted. The next year, the Jinanqiao hydropower station was ordered not to start operations because it had not yet obtained NDRC approval. In 2009, the owners of the Ludila and Longkaikou dams, also on the Jinsha, did not learn from this either: they didn't submit their environmental impact assessment (EIA) reports to the MEP until *after* they had finished damming the river.

However, once the so-called 'EIA storms' – political attempts to force companies to follow the law on EIAs – had blown over, the hydropower companies simply paid minuscule fines. (For example, the Xiluodu Dam builders were fined 200,000 yuan, around $32,000). Without a single exception, the projects were all resuscitated after the penalty was paid. Work on the Jinanqiao hydropower station started in 2003, but it wasn't approved until 2010. Just eight months later, it began operating.

Chen Kaiqi is the deputy chief engineer of the environmental impact assessment centre under the MEP. He believes that all this disorderly development is characterised by a 'scramble' to develop large hydropower and by 'construction work starting before approval is given' – and that this is causing a serious disturbance to the local environment. The transformation of big, natural rivers into channels, the increasing destruction of the environment, the emergence of water problems, the flooding of people's homes from reservoir construction, and the inadequate provision of new homes for the displaced have led to social problems and secondary environmental disasters.

But it doesn't matter how unlawful these dams are, there is ferocious momentum behind this round of dam construction and it seems to be unstoppable. For example, on the middle reaches of the Jinsha River there is now a plan to develop an eight-dam cascade at Tiger Leaping Gorge, Liangjiaren, Liyuan, Ahai, Jinanqiao, Longkaikou, Ludila and Guanyinyan, with a total installed capacity greater than the Three Gorges Dam. Apart from the dam at Tiger Leaping Gorge, these dams are either finished or under construction. Without exception, the dams started without approval.

Although the hydropower companies have long wanted to dam Tiger Leaping Gorge, work here has never started. That gorge has become like a nail stuck in the companies' throat. The campaign to protect Tiger Leaping Gorge, which ran from 2004 to 2006, not only safeguarded one of China's most magnificent landscapes, but it also saved the homes of more than 100,000 ethnic minority peoples, making the campaign one of the biggest success stories of the past decade for China's green defenders.

The Three Gorges myth

How did I end up covering this story? In 2004, I was working as a reporter for the Guangzhou-based newspaper *Southern Weekend*. One day in early September I received a call from my colleague at the newspaper, Nan Xianghong. She said that she had been asked to report on the news that a hydroelectric company was going to build a dam on the Jinsha River at Tiger Leaping Gorge, in Yunnan province, but she was too busy. Did I have time to write the story instead?

I was delighted to accept. In the previous three months, I had been reporting on the Three Gorges Dam project. Seeing the darker side of this project had got me interested in exploring the problems with China's dams.

I certainly wasn't the first to write about the Three Gorges Dam, but it's possible that I was one of the first journalists to report about its negative impacts. In that report, I wrote about the sediment accumulation caused by the dam – and how this had destroyed the port at one of China's most important inland docks in Chongqing.

During the initial stages of the Three Gorges project, the dam builders had always stressed that the rise in water levels by at least 150 metres along the 660-kilometre stretch of the Yangtze River would greatly increase shipping capacity. It would mean that 10,000-tonne ships would be able to pass directly to Chongqing, and one-way capacity would increase from 10 million tonnes a year to 50 million tonnes, with shipping costs reduced by between 35 and 37 per cent. But what I saw with my own eyes was that the Three Gorges Dam had become a noose wrapped tightly around the neck of the Yangtze River shipping industry. Many big ships could now no longer pass through the locks. I saw that big trucks needed to roll off ships before they reached the dam, roar past the dam and then board again once they were past. At best, it would take three hours and 20 minutes to pass through the locks. Sometimes it would take several days and nights. During the Spring Festival in 2004, ships from Chongqing loaded with live pigs, oranges and vegetables were held up for so long that the perishable goods started to rot and some of the pigs starved to death. People quickly started to realise that the dam was not as easy to pass through as had been predicted. Its annual capacity has never come close to reaching the 50 million tonnes it was designed for, and not one 10,000-tonne ship has ever been able to reach Chongqing directly.

Once I had finished all my interviews I sent the Three Gorges Project Corporation a draft copy of my report. This had been agreed beforehand: they would only accept my interview requests if I agreed to send them a draft for them to review and check for errors. Then I took the boat out of town. That night, they called me constantly. Before this, they had always lauded me as a professional and honest reporter, because I had covered all my own reporting expenses, including flight tickets, food and accommodation. Most of the journalists who reported on the dam had their expenses covered by the corporation. Now their tone became more stern and much less friendly.

The corporation didn't say that I had made any factual errors, but rather they advised me to cut out the parts about the sedimentation of Chongqing port and the transport bottleneck – for the sake of 'national interests'. Of course, this was nothing new. Many companies play the 'national interests' card in order to protect their own interests. The head of the corporation's publicity department called me and, talking as if we were friends, warned me that some of the experts who had criticised the project were 'enemies of the state' and I should not side with them. I turned off my mobile phone. I knew that many similar reports had been spiked before publication. But my article was published.

A week later I was back near the Yangtze River on an unrelated story, in Lichuan, in Hubei province. In the evening, four middle-aged men arrived at my hotel room door. They gave me a thick pile of documents signed by several hundred workers: these were people who were supposed to have received compensation payments, having been resettled because of the Three Gorges Dam, but their factory foreman had pocketed several million yuan from the fund. The workers were now penniless. It became clear to me that the propaganda surrounding the project concealed some terrible facts.

The Three Gorges Project Corporation said that the dam would bring prosperity to the local people, but it set up its own travel company which monopolised the tourism business around the dam, shutting out local travel companies. It made tourists pay large sums of money to visit the dam, even though it was funded with taxpayers' money. Still today, a part of every monthly electricity bill in China goes to the 'Three Gorges Construction Fund'.

The corporation said that the reservoir area would not cause landslides. Its report said the banks of the reservoir were stable, and that there were only 150 places where landslides might occur. As soon as the project had been approved, they quickly changed that figure to 1,500 places. Landslides have already killed many villagers. In an interview with the *Beijing News*, the former head of the Three Gorges Project Corporation, Lu Youmei, said that the water in the Three Gorges Reservoir was of Grade 2 quality and safe enough to drink. But water inspection teams found that the water quality in the main stream of the reservoir was Grade 3. Lu also said that the displaced were leading happy lives. But many of those relocated from places such as Yunyang, Fengjie and Wushan have had no choice but to return to the land near their flooded villages because they were unhappy living so far from home. One reporter who investigated the situation told me:

> Out of 159 people who were moved from Xintong village to Jiangxi province, 130 have come back to Yunyang. They have moved into ramshackle houses in the old county town, where all the old villagers can be together again. Standing in that part of the town, looking downhill all you can see to the edge of the horizon is water. Under that water are the homes that the villagers can never return to.[2]

The threat to the Jinsha

I was also keen to accept the Tiger Leaping Gorge assignment because I had missed out on reporting another campaign: the struggle to save the Nu – Asia's longest undammed river. One year earlier, this campaign against a cascade of dams had led to the first victory for China's environmental movement (see Chapter 2).

On a satellite photograph, you can trace three parallel rivers coursing from the Tibetan plateau through Yunnan province. These three rivers are the Jinsha, the Lancang (also known as the Mekong) and the Nu (or Salween). At their closest point, the Nu and the Lancang rivers are just 18.6 kilometres apart. The Lancang and the Jinsha nudge as close as 66.3 kilometres apart. The region's unusual geology means it has the richest biodiversity of the entire Eurasian continent. With its unique cultural resources, this beautiful and mysterious natural landscape is rightly recognised as a wonder of the world.

The Jinsha River rises on the plateau, flows through Tibet, Qinghai and Sichuan provinces and then thunders south into Yunnan. At Shigu, near Lijiang, it suddenly twists more than 100 degrees to the north-east, shaking off the other two rivers. Here it forms a spectacular 'V' shape: the first bend of the Yangtze River. Then at Tiger Leaping Gorge it cuts through Mount Yulong and Mount Haba, flushing out through the entire 16-kilometre length of the valley. The raging river waters are more than 3,000 metres below the mountain peaks on either side of its banks – making it one of the world's deepest and most dangerous gorges. The river is barely 60 metres wide much of the way, 30 metres at its narrowest point. Legend has it that a tiger once leapt across it – hence the name.

Tiger Leaping Gorge has one of the world's most magnificent landscapes – and for the hydropower company it would be one of the world's most profitable dams. Within a short span of 16 kilometres and a drop in elevation of around 200 metres, it is the perfect location for a dam, so the hydropower industry was determined to leap across the opposition to its plans, just like that tiger leapt across the gorge.

However, it was also around this time that Chinese society was undergoing a subtle change. With the rapid development of the Internet, chatrooms and forums, known as 'BBSs' (bulletin board systems), became important channels for exchanging news and information. Previously, the Chinese government could manage what news people could access, by controlling the newspapers, television and radio. But this monopoly had been broken. Now the information that media outlets normally could not touch was passed around online. The Chinese public's appetite for uncensored news and information online sharply increased too, after panic erupted in China in 2003 with the outbreak of severe acute respiratory syndrome (SARS).

As China entered the new century, more NGOs were springing up, and the commercial media became bolder and freer. Many journalists saw their mission as to work for the public interest, and civil society helped to open a window for public debates around major events. In 2003 a number of controversial news stories exploded in the media, such as the Sun Zhigang case, when a young graduate looking for work in Guangzhou died in police custody. Since 1989 there had not been a public sphere for discussing these big issues. When the Three Gorges Dam was being built, there had been no unobstructed, open debate about the project. But by the beginning of the new century, commercial media outlets – such as *Southern Weekend* and *Southern Metropolis Daily* – had emerged, and these helped lead discussions on public-interest issues. For the first time the Chinese public could learn about the threats posed by dam construction – in media reports, through appeals from NGOs and in news spread via Internet chatrooms.

But during the first few months of the campaign to stop the Nu River dam, I was busy writing about another public-interest story – the 'BMW incident' in Harbin, in China's north-east, when a woman from a rich, well-connected family killed a rural woman with her car, but was given a light sentence. I didn't have time to report on the Nu River. So when my colleague asked if I wanted to write about the Tiger Leaping Gorge dam on the Jinsha River, I said yes in an instant.

Premier Wen Jiabao had just called a stop to the Nu River project. But a few months later, the machinery had groaned into operation at Tiger Leaping Gorge, as another hydropower project began. On 27 July 2004, the state news agency Xinhua reported that the NDRC had reviewed and passed the *Planning Report on the Damming of the Middle Reaches of the Jinsha River*. It had recommended that work should start soon on the Tiger Leaping Gorge dam. The Xinhua report added: 'The elevation drop of Tiger Leaping Gorge is 196 metres, the ideal distance for a hydropower plant.'

In the plan, hydropower stations, forming an eight-dam cascade starting at Tiger Leaping Gorge, would be built on the middle reaches of the Jinsha River, on the first bend of the Yangtze (the Jinsha River is a tributary of the Yangtze's upper reaches). Stretching

564 kilometres, from the town of Shigu in the west to Panzhihua in the east, with a drop in elevation of 838 metres, it would pen the whole of the middle reaches of the Jinsha River. There were two proposals for the dam elevation, one at 2,018 metres and one at 2,030 metres. According to the plan's introduction, as well as generating electricity, the project also aimed to divert water across Yunnan, helping to solve drought problems and even flush out the pollution in Dianchi Lake, by the city of Kunming.

Tiger Leaping Gorge would be flooded 200 kilometres upstream, in Dechen Tibetan Autonomous Prefecture, near Benzilan. It would forcibly displace 100,000 people and almost 200,000 *mu* (around 13,333 hectares) of good agricultural land would be submerged.

The main public opponent of the dams at Tiger Leaping Gorge was a man named Xiao Liangzhong. He was an anthropologist and an editor at a Beijing-based publishing house, who hailed from the Tiger Leaping Gorge area. His grandmother, parents and brothers all still lived there. If the Tiger Leaping Gorge dam was built, his family home would be submerged. On 8 September 2004, I met with Xiao in the Sanlian Bookshop in Beijing's Wangfujing shopping street. He was 31 years old and full of energy. From his bag, he pulled out a Chinese-language edition of Patrick McCully's *Silenced Rivers: The Ecology and Politics of Large Dams* and handed it to me, explaining that it was an authoritative book.[3] He had just bought another dozen or so copies to give to friends – and he refused to take any payment for it. He started to arrange a number of interviews in the Jinsha River Valley for me and my newspaper colleague Cheng Gong.

The plan to turn the middle reaches of the Jinsha River into an eight-dam cascade had Tiger Leaping Gorge at the top, and the Jinanqiao hydropower station as the fifth dam. Jinanqiao was owned by the Beijing Huarui Investment Group, and preparatory work on the dam had been started in 2002. The dam was to be 156 metres high, with a total installed capacity of 2,500 megawatts. According to the plan, the river would be dammed by 2005.

Local villagers said they suspected that construction work on the Jinanqiao dam was illegal: that it had begun without approval from the central government. My colleague Cheng visited the construction site. The hydropower company had set up two security-guard posts at the entrance, blocking off any access. But with the help of local villagers, he walked along a horse caravan path used by the Lisu ethnic group to cross a mountain, and bypassed the guards. When he got round to the site, he saw various cargo trucks busying back and forth like ants, two of the dam's diversion tunnels starting to take shape, and the main building works, such as the cofferdam, already under construction. After he was found by guards on the site, Cheng was detained for four hours.

Cheng also found out from a government source that the town of Lijiang would earn about 4 million yuan in tax revenues from the dam – and that this was why the local government there had warmly welcomed the project, making it a priority and giving it the green light at every stage.

Back in Beijing, I also made a breakthrough: an official from the NDRC told me that this project had definitely not yet been approved, and that he was very surprised to hear that it had already been started. I telephoned an official from the State Environmental Protection Administration (SEPA, now the MEP) and he also sounded shocked: 'That's a world-famous site of natural beauty. How could anyone build a power station there?!' We had our evidence. This project had broken ground illegally.

The next morning Xiao Liangzhong gave me a big dossier of materials on the Three Parallel Rivers Region. Everything was thoroughly sourced. It wasn't until then that I realised how committed Xiao was: he really wasn't the type to sit back and watch what was happening to his home. He was willing to take risks to help a reporter – and I had really never met a source like him before. Naively I had initially regarded him as 'enthusiastic'. But after seeing the body of information he had amassed and the vast bank of online contacts that he had assembled of people connected with protecting the Three Rivers Region, I realised this went beyond enthusiasm. I began to regard him not only as an editor at a publishing house, but also as an intellectual and a social activist – a youth leader representing the poor in their struggle against powerful interest groups.

Our article was published on the front page of *Southern Weekend* on 29 September 2004, with the headline 'Emergency at Tiger Leaping Gorge'. It shocked the nation and focused public attention on the issue. Following our report, Chinese and international media began to cover the story. It became the biggest environmental story since the campaign to stop the Nu River dam.

The article quoted environmentalists who said that the Tiger Leaping Gorge dam could wipe out whole species. The resettlement of the Naxi ethnic group, who live along the banks of the Jinsha River, would mean the irreversible loss of the traditional sites and accumulated wisdom of their Dongba ritual culture. But supporters of the dam stressed its economic benefits. Director of the Management Bureau of the Three Parallel Rivers, Ma Suhong, said: 'We need to lift the people out of poverty.'

His view was challenged by Xiao Liangzhong. Land in the Jinsha River Valley above Tiger Leaping Gorge was both fertile and flat, he said. It was a traditional farming community with excellent quality soil. The compensation fund for relocation was far less than what the local people would really lose. High-quality farmland would be submerged. Clearly, the skilled farmers of this river valley would be impoverished if they were evicted from their land.

In 2007, then Premier Wen Jiabao admitted that since 1949 China had relocated a total of 22.9 million people to make way for water projects. Most have continued to live in poverty.[4] The plan for the Tiger Leaping Gorge dam estimated that 100,000 people would need to be relocated. When these people were moved, they wouldn't be able to find land as good as that they had been farming. Once-prosperous villages would sink into poverty.

Moreover, our report confirmed two important points. First, construction work on the Jinanqiao hydropower station was unlawful.

Second, the 100,000 local people hadn't been informed about what would happen to them, and were categorically opposed to being resettled.

Li Xiaoxi was an associate professor at the Air Force Command Institute, and knew an official in the office of the premier, Wen Jiabao. She called that official the day after our article was published and said that Wen should read it – and see that a dam was being built illegally at Tiger Leaping Gorge. The official replied: 'We've seen this article. It's a good story with solid facts.' Shortly afterwards, Wen Jiabao ordered the project suspended, while the NDRC investigated the situation. But this wasn't the end of the story.

Uncle Ge

Several days after our article was published, I flew to Yunnan province to interview some of the villagers. It wasn't until I arrived that I realised our story hadn't only had an effect on the central government, it also had had a huge impact on local people.

Xiao Liangzhong introduced me to a local farmer named Ge Quanxiao, a short, lively 57-year-old. Ge used to be a teacher at a local school, but later came back home to work the land. He was knowledgeable and brave, a leader among the local farmers. Ge took me along the roaring Jinsha River in a boat and we visited the villages along its banks. He gave a copy of our article to everybody he met who could read. He talked to each village chief, asking them to tell the villagers what was happening. Resolutely defend your homeland, he urged them. Do not stay quiet, make your voices heard and uphold your rights.

Ge became a local leader in 1997, when a lead-zinc ore dressing plant dumped poisonous waste directly into a pond in the village of Wuzhu, poisoning people and livestock. Thousands of people went to the township government to complain, and there was a small riot. Frightened, the township leader asked Ge for his advice: 'Uncle Ge, how would you fix this?' Without hesitation, he made three suggestions: immediately stop the factory from polluting the pond; instruct scientists to inspect the water quality; and check the villagers' health.

Ge led the township officials up a nearby mountain for a day until they found a fresh, unpolluted source of water. The township government promised to connect every household to the water source with pipes and to give them safe drinking water for their families and animals. There was one house quite a bit further from the village; rather than pay for their plumbing, the township leader wanted to quietly pay them off instead, but Ge stopped them. 'This is every householder's right,' he said. 'You have to lay that pipe.' In the end, just to connect that one house to the water source, the township government needed five tractors fully loaded with equipment.

After everything was resolved, the police arrested Ge and several other village leaders on the grounds that they had incited the farmers to oppose the government. Throughout his twenty-one days in detention an endless stream of villagers came to visit him. His guards were baffled – they had never seen a prisoner get this kind of attention. On his release, he was thronged, and a plaque was put up in a local temple to commemorate what had happened. He and three others emerged as leaders after the water pollution incident, their celebrity only enhanced by their imprisonment, and so they became de facto community leaders, including when it came to the campaign against the dam at Tiger Leaping Gorge.

'This is not sustainable development'

As we visited the villages, Ge carried with him a VCD copy of an independent documentary titled *The Voice of the Nu River*, made by the environmental activist Shi Lihong. He would screen it to villagers: it showed some of the people under threat of being displaced by the Nu River dam visiting the Manwan Dam, on the Lancang River, to see how the inhabitants of that region fared after resettlement. In the film, the visitors from the Nu River see with their own eyes the miserable conditions of those resettled people who have lost their land.

The Manwan Dam on the Lancang River had once been hailed as one of the hydropower industry's 'Five Golden Flowers'. But at the end of 2001, Yu Xiaogang, a graduate student in watershed management at the Asian Institute of Technology, headed to the Manwan Dam's reservoir area with researchers from Yunnan University and the Yunnan Academy of Social Sciences to investigate. Using the latest research methods, they conducted a social impact assessment of the reservoir, looking into the overall effect it had had on the local community.

For five years previously, the Manwan Power Plant had been named the country's top energy enterprise. The company's profits were in excess of 120 million yuan. It paid about 100 million yuan in national taxes, roughly 50 million yuan in taxes to Yunnan province, and another 50 million yuan in taxes to Yunxian, Jingdong, Nanjian and Fenqing counties in the reservoir area. It was a 'win–win' situation for the government and the corporation. Furthermore, Manwan workers were given stock options. The duty manager had an annual salary of 120,000 yuan. The power plant had its own four-star guest house, which belonged to the workers' collective. It was a 'win–win' situation for the leaders and the workers, too.

But at the relocated Tianba village, which was originally only 800 metres away from the dam, the researchers discovered that of its 240-odd residents, more than half were picking up rubbish from the power plant as a means to make a living. Some ten villagers had started suffering from mental illness after the dam was built, community-based organisations crumbled, and drug-taking, stealing and fighting had become commonplace.

The Manwan Hydropower Station was still regarded as an 'economical investment' with 'high returns' and a 'model-run' power plant. But, as Yu Xiaogang told me in an interview: 'After our investigation, we found out that one of the reasons for the so-called 'economical investment' was that the compensation payments given to relocated villagers were as low as possible. One of the reasons for the so-called 'high returns' was that the power station gave as little assistance as it could to the relocated villagers.'

Yu realised that the impacts of big hydropower projects on peoples' lives wouldn't be resolved if local people couldn't get involved, and so this kind of poverty would likely continue. Yu set up the environmental NGO Green Watershed, and from 2004 it ran many programmes in the Three Rivers Region. The most important of these took place in July 2004, when the NGO organised a special training class in the town of Lijiang. Villagers who had either been resettled or were in danger of being resettled because of a hydropower project attended the training. Yu Xiaogang said: 'We should give them the knowledge so they become insiders on hydropower development. So that they become participants rather than passive migrants.'

BOX 5.1   'China should look behind the curtain'

YU XIAOGANG is director of the NGO Green Watershed, based in the city of Kunming, in south-west China. In an interview for *chinadialogue* on 30 January 2012, he spoke to ISABEL HILTON about his concern that powerful special-interest groups in China exercise undue influence on government policy.

ISABEL HILTON   What are these special-interest groups and why are you concerned?

YU XIAOGANG   One characteristic is their monopoly. The second is the combination of their power and capital. China is in a transition period: in the state-planned economy, every big company or industry was under government control. Then we changed to the market economy, but big state-owned enterprises (SOEs) still have power and they now get the advantages of the market economy. So they use their influence with the government to ensure they are allocated the assets; then they can get resources from the stock or the bond markets.

The state benefits from this in several ways: through taxation, or because such companies listen to the government most of the time. The government can dominate the market economy because its share in some industries is much bigger than in others. In energy for instance, it is as much as 70 per cent.

IH   What impact does this have on dam building in China?

YX   The government can dominate some very critical industries, like railways, air transport, power industries and telecommunications. They like to control them, but this also creates contradictions with their ideology or the targets that the Chinese government is pursuing – targets such as a just and harmonious society. These monopoly companies go in the opposite direction.

The Chinese government wants to improve policy and reach 'political civilisation', but we think that the SOE monopolies have a triple role: they are company owners; they are decision-makers (or at least they can capture the decision-makers); and they also manage the market. So they control everything and that's not good for the free market or 'political civilisation'. Also it creates conflict with the people, because this combination of power and capital often works against the people's interests, against democracy and against public participation.

IH   Civil society managed to bring a halt to dam building under the 11th Five-Year Plan. In the 12th Five-Year Plan there seems to be a 'Great Leap Forward' in dam building in preparation. Will civil society be able to mobilise again?

YX   We have realised that the 12th Five-Year Plan was influenced by these interest groups. Before this plan was finalised, we observed a lot of academics, official insiders, like the National Energy Administration, decision-makers and think-tanks combined saying that NGOs and civil society have misled the leaders under the 11th Five-Year Plan and that hydropower's environmental and social impact was not negative. They portrayed it as a conspiracy between the international community and civil society to attack hydropower development. Also they said that because of the frozen period during the 11th Five-Year Plan, we now need a 'Great Leap Forward' in dam building.

We can see very clearly that this advocacy influenced the decision-makers and we also think that NGOs can do something. I think it's very important to deconstruct this discourse, because Chinese government decision-making is often influenced by this kind of discourse. NGOs should debate it. The special-interest groups often operate behind the curtain – people don't know about it. People think that SOEs are better than private companies because at least they operate in the interests of the taxpayer. People don't know that they are destroying the economy and the political system and hurting the taxpayers' interests. So we need to tell people about this.

Why do these interest groups not pay attention to the environmental and social impacts? Because they want the maximum profit. They don't care about the impacts. That's why I think that civil society should look at what interests there are behind the curtain; so we can understand why they don't listen to us and how they capture the government to make decisions that favour special interest groups. NGOs can investigate this and tell people the truth. Then people can perhaps find a solution individually, or campaign on projects.

IH   What would your solution be?

YX   There are many possible solutions. Some are more political. For example, some people say that these SOEs should make a profit. Many don't. They may pay their taxes but they don't share their profits. The taxpayer is the owner and should be recognised as such. The government should represent the people's view.

[First], the SOEs should make their profits transparent and share them with social security funds or foundations for poverty alleviation or some other public purpose. Second, the government should not be too dependent on them. For example, in energy saving and emissions reductions, we have hundreds of solutions and methods. We need to pay attention and invest, to develop small and medium enterprises (SMEs) that can solve this. We have many demand-side management opportunities with small technologies. There are two general approaches: restraint and counterbalancing with an increase in SMEs. The third element is checking and monitoring. We should train the SOEs to follow market rules and reduce their monopoly.

IH   Would you like to see a halt to the kind of dam building that is proposed in the 12th Five Year Plan?

YX   Of course. We think that in the last 60 years, China has built so many dams already. Very big dams were constructed, especially in the last decade. Now the remaining rivers are in seismic-risk areas, so building in these areas will be very risky to people downstream and we must assess the environmental impact. We think we must assess the full cost first.

They may say that we need energy, but we should also rationalise energy consumption. This needs investment and education and the government to change its orientation. In this way, the people can save energy and reduce consumption. Only this way can we stop the dam construction. First, tell the people the risks and then have the government pay attention to the many small approaches that can solve the problem.

At that time, Xiao Liangzhong was urging academics and NGOs to get involved with the campaign to save Tiger Leaping Gorge. He thought that Ge Quanxiao was a remarkable community leader and so he recommended that he also take part in Yu Xiaogang's training. Ge didn't then understand anything about power stations except for the government line: 'Build a power station and farmers will get rich.'

The theme of the training was 'the sustainable development of dam construction and resettlement.' At the training, Ge got to know some people who had been resettled because of the Manwan and the Xiaowan dams.

After the training was over, Ge took several of his fellow villagers to have a look at the Manwan Dam. The reality was nothing like the dam's propaganda, which claimed: 'The day the Manwan Hydro-power Station began generating power was the day the people got rich.' In fact, the people who had been resettled saw their living standards fall as the power station was constructed.

That year, Yunnan province's audit department discovered that about 5.5 million yuan had been embezzled from the government's Manwan Hydropower Station reservoir maintenance fund and the late-stage assistance fund. Part of this money was supposed to go to the people being resettled.

Ge took lots of photos and showed them to people in his village. He also invited some of the displaced people from Manwan to come to Wuzhu village and talk about their experiences. 'This is called partners in education', Ge said. After the training, he started using many new words. For example, he started saying 'community', instead of 'our village'.

Ge was now collecting all the information he could on resettle-ment and dam construction. He conscientiously studied texts such as McCully's book and the *Citizen's Guide to the World Commission on Dams*, by Aviva Imhof, Susanne Wong and Peter Bosshard.[5]

One time, when Ge was in the provincial capital of Kunming, he came across a copy of a newspaper with an article by Pan Yue, then deputy director of SEPA. Pan wrote that dams should not be built without strong scientific backing and that they should be built sustainably. Ge begged the owner of the newspaper to give it to him, and then made eighty copies of it and handed it out to all the villagers to study. Pan Yue's ideas, he said, 'were exactly the same as mine'.

'Twenty years ago, when villagers were being relocated because of the Manwan Dam, the country still lacked the necessary experi-ence,' Ge said. 'People were forced to move but they weren't given any compensation. Local governments and hydropower companies frequently say they are operating for the benefit of the state and the interests of the majority, but they leave the people in the dark, take advantage of them and ignore their rights, getting them to sign a contract that is not in their interests. By the time this has happened, lawyers can't find any applicable laws to protect the people's legal rights and interests.'

Ge continued: 'To solve this resettlement problem, we either use a planned-economy method where the local government takes responsibility for everything: for the peoples' production, work and lives. Living standards must not fall below their original levels. Or we use a market-economy method, and protect the legal rights and benefits of those being resettled. Allow the people to negotiate with the hydropower company about their living conditions and share in the benefits brought by the project.'

'All dams have a finite lifetime, and when the time comes, the dam can be torn down,' said Ge. 'But we will never get our land back. This is not sustainable development.' Thanks to the work of the NGOs, the Jinsha farmers were now armed with a wealth of knowledge and information about the law.

The imperious hydropower corporation and the government had never faced such a situation before. First, the media across the country had focused on the story of the Tiger Leaping Gorge dam. Second, there was Xiao Liangzhong, who was able to make scores of media outlets and NGOs concerned about the future of his hometown. Third, the region had become dotted with NGOs, who had educated the people in danger of being resettled. Finally, and even more importantly, the village leaders had emerged, like Ge Quanxiao. These people were willing to work to protect people's rights and interests – and exerted a far-reaching influence among the people.

The memorial

A few months later, in January 2005, Xiao Liangzhong died. He suffered a cardiac arrest at his Beijing home one night. He was only 32 years old. His wife and friends believe that he drove himself to an early death by working so hard. In his last few months, he had travelled back and forth with reporters to the Jinsha River so many times that he clocked up more than 2,500 kilometres. He had written and edited more than 80,000 words on the Jinsha River. He was constantly mobilising NGOs and the media as part of the campaign to oppose the dam and was wracked with worry about what would happen to his homeland. He told his friends that he kept having the same nightmare: the dam was built and he watched the Jinsha River overflow, drowning his beautiful hometown.

Files on his computer showed that a few days before he died, he was working until 2 or 3 a.m. Several journalists and NGO workers accompanied Xiao Liangzhong's wife to take his ashes back Chezhou village, where he was born. On 13 January, more than 1,000 villagers attended his memorial service. People from nearby villages, some of whom had never met him, carried wreaths of cypress branches. His family's garden was packed to bursting with weeping mourners. For hundreds of years along the Jinsha River, no young person had ever had such a grand funeral.

The villagers believed that he died to protect his homeland, and his death motivated them to defend it, too. Xiao had given them powerful encouragement to oppose the building of the dam. In the month before he died, his mother had asked him anxiously if he thought he was attracting the attention of the hydropower company by campaigning so hard. Xiao had responded: 'I'm not afraid even to sacrifice my life, if it's for the sake of those 100,000 farmers along the river!'

He repeatedly told Ge Quanxiao that their homes would be lost forever if they allowed the land to be submerged. It was more terrible than warfare. The villagers might think that they could talk it over with the hydropower company and negotiate conditions, but this would just give the developer an opportunity to bribe them.

Three months later, on Tomb Sweeping Day, Ge Quanxiao organised the villagers to put up a monument to Xiao at the entrance to his village. In large characters it said: 'The Son of Jinsha River'. Some of the villagers thought of him as a river spirit who could bless and protect their home. Gathered together for the occasion, Ding Changxiu, a 65-year-old farmer, said:

> Rivers on the earth are like veins in the human body. If you were to block off your own veins, you would die. The earth is the same. If you upset its balance, you're doomed to have rockfalls and mudslides. We never used to have mudslides here, because we protected our forests well. But after they began building dams these started happening. This is creating a catastrophe for the Chinese people. We're not just selfishly protecting our own interests; we want to share this wonderful environment with the other people of the world, and leave it for the next generation.

'Liangzhong was just 32 years old when he left us,' she continued. 'I'm more than 60 – I've lived long enough. If I could exchange my body of flesh and blood for the long-term peace and stability of this land, so that the Tiger Leaping Gorge dam wouldn't be built, I would be willing today to have my body smashed to pieces and my bones ground to powder.' Then, a 70-year-old grandmother pointed to the earth and said: 'If we sell this ground, it might give us enough to eat for a lifetime. But what about our sons' lifetimes? And our grandsons' lifetimes? What are they going to eat? We can't sell off what also belongs to our sons and grandsons. They would curse us.'

The death of Xiao Liangzhong caused an upsurge in local sentiment against the dam project. Ge Quanxiao and other village leaders, the NGOs and the media drew closer together. The local women, including Ding Changxiu, organised a publicity team. They wrote poems, set up a dance troupe and sang and danced at public gatherings. They wrote a poem in memory of Xiao Liangzhong ('His gentle and polite words / Rallied the people to fight for their rights') and songs about their hometown ('The Jinsha River flashes with gold / The riverbanks, our huge rice bowl / People on both sides get together / And work as one to save the Jinsha River.')

This part-performance, part-publicity women's group toured all along the river. It was the first time people had thought to use song and dance to spread a message since the Cultural Revolution thirty years earlier. It was a rare sight indeed.

The 21 March incident

The dam at Tiger Leaping Gorge was still a crucial part of local hydropower development plans: not only could it generate enormous amounts of energy, as the top dam of the cascade, upstream of seven more hydropower stations, but also it could adjust the water flow, having a significant impact on the power generated by the downstream seven. The dam builders could not give up on this one.

If it was only the media and NGOs that were blocking it, even with premier Wen Jiaobao's words of caution, sooner or later this dam would be built, like all the others before it. Chinese hydropower companies had proved this time and again – and they were confident it would go ahead. What they didn't realise was that the people here weren't like in the other places. They were more dogged even than the hydropower company.

The clash that proved this came on 21 March 2006 – and involved more than 10,000 people – a story I only learned about from the villagers in the summer of 2010. The incident started when Ding Changxiu and several other women were at Xiao Liangzhong's family's home, helping to build a wall. Suddenly, a farmer came running over from the next village. He told them that there were seven people from the hydropower station taking measurements. It looked like they were going to start rebuilding the dam. They rushed over to the hillside on the southern side of the village. It turned out the workers were from the Hydropower Exploration and Planning Institute, contracted by the hydropower station to do a preliminary investigation for the dam design.

The villagers asked them why they hadn't been asked for their consent. Had the local government not been asked for its consent before they came measuring their fields? One of the seven surveyors answered the villagers that there was no question about whether or not the dam would be built. They had better 'hurry up and find somewhere else to live,' he said. 'By this time next year, your homes will be under water.' The villagers were furious. They thought that the hydropower company and the local government had deceived them. So they kidnapped the seven surveyors and held them in a field overnight.

When several local policemen rushed to the scene, they were outnumbered by the villagers and couldn't mount any kind of rescue. Early the next morning, on 22 March, a deputy county head came to see them and helped the leader of the group of seven escape by claiming he was taking him for breakfast.

When the villagers asked him why he had helped the man escape, the official replied: 'You riverside people have been growing fat under the Communist Party. Do you want a revolution?'

The angry villagers chased the official out of the fields. As he ran, he tripped and fell into the Jinsha River and a local policeman had to fish him out. As the news spread, more and more villagers started to arrive from across the mountains. Their numbers grew to the thousands. Xiao Liangzhong's aunt arrived, carrying a basket of books on her back. After Xiao had died, his friends in the NGO movement had edited and printed these books to hand out to the villagers. Inside were reports on Tiger Leaping Gorge, articles by Xiao and information on Chinese policies concerning dam construction, compensation for relocated people and their legal rights. The article my colleague and I had written for *Southern Weekend* was reproduced in the first chapter.

Xiao Liangzhong's aunt handed out the books to the villagers. She said that the book would help them avoid being deceived by officials again. At that point, Ge Quanxiao got in a boat to the other side of the river, in order to make clear he would not join in the protests. This was a decision he reached after careful consultation with the other villagers. He needed to get well away, because he knew that a 'mass incident' might arise. The government wouldn't like that, and, as he had learned from his previous arrest, the authorities would not only want him to solve the problem, but also might punish him for it afterwards.

To stop the authorities from listening in to his conversations, Ge Quanxiao had bought a new, anonymous SIM card for his mobile phone. He was in his boat, halfway across the river, when the phone rang. On the line was somebody he didn't know, asking him whom he had called and who had called him. Ge Quanxiao hung up. He took out the SIM card and threw it in the river. 'The government are just too clever!' he told me. On the other side of the river, he entered Weixi county, deep in the mountains. He told people he was going fishing. Meanwhile, his friends would keep a careful eye on the situation.

The protestors were well informed and they were determined. The community leaders hoped that things weren't going to get out of hand, but as more and more villagers arrived their fury at the hydropower company started to boil over. Some of the villagers began to beat one of the workers from the survey team. But, after saying they would take the remaining six surveyors to Jinjiang town to be seen at the government hospital, officials helped the 'hostages' escape.

Feeling they had been tricked once again, the villagers turned their anger on the government officials themselves. They surrounded the government building in Jinjiang town. County officials came out to tell the villagers to go home. The seven men hadn't been sent by the hydropower company, they said. They were from the water resources ministry and would help the villagers with a new irrigation system. But the villagers knew well enough by now that this was another lie. The officials had lost all credibility. The protestors formed a tight cordon around the government building, while a stream of trucks of villagers from a 100-kilometre-stretch along the river kept arriving. In case armed police were called, some of the villagers had brought crowbars; others were carrying small rocks. Some even had explosives.

The number of people surrounding the government building swelled to around 10,000. The officials were hiding upstairs, too afraid to descend. Some of the village youths raced upstairs, but several dozen police had formed a human wall, blocking the top of a flight of stairs. Nighttime in March is cold along the Jinsha River. But the villagers didn't go home. They lit bonfires, giving the place the look of a battlefield. 'There were so many angry people grouped together,' one villager told me. 'Their emotions seemed to make the earth tremble.' At daybreak on 23 March, even more people arrived.

Inside, two of the higher officials held opposing views about how to resolve the situation. The first argued that they should use armed police to quell the protest, and the provincial armed police were already being mobilised. The second, a Tibetan (this was in the Dechen Tibetan Autonomous Prefecture) argued that they should do everything they could to arrive at a peaceful settlement. There was no need to cause bloodshed. He sent his subordinate officials to find Li Jianzhong, who used to be in charge of Wuzhu village, which was in Jinjiang town. Li was another unofficial local leader and a friend of Ge Quanxiao. The officials told him that if the villagers didn't end their protest then the local prefectural government would no longer be in charge; the provincial government would take over, and their armed police were already on their way. Li knew that this could end bloodily. If the protestors clashed with the police they didn't stand a chance. Any chance to negotiate with the government would be lost too, and they would have no way to stop the dam being built.

Around eighteen months earlier, something similar had happened in neighbouring Sichuan province. A hydropower company started building a dam at Pubugou, along the Dadu River, without a thought for local people's rights. When the locals protested, armed police were called in and the villagers were crushed. After such incidents, the authorities frequently portray the protesters as 'vandals', or accuse them of other crimes as an excuse to conduct an armed crackdown. The hydropower company ended up building its dam at Pubugou at lightning speed and the campaign against it failed entirely. Li Jianzhong didn't want to see the same kind of tragedy happen in his hometown. The protest had to end immediately. But he also knew that it would be very difficult to control a group of more than 10,000 angry people. The government would have to give the people a clear-cut response on the question of the dam.

The Yunnan provincial government set up a special emergency team to handle the situation. Chinese officials care deeply about 'social stability' and they are afraid of mass protests. As soon as a large-scale protest breaks out, there will be an official scapegoat for the problem – and even if he isn't fired, he will likely be passed over for promotion. Once a protest has started, the imperative becomes to end it as soon as possible. So on 23 March, the provincial government published a notice saying that if the majority of local people were opposed to the dam, then it would not be built. But no official dared to go out and tell this to the villagers, for fear of being surrounded and beaten. Trust had broken down. Having been deceived so many times, nobody would have dared believe such a promise from the government. That evening, the protesters stayed gathered around the government building.

One of the officials told Li Jianzhong that the armed police were due to arrive the following day and that the local government had already given up hope of a peaceful settlement. Li realised that they were standing on the brink of failure. He asked the officials to give him one more night to persuade the villagers to go home. The officials agreed. After midnight, Li started making calls. He had two mobile phones; while he was making calls with one phone, he would charge the other. He spoke to twenty heads of production teams and twenty women's group leaders. He spoke to every other villager who had any authority. He told them all: 'The government has already promised not to build the dam. This is an exceptional victory. We should quit while we are ahead. Let's go home or the armed police will be here – and we will lose. Hurry up and tell everyone near you to go home.' Ge Quanxiao called his wife, asking her to persuade all the people she knew to go home. By 3 a.m., of the thousands of people surrounding the township government building, everyone had left except a few dozen. By dawn, the street was completely empty. A violent conflict had been averted.

That morning, government workers pasted up the pledge not to build the dam all over the streets. The villagers were overjoyed, and many pulled down the notice to keep as evidence, in case the government went back on its word. The villagers had driven a nail through the hydropower company's plans to build a dam at Tiger Leaping Gorge.

Conclusion

Four years later, in the summer of 2010, I went back to Jinsha River. Ge Quanxiao was refurbishing his old house. From 2004 to 2006 the villagers did not dare repair their homes because the future seemed too uncertain. Their homes could end up under water, so why waste their money? Now, many people were rebuilding their homes. Their hearts were filled with new hope.

Ding Changxiu crossed over the fields to find me. She told me she had written a diary about the campaign to stop the building of the dam. She wanted me to give it to 'the nation' – she meant, I believe, the country's top officials – so that they could hear the voice of a local person. She was worried that the hydropower company would stage a comeback.

But for a short while at least, the hydropower company would think twice before returning to Tiger Leaping Gorge. They saw that they had more to fear from that campaign than the one that fought to save the Nu River. Even though the Nu River campaign was the Chinese environmental movement's first major victory, it was different: the campaign was driven by NGOs, scientists, journalists and urban folk. The half-a-million poor people of the Lisu, Nu and Tibetan ethnic minorities, who were the most directly affected by the Nu River dam proposal, weren't a part of that campaign. But the villagers at Tiger Leaping Gorge had built up a powerful force among themselves.

In January 2006, I visited the Nu River and spoke to local people. Although the campaign to stop the dam had started three years earlier, only a small number of people knew about the project, or that they could be resettled to make way for a reservoir. Even those who were aware didn't understand clearly how this might affect them. The government hadn't told them the truth or asked them for their opinions. If one day the bulldozers come rumbling past their front doors, they will have little choice but to follow orders, like those people forced to leave their native land because of the Three Gorges Dam. Without local leaders, they won't have the means to rally a large number of people and express their opinions to the government en masse.

In the examples of the Tiger Leaping Gorge campaign and the movement on the Nu River, it seems that a successful environmental campaign needs three factors. First is the involvement of NGOs: they can spread information and knowledge to local people, telling them about the environmental and social impacts of the dam. Second is press coverage: reports in the media rapidly spread news about an event, turning a local story into a national topic of public concern. Third is the attention of top government officials: for example, when Wen Jiabao saw the report on the Tiger Leaping Gorge dam and ordered an investigation into the illegal construction. These three factors play a crucial role for local residents: they can acquire knowledge, learn that they are within their rights to campaign against the dam, and know that they have the support of the public and central government. They will not feel that they are alone and helpless.

However, the movement to save the Tiger Leaping Gorge had three extra factors, which the Nu River campaign did not. First, it had someone who had grown up in the village with a sense of sacrifice and an indomitable fighting spirit. He grabbed the attention of both the media and NGOs and rallied them behind the campaign. Xiao Liangzhong was the most important person behind the whole movement. Second, it had local leaders, like Ge Quanxiao, Li Jianzhong and Ding Changxiu. These people were very effective at spreading awareness and inspiring people. With no leaders, the hydropower company and the local government would have easily been able to divide the villagers and crack down on dissent. If a 'mass incident' had broken out, it would have been difficult to bring the situation back under control. Third was the 21 March incident: this demonstrated the determination and the force of local opposition to the dam. The people were no longer silent. They had knowledge and awareness. They had the willingness and the capacity to voice their opinions. They didn't hesitate to make their voice heard in the form of a protest.

In the intervening years, these sorts of environmental protests have happened again and again across China. In 2007, residents of Xiamen took to the streets to protest a petrochemical chemical factory (see Chapter 4); in 2011, people in Dalian also marched against another PX chemical plant; and in 2012, people in Shifang, in Sichuan province, demonstrated against a copper refinery. These protests are happening because people in China now realise that with a show of strength they can win.

In 1989, many Chinese people took to the streets to fight for democracy, but they failed. Twenty years later, many Chinese people have begun to use a more complex and effective means to continue this fight. Of these, environmental protests have been the most successful. As long as democratically minded officials, scholars, reporters and other educated people become aware, democratic rights can be won in the environmental world bit by bit. Articles can be written, forums can be held, NGOs can be established and the people can become more enlightened. To a certain degree, they can block government actions and strike back at big interest groups. The government also supports environmental improvements – and so, in this regard, it will not crack down on environmental activists too harshly. This gives people more political space to take action in the environmental sphere.

The key strength of any campaign will be the participation of the people in the community who are directly affected. This strength is like a tree root, reaching deep into the soil. The deeper it goes, the taller and stronger the tree grows. The Tiger Leaping Gorge campaign only became a genuine movement when the 100,000 local people who were affected became part of the campaign. Campaigns to stop the other twenty-four dams on the Jinsha River all failed, because even though the media and NGOs both made appeals, they didn't have the force of local people power. And one by one these big dams have swallowed up the Jinsha River.

Likewise, the campaign would have failed without the media and NGOs, because they helped to spread the message. Thousands of people protested against the Pubugou Dam, on the Dadu River, but they didn't have any outside support. Left stranded and helpless, they were swiftly quashed by powerful interest groups.

The campaign to save Tiger Leaping Gorge should be the Chinese environmental movement's most cherished case. China's newly emerging social forces – commercial media, NGOs and the Internet – joined together with traditional indigenous people opposed to outside interest groups, showing what a vibrant thing a complete environmental campaign is. It demonstrated how we can find the strength to protect our beautiful natural environment, safeguard our homes, our culture and traditions in a China that is rapidly developing, as its environment and civil liberties worsen. Because of this campaign, if you go to Tiger Leaping Gorge today, you can still see the magnificent canyon, the thundering river, the mountains covered in dense forest and the many diverse cultures living along the river. And when you have been enchanted by all this, you should realise that this kind of idyll has become rare and endangered. Somewhere outside, the hydropower industry still has its eye firmly trained on it.

Notes

1. 'China to Add 38 GW Nuclear, 140 GW Hydro by 2015', Reuters, 6 January 2011, www.reuters.com/article/2011/01/06/china-power-idAFBJI 00251820110106.
2. Interviews from 2004 cited here, Liu Jianqiang, 'The Three Gorges: A Wiser Approach', *chinadialogue*, 23 October 2007.
3. Patrick McCully, *Silenced Rivers: The Ecology and Politics of Large Dams*, London: Zed Books, 2001; published in an unofficial translation as *Daba Jingjixue* 大坝经济学, Beijing: China Development Press, 2005.
4. Brahma Chellaney, 'China's Dam Frenzy', *Project Syndicate*, 2 December 2011, www.project-syndicate.org/commentary/china-s-dam-frenzy# h6Fem67R4uMV82SV.99.
5. Aviva Imhof, Susanne Wong and Peter Bosshard, *Citizen's Guide to the World Commission on Dams*, Berkeley CA: International Rivers Network, 2002.

Further reading

Liu Jianqiang, *Heavenly Beads*, Beijing: Tibet People's Publishing House, 2010. (Described by *Southern Metropolis Daily* as the best book about Tibet in Chinese, this travelogue discusses Tibet's modern history and traditional culture through stories of Tibetan environmental activists.)

Gary Marcuse, *Waking the Green Tiger: The Rise of a Green Movement in China*, film, Vancouver: Face to Face Media, 2011. (Seen through the eyes of journalists, activists and farmers, the documentary follows an extraordinary campaign to stop a massive dam project on the Upper Yangtze River.)

Tang Xiyang and Ma Xia. *Green Trip around the World*, Hohhot: Inner Mongolia People's Press, 1993. (The authors travelled around China and more than fifty other countries, surveying national parks and nature reserves; played an important role in raising awareness of Green issues among the first generation of Chinese environmental volunteers and NGOs.)

Xu Gang, *Woodcutter, Wake Up!* Changchun: Jilin People's Press, 1997. (Outlined the tragedy facing China's forests, and played a positive role in stopping deforestation and raising people's awareness of environmental protection.)

Yang Dongping, ed., *Friends of Nature's 2012 Annual Report on China's Environment and Development*, Beijing: Social Sciences Academic Press, 2012. (The eighth in a series of annual reports which look at the year's environmental situation in China from the perspective of civil society.)

About the contributors

SAM GEALL is Departmental Lecturer in Human Geography of China at the University of Oxford and executive editor of *chinadialogue*. He is an editor of *Berkshire Encyclopedia of Sustainability 7/10: China, India, and East and Southeast Asia: Assessing Sustainability* and author of *Climate-Change Journalism in China: Opportunities for International Cooperation*. Sam has written for many international publications including the *Guardian*, *Foreign Policy*, *New Humanist*, *openDemocracy*, *Index on Censorship* and *Green Futures*. He is a Fellow of the RSA.

ISABEL HILTON is a London-based writer and broadcaster, and the editor of *chinadialogue*. She has reported from China, South Asia, Latin America, Africa, the Middle East and Europe and has written and presented several documentaries for BBC radio and television. She has authored and co-authored several books and holds honorary doctorates from Bradford and Stirling universities.

OLIVIA BOYD is a London-based journalist. She is deputy editor of *chinadialogue* and has written for a range of titles including Chinese newspaper *Southern Weekend* and business magazine *Building*, where she was formerly senior reporter. Olivia studied Chinese at Oxford University, with a stint at Peking University, and has travelled extensively in East Asia.

ADAM MOSER is Assistant Director at Vermont Law School's US–China Partnership for Environmental Law, which works with Chinese scholars, government agencies, judges and lawyers to support the development of environmental rule of law in China. Moser received his B.A. from Ohio University (2001), his J.D. from the University of Cincinnati (2009), and his L.L.M. in Environmental Law from Vermont Law School (2011). He has volunteered and interned with the Center for Legal Assistance to Pollution Victims, at the China University of Politics and Law in Beijing and at Shandong University Law School's Human Rights Research Center.

JONATHAN ANSFIELD is a reporter for the *New York Times* in Beijing and an editor with the Chinese online edition of the paper. Previously he reported for *Newsweek* and Reuters from Beijing, where he has lived for more than fifteen years. He studied traditional Chinese literature at Brown University and the University of Chicago, and has written for the website *China Digital Times* and *Wallpaper* magazine, among other publications. He and his wife own and run a restaurant in Beijing.

LIU JIANQIANG is the Beijing editor of *chinadialogue*. Jianqiang was formerly a senior investigative reporter with *Southern Weekend* newspaper. He was a 2005 nominee for the State Environmental Protection Administration's 'China Environmental Protection Person of the Year' award and was awarded the 'Green expert' prize on World Environment Day at the 2011 SEE–TNC Ecological Awards. His books include the critically acclaimed *Heavenly Beads: A Tibetan Journey*, published in 2009.

Index

About Zed Books

Zed Books is a critical and dynamic publisher, committed to increasing awareness of important international issues and to promoting diversity, alternative voices and progressive social change. We publish on politics, development, gender, the environment and economics for a global audience of students, academics, activist and general readers. Run as a co-operative, we aim to operate in an ethical and environmentally sustainable way.

Find out more at
www.zedbooks.co.uk

For up-to-date news, articles, reviews
and events information visit
http://zed-books.blogspot.com

To subscribe to the monthly Zed Books e-newsletter
send an email headed 'subscribe' to marketing@zedbooks.net

We can also be found on Facebook, ZNet,
Twitter and Library Thing.